TO COMFORT
THE HEART
Women in Seventeenth-Century America

AMERICAN WOMEN
1600–1900

Series Editor: Julie Roy Jeffrey, Goucher College

TO COMFORT THE HEART

Women in Seventeenth-Century America

Paula A. Treckel

Twayne Publishers
An Imprint of Simon & Schuster Macmillan • New York

Prentice Hall International
London   Mexico City   New Delhi   Singapore
Sydney   Toronto

HQ1416
.T74
1996

To Comfort the Heart: Women in Seventeenth-Century America
Paula A. Treckel

Copyright © 1996 by Twayne Publishers

Twayne Publishers
An Imprint of Simon & Schuster Macmillan
1633 Broadway
New York, NY 10019

Library of Congress Cataloging-in-Publication Data

Treckel, Paula A.
    To comfort the heart : women in seventeenth century America / by
Paula A. Treckel.
        p.   cm.—(Twayne's history of women series)
    Includes bibliographical references and index.
    ISBN 0-8057-9917-6 (alk. paper)
    1. Women—United States—History—17th century. I. Title. II. Series.
HQ1416.T74   1996
305.4′0973′09032—dc20   95-39990
                                                                          CIP

For my mother and father

I serve for a day, for a week for a yeere,
For life time, for ever, while men dwelleth here.
For richer for poorer, from north to the south,
For honest, for hardhead, for daintie of mouth,
For wed and unwedded, in sickness and health,
For all that wel liveth, in good common wealth.
For citie, for countrie, for court and for cart,
To quiet the head and to comfort the heart.
—Thomas Tusser, *Five Hundred Points of Good Husbandry*

v

CONTENTS

LIST OF ILLUSTRATIONS   ix
FOREWORD   xi
PREFACE   xiii
ACKNOWLEDGMENTS   xv

CHAPTER ONE
English Women and English Families   *1*

CHAPTER TWO
From the Old World to the New   27

CHAPTER THREE
The Colonial "Huswife"   74

CHAPTER FOUR
Women's Rights and the Law   129

CHAPTER FIVE
Women and Religion   160

AFTERWORD   *196*
NOTES   *199*
BIBLIOGRAPHICAL ESSAY   *247*
INDEX   *261*

ILLUSTRATIONS

1. Anne Pollard

2. "The wyfe of an Herowan of Secotan"

3. "The wyfe of an Herowan of Pomeiooc"

4. "A cheife Herowans wyfe of Pomeoc and her daughter the age of. 8. or so. yeares"

5. Pocahontas, circa 1595–1617

6. Cradle, 1660–1690

7. Set of six plates, circa 1670–1690

8. The Old Plantation

9. Mrs. Elizabeth Freake and Baby Mary, circa 1671–1674

10. Dutch girl with red shoes, 1740

11. The Mason children: David, Joanna, and Abigail, 1670

12. Sampler, circa 1665–1670

13. Crewel on linen bedhangings, circa 1745

14. Sea grass rice-fanning basket

15. Pastel of Mrs. Samuel Prioleau, 1715

FOREWORD

For much of the twentieth century, American historians have explored the political, economic, social, and cultural events of the first 300 years of the nation's existence with a focus on men as historical actors. In the last 25 years, however, many scholars have concentrated on uncovering the experiences of early American women as individuals and as members of families and communities. This shift of perspective has had a dynamic impact on the study of the past. Women's history has raised new questions about the American experience, challenged the ways in which historians have conceptualized issues and problems, and even called into question the usefulness of familiar chronological divisions.

Each of the volumes in Twayne's "American Women 1600–1900," like those already published in its series "American Women in the Twentieth Century," draws upon a rich body of scholarship in women's history as the basis for an interpretive study of the lives of women of different classes and races during a specified time period. Each presents a readable narrative suitable both for undergraduates and general readers. In the extensive documentation, graduate students and those with particular research interests will also find a valuable introduction to the significant primary and secondary sources in the field and to its scholarly debates.

Paula Treckel's *To Comfort the Heart*, the first volume in the new series, explores the critical period between 1588 and 1748. During these years English settlers carved out colonies along the coast of North America and, as they did so, came into contact and often conflict with Native American tribes. The challenges of settlement led to increasing diversity in the new land as indentured workers from England and captives from Africa were imported to meet the pressing need for labor. Within the context of this story, the outlines of which are familiar, Treckel asks what meaning the colonization of North America held for the women who participated in it as willing or unwilling emigrants, or who were affected by it as settlement proceeded. She makes clear that, just as these women were different from each other, so too were their experiences. Yet she also points out that all the women experienced both change and continuity during the critical years of the seventeenth century; in fact, the concept of change and continuity serves as a unifying theme for Treckel's narrative. So too do the insightful questions that Treckel poses. She asks what, if any, were the similarities between women of different races, classes, cultures, and regions. How did the lives of daughters resemble and differ from those of their mothers? From what responsibilities and roles did women find satisfaction and comfort? Where and what were the dangers and hazards that colored their existence? As Treckel suggests the answers to these central questions, she not only provides a structure for understanding female experiences in early North America but also brings many seventeenth-century women vividly to life for her readers.

Julie Roy Jeffrey
Goucher College

PREFACE

Was seventeenth-century America a paradise for women, a "golden age" for women's rights? This question was posed by scholars who first explored American women's history early in this century. Yes, they concluded, it was. Frontier conditions in the New World generated a greater appreciation of women by colonial men, they argued. Women's scarcity meant they had their choice of marriage partners and could negotiate greater rights and freedoms for themselves in their new homeland. Thus, women in seventeenth-century America enjoyed a higher status than their English counterparts. The eighteenth century, these historians asserted, witnessed a decline in women's status, as Americans aped England's traditions regarding women's rights even as they declared their independence from their mother country. Not until the birth of the feminist movement in the nineteenth century, they claimed, did American women regain even some of the freedoms they once enjoyed on the seventeenth-century frontier.

Focusing almost exclusively on the lives of English women, these historians influenced the study of women's experience in early America for more than 50 years. In 1984 historian Mary Beth Norton disputed the basic premises of this golden age theory and challenged a new generation of scholars to devise different, more fruitful approaches for better understanding the lives of women in seventeenth-century America.[1]

This study of women in England's North American colonies from 1588 to 1740 asserts a new model for studying and understanding women's experience. Drawing on recent works in early American and women's history and identifying themes of *continuity* and *change*, I explore women's lives in their native lands—England, North America, and West Africa—as well as the varied roles they played in seventeenth-century America. For women's experience in the colonies was not monolithic; modes of settlement, race, ethnicity, religious beliefs, climate, geography, and economic development differentiated women's lives and affected them in ways they could not anticipate. Native American women faced the destruction of their culture, while African women, wrenched from their homes, adapted to endure the rigors of slavery. Although English women were generally in a more secure position, all of these women were forced to change if they were to survive.

But the women of early America—Native American, African, and European—also found a sense of purpose in the chaos of colonization by replicating that which was familiar to them from their lives before conquest, colonization, and enslavement. Their homes, the implements they used, and the clothing they wore reveal not only the scope of their responsibilities but their ideas about women's proper roles within their cultures. Living their lives to the same biological rhythms of pregnancy and childbirth, these women were comforted and empowered by their respective faiths. Ironically, these common experiences did not create bonds between the women of early America. Instead, they, like the men with whom they lived, were divided by barriers of race and class.

Women of all races courageously responded to the harsh realities of life in early America. They, and the children they bore, ensured the survival and development of North America. Bridging past and future, generations of Native American, African, and English women accommodated their desire for continuity with the need to change. And, in doing so, created a brave New World.

ACKNOWLEDGMENTS

I am indebted to the many teachers during my undergraduate and graduate days who inspired my interest in colonial America and encouraged my study of women's history, then a new field of historical inquiry. I am especially grateful to Stephen S. Webb, who by his example taught me what it means to be a historian. As a teacher now myself, I must also acknowledge the contribution of my students to this work. Their enthusiasm for women's history over the years has sustained and affirmed my own.

To my colleagues in the Department of History at Allegheny College—Jonathan E. Helmreich, Richard W. Turk—who endured my endless discussion of this work and had faith in my ability to complete it, thank you. I am especially grateful to Bruce L. Clayton, Barry Shapiro, and Stephen M. Lyons, who read portions of this manuscript and offered suggestions for its improvement, and to Demerie P. Faitler, whose professional support and friendship mean a great deal to me.

I am indebted to series editor Julie Roy Jeffrey, whose own scholarship on frontier women has inspired me and whose thoughtful criticism and patient encouragement have made this a better work.

I am grateful to the following institutions for providing illustrations and permitting their reproduction in this study: The British Museum, The National Portrait Gallery/Art Resource, The Massachusetts Historical Society, The Wadsworth Atheneum, The Worcester Art Museum, The Abby Aldrich Rockefeller Folk Art Center, The Winterthur Museum, The Fine Arts Museums of San Francisco, The Essex Institute, The Old York Historical Society, The Charleston Museum, and the Museum of Early Southern Decorative Arts. I wish to express my gratitude to Mr. Chris Loeblein at the Charleston Museum for his suggestions about South Carolina sea grass baskets and to Mr. Bradford L. Rauschenberg at the Museum of Early Southern Decorative Arts for information about artist Henrietta Johnston. I would also like to thank Cynthia Burton and Don Vrabel of the Pelletier Library at Allegheny College, as well as the reference staff at the Kent State University

Library, for their assistance in locating and acquiring resources for this project.

My family has always been there for me. My sister, Karla T. Mugler, her husband, Dale, and their children, Paul and Emily, have encouraged me, and I want to thank them for their love and support. My parents, Karl and Eleanore Treckel, have always believed in my ability to accomplish anything I dared. To them this work is dedicated.

Finally, I owe my greatest thanks to my "dear and loving husband," Herb Page, whose love enriched my life.

CHAPTER ONE

English Women and English Families

Before the first rays of sunlight brightened the sky, the English housewife awoke and began her work on this summer day in 1606. She built up the fire in the hearth from embers carefully banked the night before and began preparation of the day's meals for her family and servants. Placing her bread dough on the warm hearth to rise, she walked outside into the chill of the early morning air to gather vegetables for the stew she would serve for the midday meal. As she brushed the dew from the camomile and mint she decided to brew a tisane for her youngest daughter, who was feeling poorly.

In the predawn stillness of her garden, she heard the gentle clucking of the hens and the animals stirring in the barnyard as she contemplated the day that lay before her. First she must wake the servant girl to milk the cows and begin the day's churning before her husband and sons came down for breakfast and morning prayers. Then she must draw water from the well and put it to boil to do the week's laundry. At least her daughters and the servant girl would help her, scrubbing and rinsing the clothes, wringing them out, and hanging them to dry. She could spare her youngest daughter the heaviest work by having her do the mending, a good way to practice her needlework.

Her husband, sons, and the servant boy would work in the fields; they would come home for their midday meal and then return to the fields to make the most of the long summer day. She must also get ready to go to market on Saturday to sell the eggs she carefully collected all week and to trade the butter and cheeses

1

she made. Perhaps she would get a nice piece of wool cloth to make a new jacket for her husband. It has been so long since he had something new to wear to services on Sunday morning. She looked forward to seeing her neighbors and friends at the market, hearing the gossip about the squire and his family, and learning about the latest events in London town.

Her thoughts were interrupted by the sounds of people stirring indoors. As she turned to go inside, the sun peeped above the horizon. A new day had begun.

This seventeenth-century English woman's life was shaped by her responsibilities as a wife, a mother, and a mistress of her household, roles defined by her gender and shared by other women of her social class. As the wife of a middling farmer, she was her husband's helpmate. Her labor complemented his and together they created a family. As a mother, she nurtured and cared for her children. She educated her daughters in domestic skills so that one day they might marry and establish homes of their own. As a mistress, she trained her servants well in the ways of her household and saw to their basic needs. At the same time, this housewife's life was affected in ways she could not fathom by events far from her home and kitchen garden.

Even as this English woman surveyed her garden and contemplated the day that stretched before her, changes were occurring in the world around her.

> There was a wind over England, and it blew.
> (Have you heard the news of Virginia?)
> A west wind blowing, the wind of a western star,
> To gather men's lives like pollen and cast them forth,
> Blowing in hedge and highway and seaport town,
> Whirling dead leaf and living, but always blowing,
> A salt wind, a sea wind, a wind from the world's end,
> From the coasts that have new, wild names, from the huge unknown.[1]

The winds of change blowing over England gathered the lives of women as well as men, regardless of their social class, and swept them westward to the New World. How the women who voyaged to the American colonies fared in their new home was influenced by the land they had left behind them. Their experiences in the Old World served as the foundation for their adjustment to the New.

Most English women who migrated to America in the seventeenth century found security in trying to re-create the lives they had known in their homeland; they found meaning and comfort in replicating the responsibilities they assumed and the duties they performed in their English homes. At the same time, they encountered new and trying circumstances in the colonies that required them to change. They were forced to assume unfamiliar roles and surrender age-old assumptions about women's abilities in order to survive. How their lives were transformed by colonization and how they perceived their experience in the New World can best be understood by looking first at what their lives were like in seventeenth-century England.

THE ENGLISH FAMILY

Women's experience in both the Old World and the New was given shape and meaning by their families. The patriarchal, patrilineal nuclear family, which included the husband, his wife, and their children, was the basic unit of seventeenth-century English society. Ideas about women and their role in the nuclear family were affected by the major religious, economic, and political changes during this era. Chief among them were the Reformation and the rise of English nationalism.

With the Act of Succession in 1534, King Henry VIII broke with the Roman Catholic Church and created the Anglican Church with himself as its head. The consequences of his actions were far more sweeping than Henry could have imagined. The Reformation gave impetus to a new era of individualism in England as Protestant theologians encouraged men and women to take responsibility for their own religious education and salvation. The authority of the Church of England was challenged as people asserted their own needs. This sense of empowerment spilled over into the secular realm, fueling the growth of English nationalism and the birth of capitalism. England's wool industry flourished, and trade with Europe increased. The search for new markets prompted England to look beyond its boundaries, far across the seas, to routes and eventually colonies in the New World.

The growth in England's economy permitted greater social mobility. Although England retained its hierarchical class structure, with the nobility at the peak, the gentry class of large and middling landowners amassed wealth and political influence. Merchants, men whose fortunes came from foreign and domestic trade, began to clamor for a voice in government and policy making. Below the gentry and merchant classes were landowners known as "yeomen," small farmers called "husbandmen," and "cottagers," agricultural workers who were paid for their labor. Many of them migrated from depressed rural areas to towns and cities to find work in developing industries. In these bustling urban centers, initiative was rewarded and individualism encouraged.

England's triumph over the Spanish Armada in 1588, however, marked the beginning of a long and costly war with Spain and turmoil within the empire. The new century found England beset by high taxes, inflation, poor crops, and repeated outbreaks of the plague. The powerful gentry, an increasingly assertive Parliament, and aggressive English Puritans called for political and religious change and challenged the authority of the Stuart monarchs, James I and Charles I. By 1642 civil war erupted. Charles I was eventually forced to surrender to Parliamentary troops. He was tried, found guilty of waging war against Parliament, and executed in 1649. A commonwealth, led by the Lord Protector Oliver Cromwell, replaced the monarchy. Puritan reformers dismantled the Anglican Church and began reconstructing English society and government to reflect their religious beliefs.

The Puritans sought to return to a more primitive, "pure" Christianity. To that end, they repudiated the remnants of Catholic hierarchy and practice retained by the Anglican Church. Instead, they emphasized the local congregation and elevated Scripture—the literal word of God—as the basis for worship. Although they thought that salvation was predestined by God, they also believed it was possible that anyone could be saved by virtue of God's covenant with Abraham. Thus, they urged all to live according to God's will. The ability to do so was, they thought, evidence of salvation, citing Romans 8:30: "Whom he did predestinate, them he also called: and whom he called, them he also justified: and whom he justified, them he also glorified." Seeking wholesale reform of politics and society, the Puritans imposed their beliefs on the English people during the Commonwealth era.

In these times of dramatic religious and political change, the English family provided its members with a sense of security and continuity. Recognizing this need for certainty in men's and women's lives, the Puritans also realized the family could control and maintain order in society. Consequently, they idealized the patriarchal, patrilineal family and emphasized its importance in English life. Ironically, even as they raised fundamental questions about the role of the divine monarch and the validity of patriarchal power, they reinforced the power of fathers within households.[2]

The Puritan clergy, in accordance with what they perceived to be God's plan, exaggerated the authority of men in the family and urged the obedience of women, children, and servants to men's will. As God was absolute master of all things, men, whose authority came from God, were absolute masters of their households. As God was a loving father, so men were to be benevolent patriarchs in their homes. Wives owed husbands obedience, as Puritan ministers, citing St. Paul, made clear. Women were to submit to their husbands as they did to their Lord, for the man was head of his family as Christ was head of the church. While such views may seem harsh today, they made sense in a world turned upside down by war and civil strife. Many men and women found comfort and security in these ideas and strove to enforce them in their homes. While men were reassured by their authority over wives, children, and servants, women found solace and meaning in their rigidly prescribed roles as wives and mothers. By substituting the authority of the father for that of the deposed monarch, the Puritans achieved political change while minimizing the threat of social upheaval or revolution.[3]

Lord Protector Oliver Cromwell's death in 1658 marked the end of the Puritan Commonwealth. Parliament restored the monarchy and Charles II became king in 1660. While the radical political ideals unleashed by the Civil Wars were restrained and the religious ideas of the Puritans were repressed, Charles II supported the patriarchal order that once again lent authority to the monarchy and provided order in English life. The family remained important as a stabilizing force and a haven of security and continuity.

BELIEFS ABOUT WOMEN

Certain assumptions about women were embedded in the English family and subscribed to across class and religious lines during the seventeenth century. The most basic idea was that women were inferior to men. This pervasive and fundamental belief not only shaped women's existence in England but traveled with them to North America.

The belief in women's inferiority was ultimately derived from, and justified by, biblical Scripture. Roman Catholic, Anglican, and Puritan clergy differed in many essential respects, but all blamed Eve for Adam's fall from grace. Eve was the source of original sin and, for her temptation of Adam, was punished by God: "Unto the woman he said, I will greatly multiply thy sorrow and thy conception; in sorrow thou shalt bring forth children." Eve's weakness appeared as an obvious sign of her inferiority, and she was made subject to Adam as punishment for her sin: "and thy desire shall be to thy husband, and he shall rule over thee."[4] As Preacher William Whately pointedly reminded women, "If ever thou purpose to be a good wife, and to live comfortably, set down this with thyself: mine husband is my superior, my better; he hath authority and rule over me; nature hath given it to him . . . God hath given it to him."[5] In this way, Eve, Adam's temptress, was tamed.

Although most theologians believed women were eligible for salvation and agreed with William Austin that "in . . . the soul there is neither hees nor shees," in temporal matters they thought that women were inferior to men and should be subordinate to them.[6] John Calvin urged each woman to "be satisfied with her state of subjection and not take it amiss that she is made inferior to the more distinguished sex." Men were instructed to heed St. Peter's admonition, giving "honour unto the wive, as unto the weaker vessel, and as being heirs together of the grace of life."[7]

"Weaker vessels," women had to be protected from their own natures. Eve's transgression in the Garden of Eden appeared to prove their depravity and immorality. Men, less easily led astray, were charged with restraining and controlling women's sexuality. The belief that women were more emotional than men was also seen as a sign of their inherent weakness. Their physical vulnerability when pregnant, the pain they suffered in childbirth, and their supposedly greater susceptibility to illness and disease were offered as proof of their frailty.

The seventeenth-century scientific community reinforced this belief in female physical inferiority. Physicians theorized that from conception boys and girls developed at different rates and that boys required a longer gestation period than girls because they were biologically more complex. They believed that boys were more active in the womb than girls and were more easily delivered because they "assisted" in their own delivery.[8]

Men—theologians, scientists, and physicians—projected on women characteristics diametrically opposed to those they believed were male. By giving "masculine" attributes a positive connotation and "feminine" attributes a negative one, they revealed the qualities they feared most in themselves and claimed responsibility for regulating and defining women's lives. Men were active and strong while women were passive and physically, mentally, and morally weak. Men were ruled by their reason; women succumbed to their emotions and were incapable of governing themselves. Because women's sexual drive was thought greater than men's, they had a fearful power to lead men astray. To counter this threat, Puritan theologians taught that women's sexuality must be controlled and channeled in marriage, where its end was procreation.[9]

In seventeenth-century England and the American colonies, women's ability to bear children governed their lives, regardless of social class. It was the common denominator that linked them together and distinguished them from men. English society regarded childbearing as a way for women to atone for Eve's sin in the Garden of Eden; through suffering in childbirth women acquired grace. The New Testament lent support to this view: "Adam was not deceived, but the woman being deceived was in the transgression. Notwithstanding she shall be saved in childbearing."[10] Such an understanding suggested barren women were deficient. Many, in fact, believed that a woman's infertility was God's punishment for her sins. Samuel Hieron's prayer for barren women expressed just such a perception: "It is just, I confess, with thee, to punish my barrenness in grace, and my fruitfulness in holy things, with this want of outward increase." The prayer continued: "let me be as the fruitful Vine on the walls of my husbands house, and let (at the least) one Olive plant spring out from me, to stand about his table."[11]

The widespread belief that men were intellectually superior to women affected educational opportunities for women. Few girls received a formal education, for only the wealthy could afford to send their children to school or have them tutored at home. Some schools actually barred girls from attendance once they reached the age of nine or learned how to read. Most women never learned how to read at all, and women's literacy lagged behind that of men throughout the century. Even the quality of upper-class women's education actually declined from the sixteenth to the seventeenth century as Queen

Elizabeth's example of female intellectual proficiency faded from memory.[12]

Women's education reflected their limited sphere. Because they were barred from the professions—the ministry, the law, government, or military service—those who received an education did not learn history, grammar, and logic. Although some upper-class girls might share their brothers' tutors, or had fathers who encouraged them, the woman who publicly displayed her knowledge risked being described as having "a masculine intellect." A popular ballad of the day, "An Invective against the Pride of Women," condemned women's intellectual curiosity, relating it to Adam's fall:

> Their soaring thoughts to Books advance
> 'Tis odds that may undo 'um
> For ever since Dame Eve's mischance
> That villanous itch sticks to 'um.[13]

King James shared the widespread distrust of educated women. "To make women learned and foxes tame had the same effect," he declared: "to make them more cunning."[14]

Because reading the Bible was necessary for learning the word of God, some Puritan clerics during the Commonwealth period advocated women's literacy. They also tried to strengthen the family as a center of religious education and worship, encouraging wives to assist their husbands in the education of their children. Still, they hardly advocated an equal education for women, fearing it might encourage women to think they were men's equals and challenge men's domestic and public authority. Consequently, what education women were permitted was carefully prescribed by men and reinforced their subordination within the family.

Late in the century, after the Restoration, some well-born women lamented their inferior education and tried to bring about change. Hannah Woolley complained that "the right education of the female sex, as it is in a manner everywhere neglected, so it ought to be generally lamented. Most in this depraved later age think a woman learned and wise enough if she can distinguish her husband's bed from another's."[15] Mary Astell, like Woolley, hoped to revive and expand women's educational opportunities. Born in 1666, she grew up in Newcastle-upon-

Tyne. After moving to London, she became friends with many socially prominent, intelligent women who encouraged her ideas about female education. In *A Serious Proposal to the Ladies* (1697), Astell suggested founding a college for women of intellect. Resembling a secular convent, her proposed college was seen as a positive alternative to marriage and as a way of educating women. Although she recognized that not all women wanted to be wives and mothers, Astell never advocated that women assume the roles and responsibilities of men. Instead, she promoted complementary roles for women.[16]

Despite Woolley's and Astell's efforts to increase women's educational opportunities, virtually all English authorities agreed that a woman, regardless of her rank, should acquire characteristics that made her pleasing to men and ready her for marriage, the only real role open to women. During childhood girls learned to be submissive to their parents, especially to their fathers, and were schooled by their mothers to be pleasing mates. Young women cultivated "Modesty, reserve, purity, temperance, humility, truth, meekness, patience, courtesie, affability, charity, goodness, mercy [and] compassion."[17] Silence was hailed as a feminine virtue. Women were taught never to speak unless spoken to, never to voice their own opinions or, indeed, to have opinions that differed from those of men.

Regardless of their social class, all women belonged at home, tending to their families' needs. Lower-class, rural women trained their daughters in the skills necessary to be good housewives. Upper-class women showed their daughters how to supervise household servants. Girls of the gentry and nobility also learned social graces: dancing, singing, and instrumental music. Regardless of their social rank, however, certain qualities were necessary if girls were to be successful wives and mothers. Household advisor Gervase Markham noted that an English woman must

> be a woman of great modesty and temperance, as well inwardly as outwardly; inwardly as in her behavior and carriage towards her husband, wherein she shall shun all violence of rage, passion and humour, coveting less to direct than to be directed, appearing ever unto him pleasant, amiable and delightful; . . . outwardly as in her apparel and diet, both of which she shall proportion according to the competency of her husband's estate and calling, making her circle straight than large.[18]

Since virtually all young women planned to marry, they tried to cultivate these qualities in hopes of marrying well.

The Reformation led to a reevaluation of marriage as an institution in English life. The Anglican Church rejected the Roman Catholic belief that celibacy was a state more pure than marriage and permitted their clergy to marry. Consequently, clergymen became outspoken advocates of married life. God, they asserted, endorsed marriage when he provided Adam with a wife in the Garden of Eden. The most extreme Protestant reformers, the Puritans, also championed the married state. They agreed with John Cotton, who proclaimed: "Women are Creatures without which there is no comfortable Living for man: it is true of them what is wont to be said of Governments, *That bad ones are better than none:* They are a sort of Blasphemers then who dispise and decry them, and call them *a necessary Evil,* for they are *a necessary Good;* such as it was not good that man should be without."[19] While Puritan clergymen expressed enthusiasm for the married state, they also carefully prescribed the nature of the marriage relationship and carried these ideas to the New World.[20]

RELIGION AND THE FAMILY

Despite the virtually unlimited authority they granted men within the nuclear family, Puritan theologians urged husbands to treat their wives with loving kindness. Husbands should recognize their wives' limitations, acknowledge their immortal souls, and exercise their power justly. Women were to be honored for their ability to bear children and men were admonished to be comforting, patient, and understanding.

The Puritans' emphasis on companionship and affection within marriage benefited women, for it acknowledged that they were God's creation and deserved men's love and kindness. Charles Gerbier argued in 1651 that "God made woman not of man's head, lest she should presume to over top him, nor of his foot, lest she should be vilified by him, but from a rib near unto his heart, that she might ever be dear and entire to him."[21] Although many Puritan theologians stressed men's responsibility to use their superiority and authority wisely, they continued to believe that God had created women inferior to men. As Milton stated, "He for God; she for God in him."[22]

But Protestantism had a subversive potential. Its emphasis on understanding, faith, and the individual's responsibility for knowing whether or not he or she was damned or saved inspired some of its adherents to justify political democracy and social equality, including the equality of women and men. In fact, the most radical religious reformers in seventeenth-century England attacked the patriarchal structure of both the family and the state. They asserted individual liberty in thought and deed for women and men alike. Challenging the authority of parents over their children, teachers over their students, and husbands over their wives, these extremists argued that all people had the right to participate in society. Appealing especially to those of the lower classes, some advocated collective ownership of all land. Others even advocated sexual freedom. More moderate Puritans discredited these religious radicals, however, labeling their beliefs both sinful and dangerous.

Some women, dissatisfied by their subordinate role in English life, were attracted to the most extreme religious sects, especially those which advocated a fundamental egalitarianism that cut across traditional lines of gender and class. Indeed, women founded some of these groups; many even served as missionaries. Sects like the Society of Friends, known as the Quakers, which claimed revelation of the spirit and granted women authority to speak God's word in public, were especially attractive. Female prophecy and preaching had powerful social implications, for women who followed "the spirit within" might challenge their husbands' authority. Only a few of the most extreme religious groups, however, extended their belief in the spiritual equality of women and men into the secular realm. Moreover, once they were established denominations, they advocated the patriarchal household as a means of securing and ensuring domestic order.[23]

While the less literate listened to sermons that sketched the ideal family, the most literate and devout probably read their treatises on family life. There was a tremendous increase in the prescriptive literature published during this era. As authorities engineered the English family into a form suitable to their religious and political ends, they found a receptive audience, eager for direction in a time of change. Reformers sanctified and politicized the English family as a "little Church" and a "little Commonwealth," empowering men as patriarchs of their homes and exaggerating women's subordinate role within the family. Their ideal family provided English men and women with a sense of stability and order as they faced a world characterized by uncertainty and change.[24]

ECONOMIC CHANGE

Economic transformations also affected marriage and family life. Among yeomen, husbandmen, and cottagers, and in the English working class, marriage was fundamentally an economic union of a man and a woman with complementary skills. The family was a unit of production, children laboring with their parents and contributing to their support. Because newlyweds customarily established a household separate from their parents, couples often delayed marriage. The majority of English men and women of the lower classes could not rely on their parents for land or financial assistance. They often worked many years to save enough to support a family. Those unable to do so never married.

To secure a future for themselves, many young women and men of the lower classes fled the depressed countryside to find work in England's growing cities. London was a powerful magnet in the seventeenth century, attracting young women and men who sought economic opportunity and a chance to marry. Many unmarried women entered domestic service. Supervised by their upper-class mistresses, they learned how to run a household in return for behaving "decently, modestly, and industriously." Many women performed these duties for their lifetimes, receiving little more than room, board, and the clothing they wore as payment for their labor. Others enjoyed the social opportunities provided by urban life and found husbands. Most jobs open to unskilled women and men, however, required that they delay marriage, for just as craftsmen could not marry until they completed their apprenticeships, domestic servants were prohibited from marrying during their terms of service. Once wed, women were expected to quit their jobs, for it was assumed that their husbands would support them.[25]

MARRIAGE CUSTOMS

Because most English women and men delayed marriage until they could support themselves, the average age at marriage for women was 26. Men married, on average, between the ages of 27 and 29; many women and men remained unmarried into their 40s. Because upper-class parents subsidized their children's marriages, earlier marriage was more common among women of the nobility, gentry, and merchant classes. Women of these classes married at a younger age than their brothers, who had to receive an education or gain practical work experience before setting up their own household. These young women, therefore, often wed men much older than themselves.[26] The age gap reinforced the patriarchal nature of families in which wives were viewed and treated as children by their husbands. Women of lower economic status tended to marry men nearly the same age as themselves. They probably experienced greater equality in their marriages than women of the upper classes.[27]

Among the middle and upper classes, marriage was also considered a way to create economic alliances and solidify class lines.[28] Consequently, middle- and upper-class parents played a major role in arranging their children's marriages. Parents were believed wiser in making matches, and children were urged to bow to their wishes. This was especially true of heiresses, whose marriages often conferred great wealth on their husbands. The daughter of a marquess bitterly remarked, "People in my way are sold like slaves." Protestant Reformers required the consent of parents to marriage arrangements and specified that a couple must have their parents' permission to marry if either party was under the age of 21. It can only be hoped that parental objectives and the will of the young people involved went hand in hand. While some upper-class women refused to marry the men selected for them, most acquiesced to their fathers' wishes.[29]

Women who refused to submit to their parents' will in the selection of their mates courted danger. Elizabeth Duke, the daughter of Sir Edward Duke, defied her parents when she married Nathaniel Bacon. The couple fled her parents' wrath to Virginia, where Nathaniel led an unsuccessful rebellion against the colonial government in 1675. In his revised will, Sir Edward revoked his daughter's inheritance because she had married against his wishes. Following her husband's death in Virginia, Elizabeth returned to England and brought suit against her father's estate, claiming her original inheritance of £2000. The Lord Chancellor who heard her case admonished her for her disrespect and ruled against her. "Such an example of presumptuous disobedience highly merit[ed] such punishment," he angrily asserted, "she being only prohibited to marry with one man, by name; and nothing in the whole fair Garden of Eden would serve her turn, but this forbidden fruit."[30]

Young women with less property at stake than Elizabeth Bacon had more freedom to court and choose their husbands. Because the landless and the owners of small property were usually unable to assist their daughters, there was little reason for them to submit to their parents' demands. Young women who migrated to cities in search of employment were especially free from parental wishes. In the bustling cities they socialized with and married men of their choosing, far from their parents' anxious eyes.[31]

Customarily, a woman had a dowry or "marriage portion," which became the property of her husband or her husband's family when she married. In exchange for this dowry, her husband agreed to support her during her lifetime and in widowhood. A father might use the marriage portion of his eldest son's wife to endow his own daughters, as did Oliver Cromwell. Cromwell hoped to marry his son, Richard, to an heiress and use her marriage portion as a dowry for his own daughters, Mary and Frances. As he explained to the heiress's father, "I must insist upon that [£2000]. . . . The money I shall need for my two little wenches." Over the century, as the gentry and nobility encountered economic setbacks, parents found it increasingly difficult and expensive to find husbands for daughters who were not heiresses.[32]

Lower-class women also needed dowries if they hoped to marry, and many worked to provide themselves with marriage portions. Possibly these women, having earned their own dowries, brought a greater sense of self-worth to their marriages and wielded more authority within them than women whose portions were provided by their fathers. The dowries of the poorest women sometimes consisted of household implements, bedding, and the like, the "tools" of their domestic trade. In the lower classes, where economic alliances were less important and more freedom was permitted in mate selection, marriages based on romantic attraction were probably common even before the seventeenth century. Because the middle and upper classes viewed marriage as an economic arrangement, however, mutual affection was considered adequate as the basis for contracting a marriage. Presumably, love would grow between a couple after marriage, knitting the two into one. Even marital love was scrutinized by religious authorities, who argued that a husband's love for his wife was different from a wife's love for her husband. Love should emanate from the man and be reflected by the woman; the husband loved while the woman submitted to his loving. Although the Puritans urged husbands to love their wives, they feared a man's love for his wife made him subject to her. They warned that passionate love for one's mate precluded a preeminent love of God. Passion was a dangerous basis for marriage, for its irrational and temporary character made it an unstable foundation on which to build a family.[33]

Once marriage negotiations between the parents or guardians of a couple ended, the couple became formally espoused, pledging their intention to marry. More binding than a modern engagement, this promise was viewed as a contract to marry. Although sexual intercourse was not officially sanctioned until the couple married, it was popularly believed that an espoused couple was married and free to engage in sexual relations.

Attitudes about prenuptial sex changed over time and were affected by social class. The wealthy and the titled opposed such behavior for it affected the interests of many others: it usurped the control parents had over their children and jeopardized inheritance rights. The lower classes tolerated prenuptial sexual activity more easily because they had less property at risk. Women of all classes, however, were held to a higher standard of sexual behavior than men. Virginity was highly prized in brides, especially among the upper classes, for a bride's virginity ensured that a man's heirs were truly his own. While women were expected to be virgins on their wedding night, men were assumed to be sexually experienced. The sexual exploitation of lower-class women by upper-class men promoted this sexual double standard, reinforced class distinctions, and enabled upper-class women to remain chaste. During the Puritan Commonwealth, however, prostitution, fornication, and adultery declined in all social classes in England. Church courts punished couples for fornication before marriage. Prenuptial pregnancies and illegitimate births declined, a pattern that persisted long after the Puritan Commonwealth ended.[34]

After a couple was espoused and before the marriage took place, the Anglican Church required a public announcement of their promise to

marry. Banns were read or posted on three separate Sundays, permitting those who opposed the match to voice their objections.[35] Following
publication of the banns, the couple was formally married. Because
some Puritans believed that marriage was not a Sacrament and others
believed that parts of the religious marriage ceremony were sacrilegious,
especially the use of rings and the husband's pledge to worship his wife
with his body, the religious marriage ceremony was replaced by a civil
ceremony during the Commonwealth period.[36]

A marriage was not valid or complete until it was consummated.
Husband and wife possessed each other's bodies, and marital sex was
considered necessary for the health and happiness of both partners.
While procreation was the goal of sexual intercourse, this was an age
that also recognized and encouraged female orgasm, believing that
women had to experience orgasm if conception was to occur. Although
sexual pleasure was linked to procreation and advocated by theologians
and medical writers, it was not viewed as an appropriate end. Puritan
clergy instructed married couples that it was sinful to engage in intercourse merely to satisfy lust and urged moderation in sexual matters.[37]

Then, as today, not all marriages were happy, and some men and
women strove to end them. Annulments, granted only by church courts
in the years before the Commonwealth, were extremely rare. The most
common grounds for an annulment by the Anglican Church was a prior
contract of marriage by the man or woman. Although some continental
Protestant churches permitted divorce for adultery and allowed the
innocent party to remarry, this was not the case in England, where
Parliament did not pass the first divorce act until 1698. During the
Commonwealth influential Puritan thinkers like John Milton called for
absolute divorce. Milton, who was unhappily married himself, argued
that marriage was not just an institution for procreation but also for
companionship. Thus, couples should be permitted to divorce for incompatibility as well as adultery. Milton's ideas, however, were too
radical, and absolute divorce never became legal in Puritan England.

The unwillingness to permit divorce did not mean there were no
efforts to deal with unhappy marriages. During the seventeenth century, church courts and civil courts could order a couple to separate
"from bed and board" on the grounds of cruelty, adultery, or an inability to get along. Property was divided, and the wife was usually
awarded some kind of support by her husband. Neither, however,
could remarry, the hope being that they might one day reconcile.

Separations by couples unable to live together became more common following the Civil War. The political and religious issues that divided England during this time clearly took their toll on marriages. As Dorothy Osborne lamented in the early 1650s, "What an age do we live in, where 'tis a miracle if, in ten couples that are married, two of them live so as not to publish to the world that they cannot agree."[38]

A wife's adultery and a husband's cruelty were the most common grounds for marital separation. Men, concerned about the transfer of titles and property from one generation of men to another, depended on women to give birth to their legitimate heirs. A bride's virginity—the symbol of her sexual innocence—was a guarantee that she had known no other man. "Wives lose their value," an observer remarked, "if once known before."[39] Married women were expected to remain faithful to their husbands, their fidelity ensuring the paternity of their children. A wife's adultery, therefore, was a form of theft, depriving her husband of his "ownership" of her and jeopardizing his lineage.[40] Excessive abuse by one's spouse also provided grounds for separation from bed and board. Although the law permitted men to chastise their wives physically, society condemned excessive violence directed against wives. Any man who actually resorted to physical abuse to control his wife's behavior was essentially acknowledging his lack of real authority over her. In turning to violence he violated his responsibility as a husband.[41]

Most unhappily married men and women found it impossible to secure annulments or formal separations. The simplest way for a poor couple to end an unhappy marriage was desertion, an option exercised most often by men, leaving women with children to support and care for on their own.[42]

CHILDBEARING AND CHILDREARING

Marriage licensed the creation of families. English women usually gave birth to their first child within the first year or two after they wed. While men were more vulnerable to death in warfare or from disease, childbearing posed the greatest risk to women's health in the seventeenth century. Around 45 percent of all upper-class women died before the age of 50, one quarter from childbirth or its complications. Many more probably died of diseases and conditions brought about by constant childbearing.[43]

Maternal breastfeeding offered women some degree of control over the frequency of their pregnancies because it delayed the resumption of their fertility. Breastfeeding lengthened the interval between births, enabling women to regain their strength after childbirth. Couples also probably abstained from intercourse while the mother was nursing the infant, especially during the first few months. Throughout the seventeenth century, however, breastfeeding was unfashionable among upper-class mothers, and they employed other women, "wet nurses," to nourish their infants. Denied the temporary contraceptive effect of nursing their own infants, these women were actually pregnant more often than women of lesser rank. Despite this greater fertility among upper-class women, the families of middling farmers and husbandmen included more children. Upper-class infants reared by wet nurses had a higher mortality than infants of the lower classes nursed by their mothers.[44]

England's birth rate rose slightly during the Civil Wars but dropped during the Commonwealth period and continued to decline during the Restoration. Urbanization contributed to this decline, as the lower and middle classes found it more costly to support their children in cities. Late marriage, the disruptions of war, postwar depression, and the uncertainty of the times led to a decline in family size during the second half of the seventeenth century, when, on average, the family included between four and five children. Once English men and women achieved their desired family size, they practiced the most effective form of birth control, sexual abstinence.[45]

Throughout the seventeenth century and especially during the Commonwealth era, society placed great emphasis on the role of parents. Parents had the grave responsibility of giving children religious instruction and for teaching them to obey those in authority. Because children were viewed as fundamentally depraved, tainted from birth by original sin, physical chastisement, reinforced by threats of damnation and the fires of hell, was often used to ensure obedience. While mothers played an important role in the nurture and care of infants and toddlers, fathers were held accountable for the behavior of their children; mothers' affection for their children was supposed to be balanced by the authority of fathers.

Children of the gentry and upper classes saw little of their parents during their formative years. Cared for by nurses and educated by tutors until they reached the age of ten, they were then sent away to boarding schools or to live with relatives. Their physical and emotional distance from their parents, especially their fathers, reinforced parental authority and control over them. Among the upper classes children called their parents "Sir" or "Madame" and were taught to show deference to them by standing or kneeling in their presence. Children of the lower classes also learned to submit to the will of their parents. They were required to work at home or in the fields at a very early age. Some, as they grew older, were sent away from home to become domestic servants or apprentices. In this way they learned skills to maintain themselves and contribute to the support of their family.

Beginning in the late seventeenth century and early eighteenth century, the decline in Puritan religious influence led to the emergence of a more affectionate, mother-centered mode of childrearing among the upper classes in England. Praise for good behavior replaced punishment for bad behavior, and the view of children as innocents began to replace the belief in infant depravity. Women of the upper classes also began to breastfeed their children and develop an emotional bond with them. As a result, infant mortality declined among the gentry and nobility. These changes in childrearing philosophy and custom were slow to reach the lower classes, however, which practiced more authoritarian methods well into the eighteenth century.[46]

DOMESTIC RESPONSIBILITIES

While childbearing and childrearing were the focal point of women's lives in England, their responsibilities within the household complemented those of their husbands, regardless of social class. The wife was to care for the children and perform domestic tasks, while the husband was to support and maintain his family. Household advisor Edmund Tilney sketched out the norms for husbands and wives:

> The office of the husband is to bring in necessaries: of the wife, well to keep them. The office of the husband is, to be abroad in matters of profit: of the wife, to tarry at home, and see all be well there. The office of the husband is, to provide money, of the wife, not wastefully to spend it.

> The office of the husband is, to deal, and bargain with all men, of the wife, to meddle or make with no man. . . . The office of the husband is, to be Lord of all, of the wife, to give account of all, and finally, I say, that the office of the husband is to maintain well his livelihood, and the office of the woman is, to govern well the household.[47]

As Tilney's description suggests, a married man's responsibilities took him into the wider, public world of commerce and trade, while his wife's tasks customarily centered in the private sphere of the home.

The wife of a middling farmer cooked for her family or household, kept her home as clean as she was able, laundered and maintained her family's clothing, and cared for her children. She served as her family's principal health-care provider and was responsible for a great deal of domestic production. Her duties might include cultivating fruits and vegetables, preserving foods for later consumption, dairying, raising poultry, and spinning and weaving. At a very early age, girls assisted their mothers in their daily chores. They learned how to sew, cook, clean, launder, tend the kitchen garden, and preserve foods by following their mother's example. Girls also aided their mothers in caring for their younger sisters and brothers. The bonds between mothers and daughters were often close as they worked together to perform these domestic duties. For the most part, a woman's domestic industry benefited her family and was not rewarded by monetary compensation.

On small farms where women and men both had to labor to support the family, women often performed what was traditionally considered men's work. Farmers' wives helped at harvest time when labor demands were most intense or if the family was too poor to hire male laborers. Women might plant and weed the crops, even shear sheep. As one household advisor explained, it was a farm wife's duty to "winow al maner of cornes, to make malte wash and wring, to make hey, to shere corne, and in time of nede to helpe her husband to fyll the mucke wayne or donge carte, dryve the plough, to lode hey, corne & such other."[48] In fact, there was little agricultural work women did not perform when necessary. Women, therefore, had to be flexible enough to assist their husbands and to perform their traditional domestic jobs as well. While women often assisted men at their work, it was unusual for men to assist women at theirs. Women were their husbands' helpmates. Men's duties and responsibilities superseded theirs, a clear reflection of the greater importance and value assigned to men and men's work.

The popular works of household advisor Thomas Tusser paint a vivid portrait of life in seventeenth-century England. In *Five Hundred Points of Good Husbandry*, Tusser described the activities of the English farmer and his wife and offered advice on how they might improve their lives. His work illuminates the different rhythms that governed the lives of women and men in an agricultural society: while men's work was varied and seasonal, women's work was repetitive and daily, and their lives were governed by the needs of others. In a poem describing the duties of the ideal English "huswife," Tusser captured the essence of women's experience in seventeenth-century England:

> I serve for a day, for a week for a yeere,
> For life time, for ever, while men dwelleth
>   here.
> For richer for poorer, from north to the south,
> For honest, for hardhead for daintie of mouth,
> For wed and unwedded, in sickness and
>   health,
> For all that wel liveth, in good common
>   wealth.
> For citie, for countrie, for court and for cart,
> To quiet the head and to comfort the heart.[49]

While most seventeenth-century marriages, regardless of the couple's social or economic status, reflected this complementary division of labor, women often had to assume their partner's role and responsibilities. Wives performed some of their husbands' duties if they were absent for a period of time, and, even among the upper classes, wives acted in their absent husbands' stead, handling business matters and running estates, especially during the period of the Civil Wars. It was made clear, however, that such women were acting at their husbands' request, not in their own behalf. As their husbands' surrogates, they were protecting their families' interests.[50]

WOMEN AND THE MARKETPLACE

Women also played a visible role in the marketplace. As Sir Anthony Fitzherbert remarked in his *Book of Husbandrye* (1555): "It is a wiues occupacion to . . . ride to the market to sell butter, chese, mylke, egges, chekens, kapons, hennes, pygges, gees and al maner of corne. And also to bye al maner of necessary thinges belonging to a houshold, and to make a true rekening & accompt to her husband what she hath receyued and what she hathe payed." Rural women, skilled at dairying, baking, brewing, or weaving, for example, bartered the products of their labor for goods and services they were unable or unwilling to produce for their families. "Fishwives" hawked their husbands' catch or sold the shellfish they themselves had collected along the shore.

In this manner women contributed to their families' maintenance and extended the parameters of their world beyond the house and garden. The marketplace was a social as well as an economic center where women as producers, buyers, and sellers met and interacted, creating a sense of community.[51]

In towns and cities, the wives of craftsmen also assisted their husbands at their work. Because most craftsmen's shops were in their homes, women supervised their husbands' apprentices and journeymen while caring for their children and performing their traditional domestic roles. Some craftsmen relied on their wives to sell their wares, keep the shop books, purchase raw materials, and collect debts, and it was not unusual for the daughters of craftsmen to learn their fathers' trades.[52] Craftsmen's widows were often permitted to continue their husbands' businesses, a testimony to the skills they learned while working with them. As a result, a few women acted as printers and bookbinders, tailors, glovemakers, and tanners of leather in England's growing urban centers.[53]

Some trades, usually extensions of their traditional domestic role, were almost exclusively identified with women. During the seventeenth century women were an elemental part of the English textile industry, spinning and weaving cloth. Many purchased wool at market, spun it into thread at home, and sold the yarn to manufacturers of cloth, while others were supplied with wool by "clothiers" and received piece wages for their work. Spinning for the marketplace enabled women, and the daughters they trained, to augment the family income as they performed their domestic duties. Women were also wax-chandlers, upholsterers, milliners, and mantua makers, and they excelled at the needlework trades. Other women profited from their traditional identification as homemakers by taking in boarders or operating bakery shops in their homes. Brewing was almost exclusively a woman's occupation because housewives brewed beer for their families' consumption. Skilled in the production of the beverage, they dominated its manufacture and trade, and some women operated taverns where they sold their wares.[54]

Women also exploited their traditional association with the healing arts by working as nurses and midwives. Responsible for the care of family members during times of sickness, young women learned rudimentary nursing skills from their mothers. Most housewives knew how to treat minor ailments and create medicines to aid in the cure of illnesses. Virtually all household manuals contained instructions for making medicines and brewing cordials, in addition to recipes for preserving fruits and vegetables. Many women concocted drugs from herbs grown in their kitchen gardens and processed in their own distilleries. While women with these skills were often highly respected in their communities, the power they wielded to cure the sick brought with it the possibility of witchcraft accusation.[55]

Midwifery was one of the most important public professions practiced by women. Women dominated the birth process because men were excluded from childbirth. Most midwives learned their skills through apprenticeship with another midwife. Once trained, there were many calls for their assistance. The demand for midwives cut across class lines; women of all classes served their friends and neighbors in this capacity. Midwives of exceptional intelligence and skill commanded high wages for their services.[56]

As the seventeenth century progressed, expanding markets and growing networks of trade transformed the self-contained economies of England's rural villages and required more efficient methods of production. Labor became more specialized and competitive, and the terms of entry into a craft or trade were formalized and more rigorously enforced. These changes had an adverse affect on many women. Those who informally assisted their fathers and husbands in the workshop or supervised apprentices now discovered that their opportunity to practice a craft was limited. Women were prohibited from learning new production techniques and the use of new tools of the trade. By the end of the century it became less common than before for a widow, or her spinster daughter, to operate her husband's or father's business on his death.[57]

Since divorce and separation were so rare, the majority of marriages ended with the death of the husband or wife. In seventeenth-century England, life expectancy at birth was, on average, 35 years.[58] Because the family was the principle economic unit of production, a husband's death was often economically devastating to his surviving wife. From society's perspective, widows outside the immediate control of men were problematic. They were out of place in a society that defined women as subordinate to, and dependent on, their fathers or husbands.

WOMEN'S LEGAL STATUS

The common law, which evolved in England during the Middle Ages, reinforced male authority and clearly reflected the subordinate, dependent position of women. Established by Henry II during the twelfth century, the common law was born in courts, where judges created legal precedent based on the customs of the people. Their rulings gradually emerged as one law, common to all England and most of its North American colonies during the seventeenth century. Under this law, women's rights were subsumed within those of their fathers, guardians, or husbands. *The Lawes and Resolutions*, written at the end of the sixteenth century and published in 1632, stated that "All [women] are either married or to be married."[59] Eighteenth-century legal commentator William Blackstone, summarizing the position of women in the common law, concluded that with marriage, "the husband and wife are one, and the husband is that one."

With marriage, the woman's possessions became her husband's, and he had lifetime use of her property. He, in turn, had a legal obligation to support her during her lifetime. Under the common law, a widow was entitled to dower rights in one-third of her husband's lands if he died without a will. She was entitled to use this land during her lifetime for her support, but upon her death it descended to her husband's male heirs. In this way, wealth, most frequently defined as land, was transmitted from one generation of men to another.[60]

Because most women found it difficult, if not impossible, to support themselves or their families on their own, the remarriage of widows was customary in England. These women needed the assistance of a husband and wanted the security of marriage. As a result, nearly a quarter of all marriages during the century were remarriages for either the man or the woman. This was especially true among the upper classes, where property was of vital importance in the arrangement of marriages.[61]

Jointures minimized problems in dividing large estates for the support of the widow. The jointure, settled on before the husband's death, gave his widow specific lands or income rather than her "third." Men could not sell or mortgage their wives' dower or jointure lands without their consent. If, however, the value of the jointure fell to less than one-third of the husband's estate, the widow was deprived of an income comparable to dower. She then had the right to choose between the property granted in her jointure or her dower rights.[62]

Women of the upper classes benefited from the creation of equity law developed in the Court of Chancery, established during the fourteenth century. Laws of equity mitigated some of the negative effects of the common law on women and children, especially when substantial property was involved. The Chancery Court legalized trusts that ensured control of a woman's property after marriage by her father or brother and so protected her from exploitation by her husband. Although trusts provided greater economic security for women, they also reinforced the patriarchal nature of English law, permitting fathers to maintain authority over their daughters and their property even after they married.[63] Only the wealthiest women had access to the Court of Chancery and its laws of equity, which were replicated in some of England's colonies during the seventeenth century; the vast majority of women in England and North America lived under the assumptions and restrictions of the common law.

Inheritance patterns in seventeenth-century England also reflected and reinforced the patriarchal nature of English society. Primogeniture was perhaps the most important custom governing the inheritance of property in England. According to its rules, a son inherited before a daughter regardless of her seniority, and the eldest son inherited before his brothers. If there were no sons, all daughters, regardless of their ages, inherited equally, and if the eldest male heir was deceased, his children, male or female, inherited before his brothers or sisters.

Entailment of lands also permitted men to extend their control of their property after their death. By granting land "in tail male," a man secured descent of his lands to his eldest son only, excluding all other sons and daughters. In many cases, as part of marriage settlements, fathers entailed property on their sons, or sons-in-law, to be passed on to their future grandsons. Primogeniture enabled men to control estates into the third generation of male heirs and beyond, and it reinforced the patriarchal and patrilineal nature of English families.[64]

Because upper-class women derived their social rank from fathers or husbands, they had every reason to support and defend the class system that gave them their position. Although English custom and tradition held women inferior to men, women of the upper classes enjoyed a status above lower-class men and women. If gender was the basic common denominator that defined all women's lives, then social class divided women in seventeenth-century England. Beneficiaries of the class system in which they lived, upper-class women willingly carried it with them to the communities they helped establish in North America. Lower-class women, who benefited least from the perpetuation of the English social structure, were more likely to challenge its transplantation to the New World.

*   *   *

During the late sixteenth and early seventeenth centuries, the economic, religious, and social problems that emerged in England led to the founding of colonies in North America. Depression in the countryside displaced women and men who for generations had made their living off the land. The nation's population increased faster than employment opportunities, requiring younger sons along with landless women and men to migrate to towns and cities in search of employment. The surplus of workers drove down the value of real wages, while inflation forced up prices. As the cost of living increased, so, too, did poverty and homelessness. The colonization of North America appeared to be a way of relieving the pressures of population growth, economic depression, and religious dissent.

Transporting English political, religious, and social beliefs to North America, colonists affirmed English values even as they were transformed by the colonizing experience. Women and men who voyaged to England's plantations in North America found security in replicating the institutions, values, and ideals of the Old World. Yet their experiences in the New World demanded that they change, embracing new ideas and values if they were to survive and thrive in their new home.

CHAPTER TWO

From the Old World to the New

She smelled the land before she saw it.

The scent of lush greenness, of life itself, wafted on the salty breeze and penetrated the dank, fetid air of the ship's hold, drawing the young woman up to the deck. The cries of sea gulls soaring overhead drew her eyes to the horizon as she searched for sight of the land that would be her new home. She deeply inhaled the fresh air that blew around her, fragrant with its promise of land. After weeks aboard the crowded ship, England and her family were far behind her, a distant memory. Now she must face her future and make the most of it.

Life in England had been hard. Her family was evicted from the land they had farmed for generations, forcing her to travel to London in search of work. But she lacked skills and wages were low. Food was dear, and she recalled the pangs of hunger that had plagued her and nearly driven her to despair.

Then she heard about someone offering free passage to any maid willing to sail to Virginia. A beautiful place, he said, where there was always plenty to eat—a paradise with so many single men eager to wed that a woman could have her choice of a husband. In return for this opportunity, she had only to agree to work as a servant for five years. Then she was free to do as she pleased. Could it be true?

She had heard the rumors. Of the many who had voyaged to Virginia only to die of disease or starvation or in attacks by the Natives. She heard her friends whisper that to travel there was to court certain death. But did she really have a choice?

What did this new land have in store for her? Hard work, of course. She was used to that. A husband? Children? A home of her own? A chance to begin again, to have the things her mother once had. And if she failed? Well, she thought, death came to everyone—in England or Virginia—and at least she could say she had tried.

She grasped the rail to steady herself as the rolling ship crested a wave. Far in the distance her eyes made out a hazy smudge, more substance than shadow.
"Land-ho! Virginia!"

This young woman who voyaged to Virginia in 1630 embodied the experience of most English women who came to the colonies in the seventeenth century. Young, single, and in search of opportunity and adventure, she reflected the hopes and desires of many who colonized North America. She and the men who traveled with her also transplanted with them ideas and attitudes about the proper role of women and the nature of the family.

If England's North American colonies were to survive, women and families had to go to the New World. Women's migration to the colonies ensured their success and helped transform them from commercial outposts to permanent agricultural settlements. English women's work as wives and indentured servants, aided by the labor of African slave women, enabled colonial economies to grow and prosper. Mothers to a new generation, they helped create English families in the New World. As English women "civilized" the New World, they measured themselves against the Native American women they encountered and the African women they enslaved. They distinguished themselves from women of other races and elevated themselves above them, helping perpetuate the patriarchal, patrilineal culture of the Old World in the New.

English women's values were also challenged as they confronted life in North America. Frontier conditions in most colonies during the seventeenth century demanded flexibility in wives, mothers, and workers. While these women found security in replicating the values of the Old World, they faced the harsh realities of the New World. They must adapt if they were to survive in their new home.

Native American women also tried to maintain the culture and customs of their homeland in the face of English colonization. The colonists underestimated them and derided them for the labor they performed. Ironically, because the importance of Native American women among their own people was devalued by the English, they were perhaps better able than Native American men to defend and preserve their cultural traditions. Nonetheless, as they confronted the destruction of their lands, the violence of war, and the horrors of disease, they, too, were forced to change.

African women struggled to perpetuate the traditions of the land from which they were stolen. Transported to the New World against their will, they tried to re-create life as they had known it in Africa. Adapting to a new environment and adjusting to slavery, they established family ties despite the harsh conditions of their enslavement. Thus, the lives of English, Native American, and African women, linked by continuity and change, divided by race and class, became inextricably intertwined with England's colonization of North America.

REASONS FOR COLONIZATION

During the fifteenth and sixteenth centuries, England authorized voyages of exploration to the New World and laid claim to vast regions of North America, but settlement had to wait until the late sixteenth century. Economic depression and fears of overpopulation prompted England's colonization of the New World. The burgeoning of England's population outpaced economic growth, causing the price of food, clothing, and goods to rise as the value of real wages fell. Property owners evicted tenant farmers and their families from the land, consolidating and enclosing their fields. People who for generations had made their living growing crops were uprooted from the soil. Homeless people searching for work and shelter in cities and towns soon clogged the nation's roads. London, especially, was a powerful magnet attracting those in search of new beginnings.[1]

The disruption of England's economy and the dislocation of its people led many of the upper classes to fear social unrest, especially in the west country and East Anglia—Essex, Suffolk, and Norfolk—centers of the depressed woolen trade. Government officials believed that overpopulation was the cause of England's problems and promoted North America's colonization to siphon off the "surplus population" and prevent disorder.

Well-educated younger sons of English landowners were also enthusiastic about North American colonization. Inheritance customs favored the eldest son, and as the price of land rose it became expensive for parents to purchase property for their younger sons, who then had to provide for themselves. Some joined the military; others chose the law, medicine, the church, or government administration, but many sought their fortunes in the New World. Humphrey Gilbert, Walter Raleigh, John Hawkins, and Francis Drake knew they had to make their way in the world and did so through exploration and colonization abroad.[2]

ENGLAND'S FIRST COLONY

In 1578, Humphrey Gilbert, a soldier who served Queen Elizabeth in the conquest of Ireland, received a patent from her granting him permission to colonize North America. Gilbert's plan included sending Englishmen as well as women and children to the New World. He believed that a successful colony must be self-sufficient and that families would be the source of that self-sufficiency. When Gilbert's plans for establishing a colony in North America were cut short by his death, his half-brother, Sir Walter Raleigh, kept his colonial dream alive.

In 1584 Queen Elizabeth granted Raleigh his brother's patent to colonize North America. While she permitted Raleigh to name his North American lands, known as Windgancon, Virginia in her honor as the virgin queen, she refused to fund his efforts, and he turned to private investors to subsidize his venture. In 1585, Raleigh sent 300–400 soldiers to Virginia under the direction of Captain Ralph Lane. Lacking expert agricultural knowledge and inadequately supplied, they were forced to depend on the Native Americans for food. When the Native Americans' own supplies ran low, warfare resulted, and Lane and his men returned to England in 1586.

The first English women who voyaged to America were sent to Roanoke by Raleigh in 1587. They traveled with their families under the leadership of the colony's governor, the artist John White. Raleigh's decision to send women and families to Roanoke reflected his desire to make the colony agriculturally self-supporting. He promised prospective colonists 500 acres, and men with families were promised even more. Because farming in England was a family enterprise requiring everyone's labor, women were vital to the colony's future. Those who voyaged to Roanoke planned to live there permanently, establishing farms, raising families, and re-creating English society.

Ninety-one men, 17 women, and 9 children arrived in Roanoke in 1587. There were 14 families in this group of settlers, 4 of them composed of a mother, father, and child, and 6 married couples without children. Four men traveled to Virginia with their sons; their wives and daughters planned to join them later. Seven women who came to the colony had no family and were probably servants. John White was accompanied by his daughter, Eleanor, and her husband, tiler and bricklayer Ananias Dare. Eleanor Dare and Margaret Harvie gave birth shortly after arriving in the colony. Dare's daughter, Virginia, was the first English child born in North America.[3]

No one knows what happened to this small, brave band of English settlers, the first to include both women and children. Soon after their arrival at Roanoke, White set sail for England to secure supplies. On his return in 1590, he discovered the settlement abandoned and everyone mysteriously gone. The colonists probably left Roanoke to live with the Croatoan tribe on a nearby island until relief ships arrived, but because White was unable to search for them, they were lost.[4]

The disappearance of the tiny settlement at Roanoke was a setback for English colonization. Although Raleigh understood the importance of women for social and economic growth, it was years before his model of family settlement was adopted by others.[5] The colony established by the Virginia Company of London at Jamestown, Virginia, in 1607 was nearly lost because investors desired immediate profits. Only when company officials recognized that the future of Virginia depended on agriculture, and that women and families were necessary for settlement, was the colony's survival ensured. The transportation of women to Virginia as wives and workers marked a major change in England's North American policy. As Lord Bacon remarked, "When the plantation grows to strength, then it is time to plant with women as well as with men; that the plantation may spread into generations, and not be ever pieced from without."[6]

Even after women's importance in colonizing the New World was acknowledged, Virginia was slow to develop as an outpost of English families. It was not until the end of the seventeenth century that its population grew naturally rather than through immigration. During most of the seventeenth century, the shortage of English women, the hard labor required of them, and the unhealthy environment retarded family formation in the region. With laborers always in short supply, the English family farm was barely able to meet the demands of investors who subsidized colonization. As a result, Africans were imported to work the lands and plantation slavery was introduced to North America.

WOMEN AND FAMILIES IN VIRGINIA

Virginia was colonized in 1607 when 105 English soldiers and adventurers built a fort and trading post at the mouth of the James River. Financed by the Virginia Company of London, the garrison was intended to make money for the company through trade with Native Americans. Men were sent there to discover the Northwest Passage, search for mines of precious metals, and convert the "heathen savages." The reality of Virginia belied these ambitions. The company's men were ill-equipped to meet the rigors of frontier life; inadequately supplied, plagued by disease, and attacked by hostile Powhatan Natives, they had few skills to ensure their survival in the New World.

The first English women arrived at Jamestown in October 1608. Mrs. Forrest and Ann Burras, her maid, typified the kinds of English women—wives and servants—who sailed to Virginia during the seventeenth century. Mrs. Forrest accompanied her husband, artisan Thomas Forrest, to Virginia to make it her home. Anne Burras traveled with her mistress but soon after her arrival married John Laydon, a laborer. In the autumn of 1609 she gave birth to the first English child born at Jamestown. At that time there were only 20 women and children at the garrison/trading post out of a population of 490. Women were scarce because the objectives of the Virginia Company—to trade with Native Americans and to explore the land—did not require their presence. Ill-prepared, ill-supplied, and ill-housed, the colonists quickly deteriorated. In the winter of 1609–10 these harsh conditions took their toll on everyone in the colony.

During the so-called Starving Time of 1609–10, one of the few women in Virginia lost her life. The horror of her death and mutilation was related by Captain John Smith: "[o]ne amongst the rest did kill his wife, powdered her, and had eaten part of her before it was knowne; for which he was executed, as hee well deserved."[7] George Percy claimed that the woman was pregnant and that her husband had "ripped the child out of her womb and threw it into the river, and after chopped the mother in pieces and salted her for his food."[8] Conditions in the colony were brutal.

To ensure the settlement's survival, Governor Thomas Dale established a harsh code of laws acknowledging the need for Virginia to be agriculturally self-sufficient. These laws also recognized English women's presence at Jamestown and assigned and regulated their work: they were to launder, cook, clean, mend, and sew for all the colony's men. Although the laws acknowledged and valued women's skills, they also explicitly stated how women were to perform their duties. Women resented this intrusion into their lives, and Virginia's married men grumbled that were they deprived of their wives' exclusive labor. Finally, the Virginia Company decided to reward hard-working men with lands of their own, hoping that land ownership would promote self-sufficiency. Farming, however, required that more women be brought to Virginia.

In seventeenth-century England, farming was a family occupation. A wife's labor in an agricultural economy released her husband from domestic chores and permitted him to grow crops for consumption and for sale. Within this relationship, the wife was subordinate to her husband, and her labor, although vital, was auxiliary to his. Families motivated, as well as enabled, men and women to improve their holdings. Knowing that their own lives were short, parents worked for the benefit of their children: "We sow, we set, we plant, we build, not so much for ourselves as for posteritie; We practice the workes of Godliness in this life, yet shall we not see the end of our hopes before wee injoy it in the world to come. . . . They which onely are for themselves shall die in themselves, and shall not have a name among posteritie, their rootes shall be dried up beneath, and above shall perish from the earth, and they shall have no name in the streets."[9]

To create a permanent and prosperous settlement, officials of the Virginia Company had to transport women from England. Only when it was understood that women were vital to the colony's success was their scarcity seen as a liability. Women's scarcity gave them a "value" carefully delineated by the men of the company and colony. Women were needed to labor on the farms and to produce the children who would guarantee the colony's future. Their "scarcity value"—as marriage partners and mothers—defined and circumscribed their lives.[10]

The demand for women as wives and workers in Virginia was great and often illegally met. On 19 October 1618 a warrant was issued in Nethersham, England, for the arrest of Owen Evans, accused of "buying" farmers' daughters to send to Virginia. Evans's trial revealed that he offered one poor farmer 12 pence for his daughter, who was then sold into service in the colony. Evans was not the only one acting illegally. Taking advantage of the surplus of young women in the English countryside, wily entrepreneurs kidnapped, enticed, and purchased young women for service abroad.[11]

The Tobacco Brides

So great was the demand for English women in Virginia that the governor petitioned the Virginia Company to send more women. The company's minutes record that "For establishing of a perpetuitie to the Plantation . . . (it was decided) to send them over One hundreth young Maides to become wifes; that wifes, children and families might make them less moveable and settle them, together with their Posteritie in the Soile." Such women were known as Tobacco Brides, for a man fortunate to secure one as his wife was required to pay the cost of her passage, valued by the company at 120 pounds of tobacco.[12]

The Virginia Company recruited virtuous women of "good Commendacon" to be Tobacco Brides. It sought young women willing to be farmers' wives, convincing them their prospects for marriage were better in the New World than in England. Those selected were promised the right to choose their husbands from among the colony's free men. Some doubtless dreamed of marrying men of higher social status than themselves—men who had come to Virginia as adventurers and stayed to farm the land.

The Tobacco Brides were socially respectable young women. Most were daughters of the gentry and artisans, and a few were related to knights. They were required to present the company with letters of recommendation or parish documents attesting to their honesty and virtue. Many were skilled with "thread or needle," as well as in weaving, knitting, lace making, and ornamental embroidering; others were trained in baking, brewing, and making butter and cheese. Some Tobacco Brides were widows, while others were orphans. Most were between the ages of 18 and 21 and had spent some time in London. Outfitted by the Virginia Company, each received a petticoat, a waist-coat, two pairs of stockings, garters, two smocks, a pair of gloves, a hat and bands, a round band, an apron, two pairs of shoes, a towel, two coifs, and one "Croscloth." They also received bedding—six pairs of sheets, beds and bolsters, and six rugs—from the company stores.[13]

The first shipment of 90 "brides" arrived in Virginia on 27 May 1620, and in the winter of 1621 approximately 60 more arrived. By the end of 1621, nearly 150 English women had been transported as Tobacco Brides.[14] Their lives and those of the other women who came to Virginia as wives, daughters, and indentured servants were not easy; conditions were much harsher than in England. Threatened with death by disease, starvation, and attack by hostile Native Americans, they found life a challenge on the frontier.

Many of the women who came to Virginia as Tobacco Brides were probably killed in an attack on the colony by the Powhatan tribe on 22 March 1622. A total of 347 settlers, including 53 women, were killed that day. In the attack at Martin's Hundred, a James River settlement, 78 people lost their lives. Among the 78 victims of this attack, 16 were women, some no doubt Tobacco Brides. In addition to the four "maids" listed among the dead at Martin's Hundred, married women with children, like Thomas Boise's wife and "sucking childe," perished. Finally, many survivors of what became known as the Virginia Massacre died of starvation the following winter.[15]

Women were the majority of those captured for ransom during the Virginia Massacre and later wars between the colonists and Native Americans. Shortly after the attack, the Virginia Company reported that "there are none byt women in Captivitie with the Indians for the men that they took they put them to death."[16] It is possible that Native Americans realized the high value placed on women by the colonists' men and hoped they would pay the ransom demanded for their release.

Jane Dickinson and Sara Boyse were captured during an attack on the fledgling colony. Dickinson was "caried away with the Cruell salvages, amongst them Enduring much misery fir teen monthes," when her ransom was paid by the colony's physician, Dr. Pott. Pott then forced her to repay the ransom by working for him. She petitioned the Virginia Company to release her from this involuntary servitude, but her plea was ignored. Unlike Dickinson, captive Sara Boyse was described as "chief of the prisoners" by virtue of her husband's status in the colony.

Treated well by her captors, she was returned to the settlement "apparreled like one of the Indian Queens," perhaps to curry favor with the colonial government.[17]

Mistress Cicely Jordan tried to take advantage of women's scarcity in Virginia after the massacre of 1622. The colony's minister, the Reverend Greville Pooley, asked Jordan to marry him a few days after her husband's death. He claimed she said yes but wanted to delay announcing their plans until her period of mourning ended. Pooley revealed their engagement, and Jordan emphatically denied she had agreed to wed him and promptly pledged herself to another man. The angry Rev. Pooley sued Jordan for breach of promise but lost. The Virginia Council, however, tried to avert future breach of promise suits by passing a law prohibiting men and women from promising themselves to more than one person at a time. The motive was to protect men from "scheming" women who capitalized on their scarcity in Virginia.[18]

WOMEN'S SCARCITY IN THE CHESAPEAKE

Throughout the seventeenth century, English women remained scarce in the Chesapeake colonies of Virginia and Maryland, founded in 1634 by the Calvert family as a refuge for Roman Catholics, and in South Carolina, settled in 1670. The great number of male immigrants to the southern colonies impeded family formation and hindered natural population growth. To encourage the formation of families, single women were offered 100 acres of land to migrate to Maryland. The colony's men resented this policy when they discovered that some women came to Maryland but remained single. The Maryland Assembly passed a law in 1634 restricting unmarried women's right to own property. A single woman complained that the law "prevented that noe woman here vow chastety in the world, unless she marry within seven years after land shall fall to hir, she must either dispose away of her land, or else she shall forfeite it to the nexte of kinne, and if she have but one Mannor, whereas she canne not alienate it, it is gonne unlesse she git a husband."[19] Single women were also offered land as an incentive to emigrate to South Carolina, and servant women were granted land at the expiration of their indentures there.

During the first decade of Maryland's colonization, men outnumbered women six to one, and from 1650 until the 1680s the ratio of male to female immigrants was three to one. Male immigration to the Chesapeake declined in the 1680s, and the proportion of women to men begin to increase, although at the turn of the century male immigrants surpassed female immigrants by a margin of two and one half to one. It was not until the end of the century that the numbers of women and men in the region began to equalize.[20]

SERVITUDE IN THE CHESAPEAKE

Nearly three-quarters of the English women who migrated to the Chesapeake colonies in the seventeenth century were indentured servants, and they made up one-quarter of the region's servant population.[21] The usual term of service for an indentured servant in the Chesapeake was four or five years. Most servant women were in their early 20s, and many were certainly attracted by the greater chance to marry there than in England.[22] The English women who volunteered for service in South Carolina were enticed by the promise that "If any Maid or single Woman had a desire to go over, they will think themselves in the Golden Age, when Men paid a Dowry for their Wives; for if they be but Civil, and under 50 years of Age, some honest Man or other, will purchase them for their wives."[23]

In 1656 John Hammond published a promotional tract entitled *Leah and Rachel, or, the Two Fruitfull Sisters, Virginia and Maryland*, in which he wrote glowingly of the opportunities for women in the Chesapeake colonies. The women who paid their own passage, he warned, should "sojourn in a house of honest repute, for by their good carriage, they may advance themselves in marriage, by their ill, overthrow their fortunes; and although loose persons seldome live long unmarried if free; yet they match with as desolate as themselves and never live handsomly or are ever respected." Women who signed on as indentured servants could expect to work for a term of four years and then receive a year's supply of corne, "dubble apparrell," and implements to support themselves. Hammond reassured his female readers that "The Women are not (as is reported) put into the ground to worke, but occupie such domestique imployments and housewifery as in *England*, . . . yet som wenches that are nasty, beastly and not fit to be so imployed are put into the ground, for reason tells us they must not at charge be transported and then maintained for nothing."[24]

Despite Hammond's assurances, many women who traveled to the Chesapeake found themselves "put into the ground." Because men were in great demand as laborers in the tobacco fields, the price of their indenture was higher than that of women. A planter unable to afford the labor of a man might instead hire a woman. Prior to 1684, 25 percent of indentured women worked for poor planters and were either their only servant or one of two.[25] A female servant in Ebenezer Cook's satire of life in early Maryland, *The Sot-Weed Factor*, lamented:

> In better Times, ere to this Land
> I was unhappily Trappaned,
> Perchance as well I did appear
> As any lord or lady here.
> Not then a slave for twice two year.
> My cloaths were fashionably new,
> Nor were my shifts of Linnen blue;
> But things are changed, now at the Hoe
> I daily work and barefoot go.
> In weeding corn, or feeding swine,
> I spend my melancholy time.
> Kidnap'd and fool'd I hither fled,
> To shun a hated nuptial Bed.
> And to my cost already find
> Worst Plagues than those I left
>   behind.[26]

Servants were often brutally treated by masters intent on getting the most work from them. Sarah Taylor ran away from Captain and Mrs. Thomas Bradnox of Maryland because they abused her. When she was returned to them, she was whipped with a knotted rope. She ran away again and lived in the woods until she was caught and returned to them once more. Finally, unable to endure her treatment any longer, Sarah took the Bradnoxes to court. She testified that while working in the kitchen, her master and mistress "suddenly fell upon her." While Mrs. Bradnox held her, the Captain beat her "with a great rope's end . . . and so unreasonably that there is twenty-one impressions of blows, small and great, upon her back and arms." As proof of the abuse she endured, Sarah revealed to the court the bruises that covered her body.

Witnesses testified that Captain Bradnox beat the girl for reading and that he exclaimed, "You dissembling jade, what do you with a book in your hand?" Hearing this evidence against the Bradnoxes, the court found in Sarah's favor. Because of "the imminent danger likely to ensue by the inveterate malice of her master and mistress toward her," she was freed from her indenture.

Ann Beetle was less fortunate than Sarah Taylor. Severely beaten by her master and mistress, neighbors testified she suffered a cut over her eye and that her face and clothing were covered with blood. The next day, desperate to escape such cruel treatment, she took her own life. An inquest into her death found that "she drowned herself." The coroner's jury compounded Anne's tragedy by indicting the dead woman for "not having the fear of God before her eyes [and] wilfully murdering herself."[27]

If life in the Chesapeake colonies meant hard work and brutal treatment for many female servants, it also meant the risk of pregnancy. Nearly 20 percent of all indentured women became pregnant during their term of service. Doubtless some of these women were sexually exploited by their masters. Such was the case of Elizabeth Wild, a servant employed by Jacob Lumbrozo. She testified that he took her against her will several times. When she cried out, he covered her mouth with his hand or with a handkerchief, and when she became pregnant with his child, he gave her a potion to induce a miscarriage. Although Lumbrozo was brought before the court for his treatment of Elizabeth, there is no further reference to his case. Later records reveal that he married her, perhaps to prevent her, as his wife, from testifying against him.[28]

Most servant women, however, were probably not sexually exploited by their masters. The work they performed was too valuable to lose. Free from parental supervision and prohibited from marrying during their term of service, these women most likely gave in to sexual coercion and temptation with fellow servants. Pregnancy did not shorten their term of service. If they did not complete their indenture by the time their infants were weaned, their children were bound out by the courts. Unless they compensated their masters for the labor their pregnancy cost them, women were prohibited from marrying and fined for violating the terms of their indenture. Those unable to pay were whipped and sentenced to serve their masters an additional year or more. Because most women or their partners could not compensate their masters and pay their fines, the illegitimate birth rate was high among servant women in the Chesapeake.[29]

Some desperate servant women were accused of murdering their illegitimate children. Maryland servant Elizabeth Harris was tried for killing her baby boy. A witness claimed that he saw her throw a bundle into a river and that when he fished the bundle out of the water, he found a dead infant inside. Margaret Marshguy, a servant in Elizabeth's household, testified that she shared a bed with the accused and never noticed she was pregnant. The jury believed Margaret's testimony and Elizabeth was acquitted of the crime. Other female servants accused of infanticide were examined by a jury of women for evidence that they had recently given birth. If, as in the case of Hannah Jenkins, these women found that she "never had a child to the best of their knowledge," the woman was cleared of all charges against her.[30]

While virtually all single women who migrated to the southern colonies eventually married, most did not wed until they were 24 or 25 years of age, owing to the fact they were barred from marrying while in service.[31] Once married, many discovered that the quality of their lives and their working conditions declined. Because most wed men poorer than their former masters, they worked harder than ever before. Unable to afford the assistance of servants or, later, slaves, these women performed all domestic chores for their families and worked in the fields as well.[32]

MARRIAGE, FAMILY, AND WOMEN'S ROLE IN THE CHESAPEAKE

The English women who settled the Chesapeake had small families. Their fertility was affected by the difficulty of their work, their age at marriage, the prevalence of endemic and epidemic diseases, especially malaria, and the complications of childbirth. The first generation of women settlers, including those who came to the region with their husbands, did not bear their first child until relatively late in their reproductive lives. Most had no more than three or four children.[33] Their daughters married between the ages of 16 and 19 and, consequently, gave birth to one or two children more than their mothers. Because the first generation of Chesapeake women married later than the second generation and risked their lives less often in childbirth, mothers lived slightly longer than their daughters.[34]

During the seventeenth century, the life expectancy of the average woman born in the Chesapeake was 39 years. She married, usually at the age of 20, a man four years older than herself. She bore between four and six children, four or five of whom survived to adulthood. Her first child was usually born during the first year of marriage; subsequent children were born when she was 24, 30, 34, and 37 years of age, taking into account the likelihood of miscarriage and infant mortality. Upon her death at the age of 39, she left young children in her husband's care. He usually remarried a younger woman with children of her own, and they had children together. Because life expectancy for men in the Chesapeake during the seventeenth century was 48 years, a man in his second marriage often left behind upon his death a widow with small children to rear. Life was tenuous and families were fragile.[35]

Although English men outlived women in the region, women were more often widowed because they usually married men older than themselves. The daughters of immigrant women were even more likely than their mothers to marry older men, virtually ensuring their widowhood.[36] Women born in the Chesapeake were freer to choose their husbands than their English counterparts because their parents often did not live long enough to help them select their mates. Some young women, especially heiresses, were victimized by men eager to gain their property, while others married men much older than themselves, the age difference probably exaggerating their husbands' authority over them.[37]

The high mortality meant that men had to trust their wives with their estates. Widows were named executors and willed property, outright, during most of the seventeenth century. Routinely granted far more than the "third" allotted them under English common law, widows were also named guardians of minor children more frequently in the southern colonies.

For many women with children to support, widowhood meant destitution. When Maryland colonist Andrew Hanson died, he left behind four small children. His wife was "big with child with the fifth." Unable to provide for her children, Mrs. Hanson indentured some of them to her friends. The eldest child, nine-year-old Hance, was bound over to Captain Joseph Wickes, who promised to feed, clothe, shelter, and educate the boy. Most widows, concerned that their own death might place their children at risk, quickly remarried.[38]

The experiences of Affra Harleston Coming and Judith Giton reflect the harsh conditions and the opportunities many women found in the southern colonies during the seventeenth century. Affra Harleston was one of the first English women to voyage to South Carolina. A gentleman's daughter, she traveled to the colony as a "servant" with the family of Joseph Dalton. Shortly after her arrival, she married John Coming, first mate of the ship on which she had sailed. Like earlier settlers in the Chesapeake, Affra Coming found South Carolina's climate unhealthy and frontier conditions appalling. She wrote to her sister in Dublin lamenting that "the whole country is full of trouble and sickness, 'tis the Small pox which has been mortal to all sorts of the inhabitants." She reported that the settlement experienced an earthquake and a fire that had destroyed buildings and livestock, including some of her own cattle, and concluded that these events made "the place look with a terrible aspect & none knows what will be the end of it."[39] Because her husband was often at sea, Affra managed the couple's estate. Over a nine-year period she and her husband acquired 1,760 acres of land. They received 325 acres more in trade for their property at Oyster Point, a spit of land between the Ashley and Cooper Rivers, that became the site of Charles Town, the colony's capital.

Judith Giton, a young French Huguenot, left a vivid account of the hard labor required of women on the southern frontier. Born in France to a wealthy family, at the age of 20 she fled religious persecution following the revocation of the Edict of Nantes and with her family sought passage to Carolina in 1685. Shortly after her arrival, Judith married a fellow émigré, Noe Royer. She and her husband felled trees and cultivated their land, earning enough to purchase a lot in Charles Town. This gently reared young woman described the harsh conditions she found in North America: "After our arrival in Carolina we suffered all sorts of evils. . . . We . . . have been exposed, since leaving France, to all kinds of afflictions, in the forms of sickness, pestilence, famine, poverty and the roughest labor. I have been for six months at a time in this country without tasting bread laboring meanwhile like a slave in tilling the ground. Indeed I have spent three or four years without knowing what it was to eat bread whenever I wanted it."[40]

When her husband died in 1699, Judith married another émigré of good family, Pierre Manigault, and in 1704 gave birth to the couple's only son, Gabriel. While her husband operated a distillery and cooperage in Charles Town, Judith took in boarders to supplement their income. By the time of her death in 1711, Judith and Pierre Manigault had established the foundations of one of the greatest fortunes in colonial America.[41]

Although the ease and profitability of tobacco cultivation attracted great numbers from England, the Chesapeake's economy changed over the course of the seventeenth century. Overproduction of tobacco and falling prices required planters to diversify. The demand for workers remained high, but fewer men were attracted to the region as servants because they found less opportunity for advancement there. Those who came commanded shorter terms of service and higher "freedom dues." Many men, completing their terms of service, left the region to seek their fortunes elsewhere. Planters who could afford to do so replaced their servants with African slaves. While the majority of colonists continued to rely on the labor of their families and hired servants and perhaps a slave or two, a few wealthy planters invested heavily in slave labor and quickly outdistanced their neighbors.[42]

The growing dependence of planters on African labor led to the creation of a social and racial hierarchy in the southern colonies. Women whose husbands employed servants or purchased slaves were freed from laboring in the fields and distinguished their work from that of Africans. They turned their attention to the duties of the traditional English "huswife," spinning and weaving and cheese and butter making. Some taught these skills to slave women, supervising them at their labor. The nature of a woman's work became the measure of her husband's status and wealth. Poor white women strove to emulate wealthier women, whose lives, at least on the surface, appeared easier than their own.

By the early eighteenth century, English colonists were finally able to implement the "domestic patriarchalism" of their mother country. As the children of the first colonists grew to adulthood and had children of their own, the sex ratio in the Chesapeake colonies began to equalize, life expectancy increased, and the region's white population began to naturally grow.[43] Men lived longer and were able to assert their authority over wives and children as they had in England. Willing labor and land to their sons, wealthy men created a foundation for a colonial aristocracy of inherited wealth and power, the English patriarchal family.[44] Because it was no longer necessary for women to serve as their husbands' executors and as guardians of their children, upper-class women returned to the legally dependent, "protected" position typical in England.[45]

THE SETTLEMENT OF NEW ENGLAND

In contrast to those who settled the southern colonies, women who voyaged to the New England colonies during the seventeenth century were able to more quickly replicate the world they had left behind in England. New England was colonized by religious dissenters, seeking freedom from persecution, and Puritans, hoping to establish a model religious community. Recognizing that women were necessary for implementing their "mission in the wilderness," religious leaders encouraged their migration. As a result, many more women migrated to New England than to the southern colonies during the seventeenth century. Their number and their acknowledged importance in the colonial enterprise affected their experience in the New England colonies.

The majority of women who traveled to the Puritan colonies of Plymouth, Massachusetts, Connecticut, and New Hampshire came as members of patriarchal families. Most accompanied their husbands and fathers to New England or joined them after they had established homes. There they lived under the supervision of men, guided by the religious beliefs of their leaders. The resulting families gave New England a stability and order absent in the southern colonies, permitting the reconstruction of the world left behind. The many children they bore defined the parameters of New England women's lives and provided the foundation for the region's prosperity and growth.

The settlement of New England began with the founding of Plymouth Colony in 1620 by a band of English "separatists," known as the Pilgrims. A radical, nonconformist group that developed in England during the 1570s, the Pilgrims espoused greater religious individualism and desired a more direct relationship with God than the Anglican Church allowed. Although loyal to the English government, they broke away—separated—from the Anglican Church, which they deemed too Catholic, impure and beyond hope of reform, and created their own simple churches where they practiced their faith. For their actions, they were persecuted, fined, and imprisoned by the English government, especially during the reign of James I.

Seeking freedom to practice their faith undisturbed, Separatists from the small village of Scrooby in Nottinghamshire fled England for the Netherlands in 1607. There, under the leadership of William Brewster and William Bradford, these artisans, farmers, craftsmen, and their families lived first in Amsterdam and later in Leyden, where they worshipped in peace. In time, however, these simple men and women feared their children were being corrupted by the worldliness of Leyden. They resolved to leave the Netherlands and move to North America, where they might live free from persecution and temptation.[46]

On 16 September 1620, 102 colonists set sail from Southampton, England, on board the *Mayflower*, destined for Virginia. Eighty-seven were Separatists or members of Separatist families. The journey lasted more than nine weeks, and by the time the ship made landfall at what is now Provincetown on Cape Cod, virtually all on board were ill. William Bradford, the group's leader, took part in a reconnaissance voyage around the Cape. When he returned to the anchored ship he discovered that his wife, Dorothy May Bradford, had drowned. Although he later wrote that his "dearest consort, accidentally falling overboard, was drowned in the harbor," it is probable that Bradford's wife committed suicide. One can only wonder what Dorothy Bradford thought as she gazed upon the bleak winter shoreline of the Cape and contemplated her future in the New World.[47] Ill with scurvy and weak from malnutrition, the Pilgrims were unprepared for their first New England winter. By the spring of 1621, nearly half had perished. Members of the Wampanoag tribe, whose villages had been decimated by disease before the Pilgrims arrived, shared their food with the starving settlers and taught them how to survive.

Initially, Plymouth Colony's residents worked together for the benefit of all. Their leaders believed that "the taking away of property and bringing in community into a commonwealth would make them happy and flourishing." This experiment at a "common course" failed, however, because the colony's men "did repine that they should spend their time and strength to work for other men's wives and children without recompense." The women also resented having to work for all the men and made their displeasure known: "for men's wives to be commanded to do service of other men, as dressing their meat, washing their clothes, etc., they deemed it a kind of slavery, neither could many husbands well brook it." Finally, the leaders conceded defeat and divided the lands among the families present. Husbands and wives then worked together to provide for their children as they had in England, and women shouldered responsibilities that they had refused to perform. Governor Bradford noted: "The women now went willingly into the field, and took their little ones with them to set corn; which before would allege weakness and inability; whom to have compelled would have been thought great tyranny and oppression."[48]

The survival of the Separatists at Plymouth and the religious persecution of other nonconformists in England prompted a massive migration of men and women to New England in the decades that followed. In 1628, a group of Congregationalists established a settlement at Cape Ann, north of Cape Cod, and the following year more than a thousand souls traveled to the colony of Massachusetts, most settling in or near the town of Boston. Led by Governor John Winthrop and the Reverend John Cotton, they worked to create a model Christian community in New England, and by 1643 nearly 20,000 had joined them there.

NEW ENGLAND WOMEN'S LIVES

New England's colonists were far more successful in surviving the rigors of the American frontier than those in the Chesapeake. By 1700, the two regions had roughly the same population, although seven or eight times as many settlers had voyaged to Maryland and Virginia than to the northern colonies. Where women's scarcity and the high mortality rate had retarded population growth in the southern colonies during the seventeenth century, the many women who migrated to New England coupled with its low mortality rate ensured rapid population growth. The life experience of New England women contrasted dramatically with that of women who remained in England or journeyed to the Chesapeake. Unlike the first generation of women new to the southern colonies, Plymouth's women married much earlier; by the end of the century the average age of women at marriage was only 22.[49]

Because the New England climate was healthier, northern mothers lost fewer children to miscarriage, stillbirth, and infant death than southern mothers. The first generation of Plymouth women bore an average of 7.8 children, 7.2 of whom lived to maturity. Their daughters gave birth to an average of 8.6 children and saw 7.5 live to adulthood, while their granddaughters averaged 9.3 children, 7.9 surviving to the age of 21. While 40–55 percent of all children born in the Chesapeake died before they reached adulthood, nearly 80 percent of all children born in New England survived to the age of 20.[50] Because few women came to New England as indentured servants who were prohibited from marrying while under contract, premarital pregnancy and illegitimate birth rates were low. At the same time, the religious beliefs of the early settlers also discouraged prenuptial sexual relations, and these beliefs were rigorously enforced for most of the century.[51]

People in New England lived longer than those in England or the southern colonies. The life expectancy of first-generation men was 71.8 years, while women lived, on average, 70.8 years. Their children, too, could expect to live long lives. New England–born men lived, on average, 64.2 years, while second-generation women had a life expectancy of 61.6 years. Women lived nearly as long as men once they survived their childbearing years, although childbirth was probably not as hazardous to women in this region and century as was once thought.[52] Women could expect to outlive men once they reached the age of 60, and nearly 40 percent of all women reached the age of 70. Consequently, elderly women were not uncommon in colonial New England (figure 1).[53]

Despite news of New England's healthier climate, not all women were eager to leave their homeland or join their husbands in the North American wilderness. In July 1632, John Winthrop, governor of Massachusetts, complained: "I have much difficultye to keepe John Gallope heere by reason his wife will not come." Winthrop did not understand Mistress Gallope's hesitation, commenting, "I marvayle at her womans weaknesse, that she will live myserably with her children [in England] when she might live comfortably with her husband here."[54]

Many women found it difficult to face the ocean voyage and the uncertainty of a new life in a strange land. The wife of minister John Dunton was reluctant to join her husband in New England, wryly remarking that she would rather be "a living wife in England than a dead one at sea."[55] Even the poet Anne Dudley Bradstreet admitted that leaving England was difficult. She recalled that she "came into this Country, where I found a new world and new manners, at which

Figure 1. Anne Pollard. *Courtesy, The Massachusetts Historical Society, Boston, Massachusetts.*

my heart rose. But after I was convinced it was the way of God, I submitted to it."[56]

John Winthrop was probably most embarrassed that his own sister, Lucy, hesitated to follow her husband, Emmanuel Downing, to New England. She managed to postpone her migration for nearly eight years. Practical doubts about the success of the enterprise, not "womanly weakness," influenced her decision to delay. She wrote to her brother John: "I must then deal plainlie with you, and let you know that many good people hear, and some that understand new Engl. resonable well . . . they do much feare the country cannot afford subsistence for many people, and that if you were not supplyed of incomes from hence, your lives would be very miserable." She also astutely remarked, "I hear not of any commodities from thence yet, as can furnish your necessities much less inrich you." Despite her misgivings, however, Lucy Downing eventually joined her husband in Massachusetts, settling in the town of Salem in 1638.[57]

QUAKER WOMEN

Like the religious dissenters who founded the New England colonies, members of the Society of Friends, also known as Quakers, brought to England's American colonies a religious philosophy that reinforced family migration and colonization.[58] The Quakers believed in the spiritual equality of women and men and encouraged mutual love as the basis for marriage. They saw marriage as a partnership rather than an authoritarian relationship and encouraged mutual respect between husband and wife. Secure in loving, egalitarian relationships and urged to be fruitful and multiply by religious leaders, Quaker women were more fertile than their non-Quaker counterparts. Their fertility often strained family finances, however, and family poverty meant that children often had to leave home at an early age to support themselves. Free from parental supervision, many children married outside the Quaker faith. Fearing the corruption of their children and the end of their religion, some Quakers with large families chose to leave England and carve out new homes in its North American colonies.[59]

Their beliefs about marriage and the importance of the family helped Quakers adapt to the New World. In Pennsylvania, a colony established by William Penn in 1681 as a refuge for practitioners of their faith, Quaker women bore between five and six children who survived to adulthood. Their families were somewhat smaller than those of Puritan women because Pennsylvania-born women married slightly later than their New England counterparts. Quaker parents made their children financially independent when they married, customarily giving their sons land and their daughters cash. By delaying marriage, daughters received larger dowries. Consequently, women's age at marriage remained relatively constant in the region for three generations. The living conditions and the rich lands of the middle colonies shaped the lives of Quaker women and their families in North America. Cooperation between women and men, an outgrowth of their beliefs about marriage, facilitated their settlement and survival in North America.[60]

Whatever their religious beliefs, the first generation of English women in North America had reason to be anxious about life in the New World. In the early years of settlement in the Chesapeake, they faced possible death by starvation and disease, and in all the colonies they risked attack by Native Americans, resentful of the foreign intruders who stole their land, depleted their resources, and destroyed their culture.

NATIVE AMERICAN WOMEN

Long before they journeyed to the colonies, English settlers heard stories about the Natives of North America. Since the time of Columbus, tales of encounters between explorers and "Indians" circulated through the courts and coffee houses of Europe. In many ways, however, the reports that described Native Americans were deceptive. Either idealized as a gentle, childlike people or vilified as brutal savages, Native Americans were certain to be misunderstood by the English colonists who encountered them in the New World.

A report written by scientist Thomas Hariot and illustrated by John White promoting Raleigh's colony at Roanoke gave many English men and women their first glimpse of the people who inhabited North America. In addition to describing the region and listing the commodities that might be grown there for profit, Hariot's report also included observations about Native Americans. White's drawings of Roanoke's women and men, however, are more valuable than the report. Richly detailed and remarkably free of English racial bias, his art provides a portrait of these people and their culture before colonization destroyed their way of life.

The inhabitants of Roanoke Island, located on the outer banks of present-day North Carolina, were coastal Algonquins who shared a common linguistic base and culture with other tribes in the region. Depending primarily on agriculture for their survival, these Middle Atlantic tribes also fished, hunted, and gathered along the rivers and streams of their homeland. Those living near the sea harvested its riches to augment their diet; those farther inland depended on hunting to supplement the crops they raised and to provide them with resources for trade.[61]

According to Hariot's report and White's drawings, the Roanoke tribe lived in villages of around 200 people. Their leaders were housed in long, wooden-framed, arched-roofed structures, some nearly 30 feet in length, arranged around a commons and surrounded by a palisade. The walls of their homes were made of mats woven by the women, which could be rolled up or down for ventilation. A hearth for cooking and heating was located in the middle of each building. The rest of the tribe lived in similar structures outside the fenced area, close to the fields where their crops were grown.

The Roanoke people farmed their lands. While both women and men prepared the fields for planting, White's watercolors show the women growing the maize, beans, pumpkins, sunflowers, gourds, and herbs that fed their people. Roanoke women planted and harvested three successive crops during the growing season, from May until September. The men hunted or fished to supplement their diet, and grew and cured the tobacco used for medicinal, recreational, and religious purposes.

White's richly detailed drawings of the women demonstrate his fascination with their activities and appearance. His portraits of important women illustrate how their attire reflected their age, position, and tribal affiliation. To indicate their status and their tribe, women adorned their bodies with painted and tattooed ornamentation in the form of necklaces, bracelets, and headbands. They tied up their long hair with leather thongs decorated with shells and feathers (figure 2).

Unlike their English counterparts, Roanoke women wore little clothing. In warm weather, most wore only a cloth or dressed skin wrapped

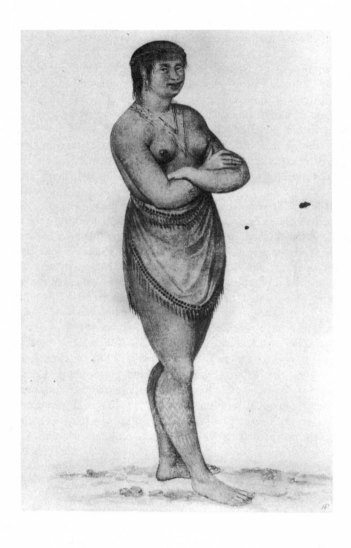

Figure 2. "The wyfe of an Herowan of Secotan." Artist: John White, circa 1585. *Courtesy, the Trustees of the British Museum.*

around their waists, enabling them to move freely. Their breasts were bare. Hariot commented favorably on the modesty of the women, revealing his assumption that nudity and immodesty went hand in hand.

White's drawings depicted the women as loving mothers who placed their infants in cradleboards shortly after birth. This permitted them to carry their infants to the fields and tend them while they worked. One watercolor shows a woman carrying a toddler on her back (figure 3), while another pictures a young girl, diapered in moss, holding an English doll made for her by one of the colonists (figure 4). According to White, Native American children of both sexes wore no clothing at all during the warm months until they reached the age of ten. Hariot's report and White's drawings provide us with a rare look at women's lives within Native American culture before England's conquest and colonization of the region.[62]

Most agricultural Algonquin tribes—from the Hurons of southern Ontario to the Creeks of what is now Alabama and including the Roanoke Natives—were matrilineal. This is because the biological tie between a mother and her child was incontrovertible, while the paternity of a child was less certain. Native Americans viewed female sexuality differently from Europeans. Bridal virginity and a woman's marital fidelity, devised to ensure paternal lineage in England, were unimportant to them. Most Algonquin women were sexually active before they married, their fertility far more important than the paternity of their children.[63]

Because men were often away hunting, fighting, and trading for lengthy periods, women, tied to the soil, provided stability and cultural continuity. Children were born into their mother's clan and reared with their cousins. Their mother's people—her mother or sisters, for example—were their closest kin. In the absence of their biological fathers, their maternal uncles were the most important men in their lives.

In most Algonquin tribes, women preserved the traditions of their society and provided stability for their people. Their authority was greater in agricultural tribes than among hunters, because they were responsible for feeding their people. They also wielded more authority at the village level, where their daily contributions were acknowledged and respected. Leadership in matrilineal clans was determined by a man's maternity; a woman's eldest son usually assumed the mantle of

Figure 3. "The wyfe of an Herowan of Pomeiooc." Artist: John White, circa 1585. *Courtesy, the Trustees of the British Museum.*

Figure 4. "A cheife Herowans wyfe of Pomeoc and her daughter the age of. 8. or. so. yeares." Artist: John White, circa 1585. *Courtesy, the Trustees of the British Museum.*

authority. Often women elders selected the village leaders, most of whom were men. Women frequently decided whether to avenge the death of a clan member or adopt a captive into their clan. In this way they influenced matters of war and peace. They also could undermine men's decision to wage war by refusing to supply warriors with moccasins or provisions. While at the tribal level only the Iroquois formally institutionalized the role of women elders, empowering them to nominate or depose chiefs, in a few coastal Algonquin tribes women actually inherited the office of chief. The English identified these women sachems as the sisters or wives of male leaders, assuming they inherited their brothers' or husbands' authority. More likely, however, the men's authority was derived from their relationships to the women.[64]

Their practice of spiritual and healing arts also qualified Native American women for leadership in their villages. At the time of European contact, Native American men did not completely control the sacred in their culture; the only coastal Algonquin culture with a formalized male priesthood was in the Chesapeake. Virtually everywhere else, women participated actively in the religious life of their tribes and wielded spiritual authority.[65]

Native American women also enjoyed indirect power as the wives of leaders, who often married more than one woman to cement kinship ties with other tribes. A leader's first wife was usually the most important, and it was imperative that she come from a highly ranked lineage. Other wives from other lineages strengthened and united the tribe.[66]

Much of our knowledge of Native American culture comes from the observations of European men. Because English authorities most often had contact with tribal leaders, usually male, they assumed that men held all positions of authority. The English did not understand Native American kinship systems and, consequently, underestimated the importance of Native American women in tribal life. At the same time, they viewed Native Americans through the gender bias of their own culture, distorting what they saw.

Beginning in the sixteenth century, contact with the English changed the lives of Native Americans, and altered the role of women within their communities. As trade between these peoples grew, Native economies were transformed. The English desire for furs required that Native American men spend more time away from their villages hunting. As a result, the lives of Native Americans became even more segregated.

In agricultural villages, women assumed the responsibilities of the absent men. At the same time, however, the increased emphasis on hunting skills as a result of the English fur trade diminished women's economic importance in their tribes.[67]

The English in North America were greatly outnumbered by the Native Americans. Unwilling to admit they had much to learn from those whose land they seized, the colonists searched for ways to justify their conquest. English men and women believed their culture to be far superior to that of the Natives and were unwilling to see the similarities between their cultures or the weaknesses of their own. And they were especially incapable of appreciating the role of Native American women in their own culture.

English men compared Native American women with their English counterparts and found them wanting in every way. Native American women built houses, tended crops, gathered wood, and hauled heavy loads. In England, this was considered men's work, and men claimed superiority over women because they performed it.[68] That Native American women capably performed these jobs challenged English men's sense of masculinity and their fundamental beliefs. English men criticized Native American men for permitting women to do this work. John Smith observed: "The men bestow their times in fishing, hunting, warres, and such man-like exercises, scorning to be seen in any woman-like exercise, which is the cause that the women be very painefull, and the men often idle. The women and children doe the rest of the worke. They make mats, baskets, pots, mortars, pound their corne, make their bread, prepare their victuals, plant their corne, gather their corne, beare all kinds of burdens, and such like."[69]

English women also criticized the work Native American women performed. Defining themselves in terms of the domestic sphere of house and kitchen garden, English women disparaged Native American women for their work in the fields. To work like a "squaw" was thought the ultimate degradation by English women, incapable of understanding or appreciating the authority Native American women derived from their work. Certainly English women did not wish to emulate the Native women they encountered in North America.

Most English men were quick to note the physical differences between Native American and English women. While a few commented favorably on the former's appearance, most found their darker skin unattractive, attributing its tawny color to the application of dyes and excessive exposure to the sun. Valuing whiteness as evidence of racial superiority and moral purity, the colonists saw Native Americans as "discolored" and racially inferior to themselves. Native American women were thought ugly and immoral in contrast to white-skinned, "moral" English women. The ideal English woman was a virgin before marriage and faithful thereafter; Native American women were libidinous, provocative, and sexually promiscuous. Projecting on Native American women their own sexual fantasies and anxieties, English men debased them.[70]

Despite, or perhaps because of, these views of Native American women, informal liaisons between them and English men were probably more common than is known throughout the colonial period. Many tribes provided distinguished visitors with "a woman fresh painted red with *Pocones* and oile to be his bedfellow." In most coastal Algonquin tribes, married women were free to choose their sexual partners, a fact that English men had difficulty comprehending. Such sexual freedom was quite different from the behavior they demanded of women at home. Assuming, therefore, that all Native American women were available sexual partners, English men probably took them against their will. Virginia's "Lawes Divine, Moral, and Martiall" punished the rape of any woman, "maid or Indian," with death, reflecting fears about the male colonists' conduct and the desire to protect the colony from attack by Native American men.[71]

The English government condemned intermarriage with Native American women, and few marriages between the two races were recorded throughout the seventeenth century. The absence of interracial marriages is especially noteworthy in the southern colonies, where English women were scarce and the potential for miscegenation was great. English men's fear of Native Americans and their anxiety about survival militated against marriage with Native American women, especially those of the Powhatan tribe encountered at Jamestown.

POCAHONTAS

The Powhatan Confederacy was a loose alliance of Algonquin tribes in the Chesapeake forged by the sachem Wahunsunacock, more commonly known as Powhatan, just before England's colonization of Virginia in 1607. Captain John Smith respected Powhatan and sought an understanding of his people to ensure the survival of the colony. A careful, although biased, observer of Native American culture, Smith was one of the few English men to recognize the importance of women in Powhatan society. He acknowledged a woman chief among the Powhatans whom he called the "Queene of Appamatuck." The elder sister of Powhatan, she attended several tribal councils, including the one that allegedly sentenced the captured Smith to death. His life was saved by Powhatan's daughter, Matoaks, also known as Pocahontas. As Smith remembered: "as many as could layd hands on him, dragged him to them, and thereon laid his head, and being ready with their clubs, to beate out his braines, Pocahontas the Kings dearest daughter, when no intreaty could prevaile, got his head in her armes, and laid her owne upon his to save him from death: whereat the Emperour was contented he should live to make him hatchets and her bells, beads, and copper."[72]

The life of Pocahontas has been obscured by myth and romance. A favorite of John Smith, who first met her when she visited Jamestown as "a child of tenne years old," Pocahontas played freely in the town's streets and learned the English language. When war with the Powhatans threatened in 1613, she was kidnapped and held hostage in Jamestown to ensure peace. There Pocahontas was baptized in the Anglican faith and given the baptismal name Rebecca, derived from the Hebrew word for "binding." Her conversion was part of the colonists' strategy to ally themselves with Powhatan and suggests that some English leaders recognized her position in her tribe.[73]

During her captivity in Jamestown, John Rolfe resolved to marry Pocahontas. Theirs was one of the few sanctioned marriages between an English man and a Native American woman during the seventeenth century. Rolfe's decision to marry Pocahontas created an ugly controversy in the colony, and he was required to seek permission from the Virginia Company in England. Rolfe assured the company that he wished to wed "for the good of this plantation, for the honor of our country, for the glory of God, for my own salvation, and for the converting to the true knowledge of God and Jesus Christ [of] an unbelieving creature, namely Pocahantas [*sic*]." He described his future wife as "one whose education hath been rude, her manners barbarous, [and] her generation accursed," revealing the English prejudice against those unlike themselves. Rolfe angrily defended himself against charges that he wished to marry Pocahontas because of "unbridled desire of carnal affection": "let them know [that] it is not [from] any hungry appetite to gorge myself with incontinency. [To be] sure, (if I would, and were so sensually inclined), I might satisfy such desire—though not without a seared conscience, yet with Christians more pleasing to the eye and less fearful in the offence unlawfully committed."[74] The stigma of inter-marriage in early Virginia was overcome only by colonists' need to secure peace with Native Americans.

Governor Dale acknowledged the diplomatic value of marriage to a Native American woman when he asked for the hand of Powhatan's youngest daughter. Powhatan bluntly refused Dale's request, stating that only if Pocahontas died was he willing to permit another daughter to marry an Englishman. Although it was customary for chiefs to have more than one wife, Powhatan probably knew that this was not true for the English. He might also have learned that Dale had a wife in England and could not marry his daughter in a Christian ceremony. Powhatan correctly deduced that Dale simply wanted to secure an additional hostage for peace in Jamestown.[75]

Unfortunately, we do not know what Pocahontas thought of John Rolfe or how she viewed her marriage. She was probably already married to a Native American and had a child when she wed Rolfe. A woman of importance in her tribe, she understood the value of an alliance with the English and performed her duty to her father and her people. In 1615, she gave birth to a son, Thomas, and the next year, with a retinue including two half-sisters, three Native women and four Native men, traveled to England with her husband. The Virginia Company of London hoped her appearance at court would promote investment in the colony.[76]

In England Pocahontas visited her old friend John Smith, who left Virginia in 1609. In his account of their meeting, Smith described this remarkable young woman as small in stature but great in spirit. A stranger in a strange land, Pocahontas criticized Smith for neglecting her and berated him for not treating her as a father would a daughter. She asked him: "Were you not afraid to come into my fathers countrie, and caused feare in him and all his people (but me) and feare you here I should call you father; I tell you then I will, and you shall call mee childe, and so I will bee for ever and ever your Countrieman."[77]

Pocahontas's portrait was painted during her visit to England. Because the English believed Christian women should modestly cover their nakedness, she wore English clothing. Although richly attired in silk and velvet ornamented with lace and gold, befitting her position as a Native "princess," Pocahontas's copper colored skin, dark eyes, and high cheekbones betray her Native American heritage (figure 5).

Tragically, while preparing to return to her homeland in 1617, Pocahontas fell ill with a respiratory ailment, possibly tuberculosis, and died. She was buried at the St. George's Parish Church in Gravesend. Her death marked the end of a peaceful era in Native American–English relations.

English Racism

Although the Native American women who accompanied Pocahontas to England were sent to the English colony of Bermuda as brides for men there, intermarriage between Native Americans and the English was discouraged by the Virginia Company and the English government. Only three other such marriages—all between Native American women and English men—were recorded, in 1644, 1684, and 1688. Perhaps another reason for the few interracial marriages was English men's fear that their Native American wives might conspire against them. Ironically acknowledging the autonomy of Native American women in their own culture, English men did not try to dominate them sexually in order to subordinate Native American men. Instead, they feared that submission to Native American women's charms might destroy their fragile hold on the New World. Finally, most Native American women were probably not attracted to English men and found little reason to abandon their own culture for another. Native American women would have found women's position in English culture inferior to their own.[78]

In 1691 the Virginia House of Burgesses forbade marriage between English settlers and the Africans, mulattoes, and Native Americans in the colony. English women were barred from marrying men of color and "tainting" the purity of their race. Whether this act was passed because miscegenation had already occurred or because white men feared it might is not known. Punishment for violating this statute was banishment from the colony. Certainly English women who embodied the gender and racial beliefs of their mother country saw alliances with

Figure 5. Pocahontas, circa 1595–1617. Unidentified Artist. *Courtesy, National Portrait Gallery, Washington, D.C./Art Resource, New York.*

Native American or African men as beneath them. There is no record of an English woman marrying a Native American in the Chesapeake during the seventeenth century, probably because white women were scarce in the region and had their choice of English men as marriage partners.[79]

The New England colonists held the same attitudes about race as their southern counterparts. They looked upon Native Americans as culturally and racially inferior to themselves, despite their dependence on Native American generosity during the first years of settlement. Colonial leaders asserted their "God-given" right to the Natives' lands and were surprised in 1636 when several New England tribes, including the Pequots, banded together to fight back. At war's end, the Pequots were defeated and the region's Native American population was reduced by 75 percent. Captive women and children were enslaved to work in colonists' homes and Native American men were shipped to England's Caribbean colonies as slaves. Subject Native Americans were forced to adopt the English way of life, wear European clothing, farm the land as the English did, and model themselves after their conquerors. Others submitted to the ministrations of Puritan missionaries, converted to Christianity, and moved into "praying Indian" towns. While those who had survived the vicious war struggled to retain their identity in the face of English expansion, the colonists' interpreted their victory as a reflection of God's will, reinforcing their sense of racial and religious superiority.[80]

In 1675 a second major war, led by the Wampanoag chief Metacomet, devastated New England. Metacomet, also known as King Philip, created an alliance of tribes to wage war against the English settlers and drive them from his lands. Fifty-two New England towns were attacked and 12 completely destroyed, and thousands of English settlers and Native Americans lost their lives before the English were victorious. In the end, Metacomet was killed and his wife and son were sold into slavery in the West Indies. Surviving Native Americans were forced to live under English supervision and adopt the behavior and values of their conquerors.[81]

Racial animosity also fueled South Carolina's trade in Native American slaves. Captured in warfare by coastal tribes allied with the English, most slaves were sold to the West Indies and the New England colonies. By 1708, the population of South Carolina included about 5,300 white settlers, 2,900 African slaves, and 1,400 Native American slaves. A bitter critic of this Native American slave trade wrote that the English slave traders "ravish the wife from the Husband, Kill the father to get the Child and to burne and Destroy the habitations of these poore people into whose Country wee were Charefully received by them, cherished and supplyed when wee are weake, or at least never have done us hurt."[82]

English women felt little sympathy for the Native American women whose homes and families were destroyed by warfare. Having lost their fathers, husbands, and sons and witnessed the destruction of their homes in the region's wars, they, too, sought the defeat of New England's Native American population. In a chilling example of racial hatred, the women of Marblehead, Maine, brutally assaulted the Native Americans who threatened their homes and families. Warfare with local tribes dragged on in the region, long after the death of Metacomet, and in 1677, two Natives, who had attacked fishing ships crewed by men from Marblehead, were captured and brought to town. On Sunday, 15 July, "the women at Marblehead, as they came out of the meeting-house, fell upon two Indians that were brought in as captives, and in a tumultuous way, very barbarously murdered them." A mariner noted that "with stones, billets of wood, and what else they might, they made an end of these Indians." The "vengeful women of Marblehead" literally tore the captives apart, flaying and beheading them. Stunned, the mariner remarked, "[s]uch was the tumultation these women made, that for my life I could not tell who these women were, or the names of any of them." These English women so violated this Englishman's assumptions about women's gentle nature that he could not or would not identify them.[83]

SLAVERY IN THE COLONIES

The racism of English women and men was made worse by the presence of African slaves in the colonies. The first Africans brought to England's North American colonies were transported by a Dutch ship and arrived at Jamestown in 1619. These women and men were probably treated as servants rather than slaves, and their indentures were sold to planters eager for their labor. By 1630, however, legal distinctions existed between Africans and white servants in Virginia, and their labor was valued differently. The popularity of African slavery grew slowly in the Chesapeake, and as late as 1671 slaves were less than 5 percent of Virginia's population. By 1700, however, they made up one-fifth of the Maryland population and were the majority of the colony's workers.[84]

African slaves were introduced to New England around the time of the Pequot War, and by 1641 slavery was encoded into Massachusetts law.[85] Although other New England colonies also acknowledged the legality of slavery, the institution grew slowly in the region during the century. In 1700, there were only about 1,000 African slaves in New England out of a total of some 90,000 residents. The first census taken in New England found 4,150 women and men of African heritage and nearly 158,000 white residents.[86]

While most slaves imported to England's North American colonies before 1695 came from the West Indies, the majority thereafter came directly from Africa. The colonies became participants in an extensive trade network that tied them to Europe and the "dark continent." Most of the slaves brought to the mainland colonies came from the west coast of Africa and its west-central region. Some areas provided greater numbers of slaves to English traders than others. Nearly 25 percent of the slaves imported to the American colonies came from the "Congo-Angola" region, north and south of the Zaire (Congo) River. Another quarter of them were from southeastern Nigeria, while an additional 15 percent came from Senegambia, the Gold Coast, Sierra Leone, and the Ivory Coast.[87]

LIFE IN WEST AFRICA

The West African peoples were linguistically, economically, and culturally diverse, and in many ways as different from each other as they were from the European people who enslaved them. To generalize about their cultures would be to diminish that rich diversity. Yet, their societies shared some basic characteristics. Their economies were usually either agricultural or pastoral; livestock was raised in areas where crops would not grow. Farmers raised rice or millet. Corn was introduced from the New World to Africa in the seventeenth century by Portuguese traders.

West African people tended to organize themselves in patrilineal extended family groups, while west-central and central African people were matrilineal. The wealthiest men in virtually all of these nations had more than one wife. The basic unit of labor for most West Africans was the household consisting of both family members and slaves. Slavery was not unknown to most West African people, but it was not the chattel slavery that developed in colonial America.

Women made up the majority of slaves in sub-Sahara Africa. Valued for their work and their ability to reproduce, they were important to the African economy and society. Because most African cultures assigned agricultural work to women, it was they who tended the crops and produced the food for their people while African men assumed responsibility for crafts and industries, duties they also performed as slaves in their native land. Some male slaves were highly trained in a particular craft or industry, such as the forging of iron or weaving; usually slaves performed the same kinds of tasks as the family members for whom they worked. Well-educated slaves even assumed professional responsibilities.[88]

Africans often acquired slaves through warfare, but those found guilty of civil or religious crimes were also enslaved. Because it was customary to remove slaves from the vicinity of their homes to minimize their chance of escape, an internal African slave trade developed as early as A.D. 700. When Europeans entered the slave trade in the fifteenth century, African traders simply diverted their slaves to the coastal forts, where they were exchanged for desired commodities. The expansion of the African slave trade to New World markets dramatically changed the nature of the institution of slavery.[89]

Nearly 10 million Africans were brought to the New World from 1450 until the middle of the nineteenth century. An estimated 450,000—nearly 7 percent of those transported across the Atlantic Ocean from 1680 until 1808—came to England's American colonies. Between two and two and a half times more African men than women were shipped to England's Chesapeake colonies, the earliest large market for slaves during the seventeenth century. Africans made up a quarter of those who came to South Carolina before 1700, and by 1708 they were a majority in the colony. In that year there were 4,080 white settlers in South Carolina and 4,100 Africans, 1,100 of whom were women.[90]

Slaves were highly valued as laborers and imported to South Carolina by immigrants familiar with their use on the sugar plantations of Barba-

dos. Lady Margaret Yeamans accompanied her husband, Sir John Yeamans, from Barbados when he was appointed governor. She brought
her slaves "old Hannah & hir children Jupeter . . . & Joane" with her.
She also took advantage of the generous head-right system in the colony
and received more than over 1,070 acres of Carolina land for slaves she
imported from her former island home.[91]

African Women and Slavery

The colonists imported African men to perform the agricultural work
undertaken by English men in their society, not realizing or caring that
in Africa this was usually women's work. As a result, the work expected
of many African men was unfamiliar to them. The demand for African
women was also high in the American colonies. Planters viewed them
as capable of almost the same work as men, although a male slave cost
more than a female slave. Some African traders were reluctant to sell
women to North American traders because they were highly valued
in Africa as agricultural workers and the bearers of children. They were
more likely to be kept in Africa as slaves than their male counterparts.[92]

While the sex ratio of African slaves in the Chesapeake mirrored that
of the region's English population, African women and men had fewer
opportunities than their owners to interact. Nearly half of all planters
in the Chesapeake had only one or two slaves during the seventeenth
century. This meant that more than half of all slaves lived on plantations
with fewer than ten slaves and that a third lived on plantations with
less than five. As a result, many African slaves in this region had little
contact with members of their own race. During the earliest years of
Chesapeake slavery, only a tenth of all African slaves actually worked
with other slaves. Instead, they often worked closely with their English
masters and mistresses or with indentured servants.[93]

Few African women in the Chesapeake colonies during the seventeenth century had any hope of developing long-term relationships with
men of their own race. The imbalance of the African sex ratio was
exaggerated by the isolation on plantations. Nineteen percent of all
African women lived on farms or plantations where there were no men
near their own age, and only 23 percent of all women lived where there
was an equal sex ratio. Fifty-three percent of all slaves lived on estates

where the adults of one sex greatly outnumbered the adults of the other sex. Immobilized by their enslavement, few women were permitted to seek out partners on other plantations. As a result, family formation by slaves in the region was impeded.[94]

Africans adapted to their new circumstances, shaping their families within the parameters permitted by their owners. Legal marriages between slaves were prohibited, but owners tolerated, even encouraged, stable sexual relationships. Slave women who gave birth increased their owners' wealth, while having the authority to separate family members gave slave owners even greater power over their slaves. Families were a mixed blessing for slaves: the support they provided enabled many slaves to endure their plight; however, many women and men thought twice about running away or defying their owners if they believed their families might suffer.[95]

In the New England colonies there were also more African men than women. Only a minority of the region's colonists owned slaves at all, and those who did owned, on average, only one or two. Because of their isolation, many never developed stable relationships with others of their race. They had even less opportunity than slaves in the southern colonies to create a supportive slave community and maintain the traditions of their homeland.

In the diverse economy of New England, African slaves performed a variety of duties. Most men were employed in farming and animal husbandry, while African women performed domestic labor. They cooked, cleaned, laundered, sewed, and cared for their owners' children. Others were trained in the making of cheese and butter, as well as in spinning and weaving. One woman was advertised for sale as being "fit for any service either in town or country," while another was described as "skilled in all household arts and especially talented in needle work." All the same, African women, like their Native American counterparts, were more likely than white indentured servant women to work in the fields when necessary.[96]

Because more Native American women were enslaved than men following the Pequot War and King Philip's War and served as servants in the homes of New England farmers, miscegenation between Native American women and African men was relatively common in the region. This alarmed colonists, who feared an alliance between the races. By the end of the century, African men trained to defend the colonies were barred from military service in New England. Miscegenation was also common between Native Americans and Africans in South Carolina, despite efforts by planters to encourage animosity between them. Children born of these unions were called "mustees."[97]

English men were also anxious about liaisons between white women and African men in all the colonies. Fearful that African men saw white women as possible sexual partners, in 1705–1706 the government of Massachusetts prohibited sexual relations or marriage between African and English residents. English men in South Carolina also revealed their anxieties about racial mixing when in 1717 they ruled that "any white women, whether free or a servant, that shall suffer herself to be got with child by a negro or other slave or free negro, . . . shall become a servant for . . . seven years." Children born of "such unnatural and inordinate copulation" were placed into service: girls until they were 18 years old, boys until they were 21.[98]

In Quaker Pennsylvania the demand for laborers was also great as ambitious men competed to purchase more and more land. Quakers, however, viewed the employment of non-Quakers as a threat to the sanctity of their families. "Nonbelievers" were seen as a source of corruption, and most Quakers preferred utilizing the labor of their children or their Quaker brethren. As a result, few slaves were owned by farmers in Pennsylvania, despite the fact that they had sufficient wealth to invest in slave labor. Anxious about that which was alien and afraid of the exotic difference of the Africans they encountered, they saw slaves as threats to their faith and their family values. Quakers also feared the oppressive nature of slavery might lead to slave revolt and require them to take up arms—a violation of their religious beliefs. One Quaker man, however, expressed more basic fears: "What if I should have a bad one of them, that must be corrected, or would run away, or when I went from home and leave him with a woman or maid, and he should desire to commit wickedness[?]" By the end of the seventeenth century, such fears resulted in a ban on the importation and purchase of slaves in the colony.[99]

Women's experience as wives and mothers in West Africa helped them survive the rigors of slavery in North America. In many West African cultures, women and children lived in separate quarters from men. Children were cooperatively raised by women kin, and fathers had little to do with childrearing. As in many Native American societies, the most important men in African children's lives were often their mothers' brothers. In the colonies, African men assumed the role of "uncle" for children whose biological father might reside on another plantation, adapting an African custom to the circumstances of the New World.[100]

Because they lacked control over their lives, African women enslaved by the English could not exactly re-create the kinship networks of their homeland. They did extend the boundaries of their biological families to include others on their plantations as kin. These women and men acted as a safety net, caring for children if their families were separated. By sharing childrearing responsibilities, women developed emotional bonds to ensure their children's care if they were parted.

The African population, like that of whites in the southern colonies, did not increase naturally but instead through importation during most of the century. African women had fewer children than their English counterparts. The disproportionate number of African men in the slave population negatively affected the birth rate of first-generation slave women. Their physical condition, the perpetuation of African child-rearing customs, and their emotional alienation also limited their fertility. The conditions of their enslavement—the hard work expected of them, their exposure to new and disabling diseases—probably led to higher maternal and infant mortality rates than in the English population. Many women also practiced the West African custom of nursing their infants for three years or more and abstained from sexual relations until they were weaned. Finally, stolen from their homes in West Africa, some women doubtlessly rebelled against enslavement by choosing not to bear children. All of these factors led to low fertility among African slaves living in the Chesapeake in the seventeenth century.[101]

By the early eighteenth century, the region's slave population began to grow, despite the fact that African men outnumbered women by a margin of nearly two to one among first-generation slaves.[102] American-born slaves gave birth to their first child at a much earlier age than their African-born mothers, who usually waited two or three years before "marrying." These young women probably bore their first child between the ages of 17 and 19 as proof of their fertility, ensuring their value to their master. It is likely there was a gap of a few years between the birth of the woman's first and second child, the second child born after a "marriage" had taken place. Over the course of their lifetimes, African-American women gave birth to more children than their mothers and more of their children survived infancy. The improved fertility of African-American women demonstrated to their masters how natural reproduction increased the slave population. Masters began to encourage family formation and the creation of support networks for their slaves, making slavery more tolerable for its victims.[103]

Slave women born in the American colonies probably preferred to "marry" African-American men able to speak English and familiar with living in slavery rather than first-generation slaves. This, in combination with the continued preference for male slaves, meant that many African men never had the opportunity to "marry." Some white men, with little chance of finding a white woman to marry in the southern colonies, took African-American slave women as their common-law wives. Many more, however, abused their power as masters and men and sexually exploited their slaves.

African and African-American women resisted slavery throughout the century. Some, especially those of Ibo origin, ran away. These women came from a culture that encouraged them to be independent and assertive. Among the Ibo, women were responsible for trading and selling goods at market. They often traveled from village to village and were not bound to their homes, as were many tribal women. They chafed at the restrictions of slavery and English domesticity imposed on them by their owners. They sought freedom by running away.[104]

Most African women were reluctant to run away and leave their children behind. Masters recognized this, and by encouraging the fertility of their slaves and keeping mothers and children together they minimized the runaway problem. Because female slaves were, in general, less mobile than their male counterparts and less familiar with the geography of the colonies, they also lacked the knowledge necessary for successful escape. Instead, they developed other, more subtle, methods of resistance. Many were truant, absenting themselves without permission to visit friends or families on other farms or plantations, eventually returning. Others slowed their rate of work or feigned ignorance of their instructions. African women were also less likely than men to violently resist their plight, although in their capacity as cooks and nurses they had the knowledge and power to poison their owners.[105]

* * *

Greatly outnumbered by the men of their own race during most of the seventeenth century, vulnerable to diseases that threatened their lives and the lives of their children, required to labor at tasks unfamiliar to them in their native lands, English and African women found the New World a harsh place. Of course, the majority of English women, while they might have regretted their decision, voluntarily traveled to the colonies. African women were given no choice. Their adaptation to, and survival in, England's North American colonies is even more remarkable.

Native American, African, and English women strove valiantly to preserve the familiar in their North American homes. While Native American women tried to protect their tribes and their culture from destruction, English women tried to re-create in the New World the lives they had known in their mother country. African women, brought to the colonies by force, endeavored to preserve their heritage as they grappled with the horrors of slavery. These women all saw themselves as mothers of their people, the source of families, and the repositories of their culture. All confronted disease and warfare and frequently performed the same work, often side by side. Thus, in their desire to perpetuate the values of their peoples in seventeenth-century America, Native American, English, and African women were remarkably alike.

Yet, in protecting and preserving they things they valued most in their own cultures, they ignored the ways in which gender made their lives similar. Although these women of all races and cultures experienced pregnancy, childbirth, and death, they did not see each other as sisters. Instead, as a way of defining themselves, they focused on their differences. The lack of shared experience between Native American, English, and African women arose from their desire to perpetuate the worlds they had lost.

England's colonization of North America also required women— Native American, English, and African—to change. Forced to compromise their cultures' views of women if they were to survive, they proved to be remarkably resilient. Native American women adapted to changes in their economy and society caused by trade and warfare with Europeans who took their lands and undermined their culture. African women, enslaved by the English, learned skills to enhance their value and provide some leverage with their masters and mistresses. They devised methods of resistance that enabled them to exert some control over their lives. And they struggled to create families, developing ways to ensure their children's care in case of separation. They taught their children, by example, how to cope with the uncertainties of bondage, and they endured. English women also performed work they were unaccustomed to in their native land. Their labor, and that of their families, proved vital to the successful colonization of the New World. Widowed, they faced additional responsibilities as executors of their husbands' estates and guardians of their children. They, too, proved remarkably resilient, adapting to the circumstances they faced.

Although English, Native American, and African women altered their assumptions about women's abilities and responsibilities when their cultures clashed in colonial America, they did so reluctantly. They longed for the familiar and, whenever possible, attempted to re-create the worlds they once knew. All courageously faced the challenges before them on the seventeenth-century American frontier.

CHAPTER THREE

The Colonial "Huswife"

The young girl sat hunched over the scrap of linen in her lap. Her needle flashed in the bright sunlight streaming through the open door as she took one small stitch and then another, over and over again. She sighed. Working on her sampler was so boring. Her back and shoulders ached, and her thread always snarled in knots that she must painstakingly unravel.

She'd much rather be outside on this sunny spring day, weeding the garden, playing with the new calf, or helping Papa and her brothers prepare the land for plowing. But Mama insisted she stay inside and work on her sampler.

Mama said that all her daughters must learn how to sew. Sewing taught girls patience and self-control, qualities she would need as a wife and mother some day. And besides, Mama needed help making and mending all the family's clothes. With five children and the baby on the way, her Mama had her hands full. As the eldest girl, she was expected to look after the little ones and keep them out of mischief while Mama made the butter and cheeses that would be traded to their neighbor for cloth.

When Mama was a girl in England, her mother taught her how to sew. Mama pulled her old sampler out of her workbox and unrolled it to display all the fine stitches that she learned when she was young. When she was a girl, Mama said, she stayed indoors and minded her mother. She helped her mother in the dairy and looked after her younger brothers and sisters. She didn't run outside in the fields with her brothers like a wild Indian.

Mama was always talking about the way things were when she was a girl in England. Sometimes she got a dreamy, sad look on her face when she spoke about her old home and family there. But then she married Papa and they came to the colonies seeking their fortune. Life here was harder than they thought it would be. Mama worked in the fields with Papa because they couldn't afford a hired hand or a slave. But together they built a place of their own and a home for their children.

Mama said she had worked hard so that her daughters would never have to work in the fields as she had. She wanted them to be good housewives and learn their manners so they might marry men with lots of land and have nice homes of their own. Someday they might even wear silk gowns instead of homespun and have servants or slaves do their housework for them!

It would be nice to have a big house with lots of windows and china plates with silver spoons and knives, the girl thought. And a bed of her very own— one she didn't have to share with her little sisters. They always squirmed and stole the covers. And a gown of sky-blue silk with a beautiful lace collar would be nice, too. . . . But first, she must stop her woolgathering and learn to garden, cook, and clean. And sew.

She hunched over her sampler again. Taking one small stitch and then another, she dreamed of her future and of finer things in the bright spring sunshine.

For this young girl, born and raised in the American colonies, England was a place her mother remembered but that she had never known. Her mother recalled England as a place of civility and order and tried to re-create the way of life she once knew there. Like her own mother, she taught her American-born daughter the skills of an English "huswife." Although frontier conditions often required her to perform the work of men, she longed for the day she might resume what she remembered as her traditional role. She taught her daughters by example and passed on to them her values as well as her hopes and dreams for their future.

In the New World, even more than in the Old, women helped create and develop colonial society. During the first years of settlement in all of England's North American colonies, women tried to introduce domesticity to the frontier. Just as in England, they claimed hearth, home, and kitchen garden as their domain, although the actual work they performed was influenced by the wealth and status of their fathers, husbands, and masters. Contrasting their lives with those of Native American women, they saw themselves as "civilizers" of the wilderness.

These female pioneers also hoped their daughters and granddaughters—their "posterity"—might live better lives than they had and so taught them skills they believed necessary for their advancement in the New World.

Despite the value placed on English women's work and their civilizing influence, their relative scarcity and the slow rate of family development in the southern colonies led to the importation of indentured servants and, finally, slaves as laborers in the region. The work of African women and men contributed to a colonial class system based on family, wealth, and race. Slave ownership distinguished the experiences of southern white women from each other and from African women, and it defined their daily lives and domestic responsibilities.

In New England and the middle colonies—Pennsylvania, New York, and New Jersey—women and children were present from first settlement and households more closely resembled those in England. Colonists transplanted the English gender division of labor, enabling women to re-create their traditional role as housewives with only minor alterations. Women's industry contributed to their families' prosperity and helped promote a new hierarchy of wealth in these colonies.

By the end of the century, urbanization and the emergence of commerce and trade also altered women's lives and differentiated their experiences, especially in New England and the middle colonies. While some women assisted their menfolk at crafts and trades, others, widowed in colonial wars, sought work to support themselves and their families in urban centers. As men became preoccupied with trade and production for the marketplace, they embraced new, secular, values; competition replaced the cooperation so vital in the early years of settlement. Women came to embody the older, religious values of the original settlers and became the majority of church members.

The common experiences of pregnancy, childbirth, and childrearing defined women's existence in the American colonies throughout the century. In childbirth all women faced their own mortality, regardless of their race or class. Women living in the southern colonies faced a harsh climate that took its toll on them and the children they bore. New England women and those living in the middle colonies found a healthier environment in which to bear and rear their children. African women risked their lives to bear children while knowing that their infants were the property of their masters and might be cruelly taken from them. By the end of the century some women, freed from the work performed by earlier generations of women, devoted themselves almost exclusively to the bearing and rearing of children and to their domestic role. What their mothers and grandmothers had longed for had come to pass.

THE WORLD OF NATIVE AMERICAN WOMEN

Just as English and African women were important to the colonization process, Native American women were vital to their people. Many northern tribes relied entirely on fishing, hunting, and gathering to survive. They moved from their winter camps to the Atlantic Coast in the spring, harvesting more than half of their annual food supply from the sea or rivers. While the men fished, women and children searched for shellfish—scallops, crabs, clams, and mussels—and birds' nests, setting snares and gathering eggs throughout the summer months. They also gathered berries, nuts, and other edible and medicinal plants, preserving many of them for use in less plentiful seasons.

When autumn came, the men formed hunting parties while the women transported and constructed sapling and hide dwellings for the tribes' winter quarters. They also prepared the game, preserving the meats and curing the hides and furs the men brought back from the hunt. Women traded these hides and furs to other tribes and to the English in return for goods they could not produce themselves. Their importance in the colonial fur trade was acknowledged by English traders, who stocked up on the labor-saving items the Native American women valued: needles, awls used in the working of hides, cloth, and kettles.

The most difficult months for northern tribes were in late winter, when supplies were low and game was scarce. They survived the seasonal scarcity of food because they restrained their fertility. Native women in northern New England had fewer children than their southern counterparts, who practiced subsistence agriculture. The rigor of their lives, their diet, the custom of lengthy nursing, and the absence of men out on hunting expeditions limited the number of children they bore. As a result, population densities in this region were low, permitting the animals and plants on which the tribes relied to replenish themselves.[1]

Native American women of southern New England, the Chesapeake, and the Carolinas grew crops that sustained their tribes over the winter months. Because more than half of their diet was grains, they were less dependent on wild plants and game and could feed more people than the northern tribes. Although women in agricultural tribes also nursed their children for a long period of time and probably abstained from sexual relations while breastfeeding, their better diet and less taxing labor enabled them to have more children than their northern counterparts.

Women played an essential role in Native American agriculture. Using clamshell hoes to work the ground, they created mounds two to three feet apart, which they planted with five or six kernels of seed corn. As an observer noted: "with the corn they put in each hill three or four . . . beans. . . . When they grow up they interlace with the corn, which reaches to the height of from five to six feet; and they keep the ground very free from weeds. We saw there many squashes, and pumpkins, and tobacco, which they likewise cultivate."[2]

Native women did not use fish as a fertilizer; the English imported this custom to the New World. Instead, when the richness of their fields declined, they abandoned them for new lands. A woman tending a one- or two-acre plot of land might grow between 25 and 60 bushels of corn, enough to support a family of five for a year. Her labor accounted for nearly 75 percent of her family's needs. Because women's agricultural work was so essential, their tribes conferred on them greater esteem and authority than the English granted women in the American colonies.[3]

Roger Williams described the gender division of labor practiced by the farming tribes of southern New England:

> [t]he Women set or plant, weede, and hill, and gather and barne all the corne, and Fruites of the field: Yet sometimes the man himselfe (either out of love to his wif, or care for his Children, or being an old man) will help the Woman which (by the custome of the Countrey) they are not bound to." He observed that, "When a field is to be broken up, they have a very loving sociable speedy way to dispatch it: All the neighbors men and Women forty, fifty a hundred, &c., joyne, and come into help freely. With friendly joyning they breake up their fields, build their fort, hunt the Woods stop and kill the fish in the Rivers.[4]

Depending on their skills, age, the seasons of the year, and the urgency of the job at hand, Native American women and men shared responsibility for work in their society.

COLONIAL HEARTHS AND HOMES

Like their Native American counterparts, the English men and women who came to North America also practiced a gender division of labor. Although they hoped to replicate this system in the New World, they were forced by frontier conditions to temporarily suspend their assumptions about what was men's and women's work. Women, often expected to do the work of men, looked forward to the day when they or their daughters might return to the domestic sphere, devote themselves to the care of their homes and their families, and perform the work of traditional English housewives.

English colonists were not used to the harsh conditions they found on the frontier. As they confronted the "howling wilderness" of North America, their homes became a refuge. To reaffirm their identity and establish a sense of security in an unfamiliar world, they tried to replicate the houses they had built in England. Yet they were forced to adapt to their new environment, altering the materials and design of their homes to meet the realities of life in the colonies. In this way, their homes embodied both the continuity and the change in English values and ideals demanded of those who migrated to North America.

The colonial home was the domain of women. The model housewife was like a "tortoise, the emblem of a woman who should be a keeper at home, as the tortoise seldome peeps out of its shell."[5] The household furnishings they treasured and the domestic implements they used also reveal the quality of women's lives and the nature of their work as they struggled to make homes for their families in North America.

Although the first colonists built temporary structures similar to those lived in by the Native Americans, they soon tried to construct houses like those in England.[6] In the Chesapeake, the majority of families lived in humble cottages of only one to three rooms. Roughly constructed of posts and beams, sided with unpainted clapboards, and roofed with thatch or wood shingles, these simple houses were functional shelters. Adapted from architectural styles found in the English countryside, they evoked a feeling of the Old World, although they were built of materials found in abundance in the New World. With low ceilings, floors of dirt or planks, and no glass windows, their interiors were quite dark.

Wealthy southern planters lived in houses not much larger than those of their poorer neighbors. While their homes sometimes had brick chimneys, glass windows, and stairs to the second floor, they did not build opulent mansions as monuments to their success during the seventeenth century. Instead, a planter's prosperity was reflected in the number of outbuildings surrounding his home, each having a specific purpose. A kitchen with its own hearth was sometimes built as a separate structure to minimize the chance of fire destroying the home and to keep the main house cool during the summer months. Tobacco barns, a dairy, a hen house, and housing for servants or slaves reflected a plantation's diversity and its owner's wealth.

The more outbuildings a plantation boasted, the more servants or slaves it usually had. Removing the housewife's duties from the house to these structures and assigning them to servants or slaves signified a change in her domestic role. Instead of performing those duties herself, she supervised the work of others. Most of those planters who could afford to build substantial homes and outbuildings did not do so until the eighteenth century, however, investing their money instead in land and labor.[7]

New England colonists expanded their homes as they prospered or as their farming activities diversified. Most houses had a central "hall" or room containing a hearth for heating and the preparation of meals. Although chimneys were initially built of "wattle and daub," stacked saplings mortared together with clay, by midcentury they were constructed of brick. A second room, or parlor, might be found on the first floor, with a loft or chamber above that could be reached by ladder.

Apart from barns to house their livestock and store their produce, New England colonists did not build separate structures to house farm activities. Instead, they added rooms onto their homes, constructing the lean-to additions that characterize the saltbox shape of that region's homes. These additions accommodated the activities of colonial housewives. Some were used as butteries or sculleries; others were used as distilleries for preserving and distilling foods and elixirs and for drying herbs. Cellars to store fruits and root crops were common in the northern and middle colonies and were located beneath the lean-to for accessibility during the winter months.[8]

Small, dark, intimate places, seventeenth-century houses did not permit much individual privacy. Families were cooperative units, and the design of their homes underscored the interdependence of family members. Their homes served as a refuge from the threatening world that surrounded them, where intimacy with other members of the family was enjoyed.

The primitive houses built by settlers in all the colonies provided them with a sense of security and community in the intimidating wilderness of North America.[9]

Colonists furnished their homes with functional objects, reflecting the basic nature of women's domestic work in the early years of settlement.[10] In the smallest houses, rooms had no specialized use; all were used for eating and sleeping. Chairs were rare, but benches or stools and a table were common in the homes of most poor farmers. A house might have one bed positioned close to the hearth, curtained with bed hangings for warmth as well as privacy. Here slept the husband and wife who often shared the bed with a nursing infant or a sickly child. Infant cradles were rare in the seventeenth century (figure 6). Once weaned, children slept with their brothers and sisters on straw-filled mattresses before the hearth or in the loft. It was customary to share beds and sleeping quarters with relatives or visitors. Only the very wealthy reserved the right to a bed of their own.[11]

Clothes were hung on pegs fastened to the walls or placed in large chests or trunks in which the colonial housewife stored her family's linens. Many women's dowries included bed and table linens, often handed down from mother to daughter. Women valued them for their practical use as well as for the emotional bond they symbolized between generations of women. Anne Bradstreet mourned the loss of all her household goods in a fire that destroyed her home:

> Here stood that Trunk, and there that chest;
> There lay that store I counted best:
> My pleasant things in ashes lye,
> And them behold no more shall I.[12]

THE HOUSEWIFE'S DUTIES

The colonial housewife's domestic responsibilities, as in England, customarily included cooking, cleaning, sewing, caring for children, and tending the kitchen garden. While some women raised poultry, others managed a dairy. One visitor to the southern colonies observed women "take care of . . . cattle, make butter and cheese, spin cotton and flax, help to sow and reap corn, wind silk from the worms, gather fruit

Figure 6. Cradle, 1660–1690. Probably Plymouth Colony. Red oak, white pine, and maple, 32½ × 34½ × 18 inches. *Courtesy, Wadsworth Atheneum, Hartford, Connecticut. Wallace Nutting Collection. Gift of J. Pierpont Morgan.*

and look after the house." Much of this work was monotonous, time-consuming, and physically exhausting.[13]

    Women's daily activities in most seventeenth-century homes centered around the hall or kitchen. Here they prepared meals and served them to their families, servants, and slaves. Cooking pots, skillets, and pans were stored at the hearth, while dishes and implements, commonly made of earthenware, wood, or pewter, were placed on shelves or in cupboards until used. A "middling" farmer's wife might have "11 iron potts, 1 great Kettle, 4 kettles 2 old & 2 new, 1 bakeing pan, 1 skellet, 1 scummer, 11 frying panns, 1 iron ladle, 1 spitt, and a driping pan" at her disposal. The wife of a poor colonist might have to make do with only "one smale iron pott," "a smale scillite," and "one smale brass scimer." Many wives of Maryland's poorest planters did not even have brick ovens in which to bake their bread.[14]

Although domestic implements aided women in their work, they often added to their responsibilities. For example, the housewife with many pots, pans, and kettles prepared more foods in different ways than her neighbor with only a small pot and a skillet. Likewise, the housewife with a brick oven regularly baked bread for her family while the family of a woman who lacked an oven did without it.[15]

Eating utensils found in early American homes shed light on the kinds of food women prepared for their families. The lack of eating utensils in poor farmers' homes means they must have eaten their meals with their fingers or with "found" implements like oyster shells. Spoons were common utensil in most homes, so one-pot stews cooked all day over an open hearth were probably standard fare. Knives were less common and forks were virtually unknown in seventeenth-century America, not appearing in the inventories of middling Chesapeake planters until the early eighteenth century.

Poor families ate their meals out of a common pot or off trenchers made of wood, while more affluent families used locally made pottery. Cups and bowls carved of wood or earthenware were also shared by family members and discarded when cracked or broken. Archaeologists at Jamestown discovered that while earthenware plates for everyday use were locally made, prosperous colonists imported ornamental pottery from England and the Netherlands. In their effort to make the American colonies "English," they imported tableware and table manners to the New World. One proud colonial housewife displayed a set of six English tin-glazed earthenware plates in her home (figure 7). The plates reflected her desire to transplant English civility to the colonies, with the verse inscribed on them asserting women's importance in making the English house a home:

> What is a merrey man
> let him doe what he cane
> to entertaine his guests
> with wine and merrey jests

but if his wife doth frowne
all merriment goes downe.[16]

Household inventories reveal the priorities of men who purchased goods for use by their families. Most homes contained beds, cooking implements, and eating utensils, but items identified with cleanliness, convenience, and civility—washtubs and irons, chairs and candles, tablecloths and chamber pots—were fewer in number. The scarcity of objects identified with women's chores made it difficult for them to do the jobs expected of them. This devaluation of their work demonstrates the subordinate role they were often forced to play in the settlement process. Placing greater importance on profit than comfort and on their own work rather than that of their wives, men made women's lives more arduous in early America than it had been in England.[17]

The wives of poor farmers owned neither imported pottery nor candle molds, illuminating their small, dark homes with tallow lamps or pine knots adopted from the Native Americans: "There are such candles as the Indians commonly use, having no other, and they are nothing else but the wood of the pine tree, cloven into two little slices, something thin, which are so full of the moysture of turpentine and pitch that they burne as cleere as a torch."[18] Because they spent nearly half the day in the fields hoeing corn or tobacco, the wives and daughters of poor Chesapeake planters had little time or energy to do anything else. They seldom made candles, wove their own cloth, or brewed beer, instead purchasing these goods from others or doing without them.[19]

The homes of wealthier planters in the southern colonies and wealthier farmers in the New England and middle colonies had more implements for use by women to make candles and cloth. These objects reflected both the wealth of the household and the greater value men placed on their wives performing traditional women's work. Although having these implements meant many women worked harder than ever before, their work gave them added importance in the household economy. Their contribution was recognized by husbands who purchased mirrors, chamber pots, and linens, emblems of cleanliness and civility, for use by their wives and daughters.[20]

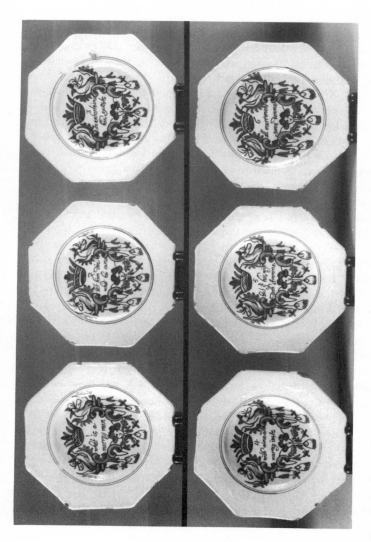

Figure 7. Set of six plates. Tin-glazed earthenware. Probably from Lambeth, England, circa 1670–1690. *Courtesy of Historic Deerfield, Inc., Deerfield, Massachusetts. Photo by Amanda Merullo.*

Women's Clothing

The clothing colonial women wore in the New World was an emblem of the civilization they had left behind. Most wore gowns consisting of a separate bodice and a skirt, divided in front to show the petticoat, sometimes elaborately embroidered, beneath. Women attached their sleeves to their gowns with laces and tucked neck cloths or fabric kerchiefs, called "whisks," into their low-cut bodices. Stomachers— stiffened garments covering the stomach and breast—were worn beneath the bodice, but few women, regardless of their wealth, wore undergarments of any kind. Middling and upper-class women wore stockings made of wool, cotton, or silk that they tied with garters and shoes made of leather or cloth. Some women wore clogs—half-slippers with wooden soles—over their shoes to protect them from the mud.

Poor women wore roughly made clothing little better than that worn by female servants and African slaves. A simple shift—a long blouse— and an ankle-length skirt were their basic attire during the summer months. To keep their skirts clean, they wore aprons, and they saved their crudely made shoes and stockings for special occasions. As the weather cooled, they layered on petticoats and shawls for warmth. In Virginia, female servants were entitled to a calico gown and apron, a shift, a handkerchief, and a pair of shoes. Those in South Carolina were given a waistcoat and petticoat, two shifts, an apron, two caps, and shoes and stockings when their period of indenture was completed.[21]

African women wore shifts of the coarsest linen or homespun wool and usually worked barefoot in the fields.[22] Prohibited from wearing traditional African dress, many women wore headcloths tied in distinctive ways as a reminder of their native land. In Africa, the color and method of tying a woman's headcloth were significant; a white headcloth denoted a woman with religious powers. An eighteenth-century painting of an African-American wedding on a Virginia plantation shows women, dressed in European garb, wearing headcloths tied in the Yoruban manner (figure 8).

Out of sight, beneath their headcloths, they continued to dress their hair in traditional African styles and designs, tying it in plaits, knotting it in bunches, and weaving it into intricate patterns. African women's appearance expressed their desire for continuity in the face of change. It was also a form of resistance against the strange new land they confronted and their enslavement as a people.[23]

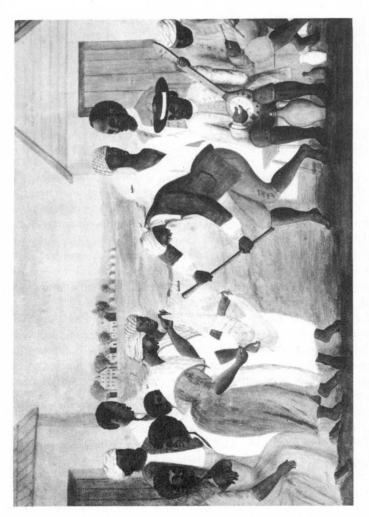

Figure 8. The Old Plantation. *Courtesy, Abby Aldrich Rockefeller Folk Art Center, Williamsburg, Virginia.*

Excavating Martin's Hundred, the Virginia settlement destroyed by Powhatans in 1622, archaeologists discovered the skeleton of an English woman who died of shock and exposure after the attack. Around her head they found a narrow iron band that foiled her attacker's attempt to scalp her. The purpose of the band puzzled them until they learned it was the remains of a fabric-padded roll over which fashionable English ladies dressed their hair. In a poignant attempt to bring some measure of civility to the rough settlement, this English woman awoke on the morning of her death and dressed her hair as she had in England. In this small, familiar act, she valiantly defied the wilds of seventeenth-century Virginia. Her efforts, however, did not protect her from attack, and she died alone, forgotten for more than three centuries.[24]

Like the woman at Martin's Hundred, other colonial women dressed their hair and wore clothing that visibly affirmed their role as "civilizers of the wilderness." Because clothing was also a reflection of social class, colonial authorities frowned on those who dressed "above" their station. As a result, the Jamestown, Virginia, cow-keeper's wife was criticized in 1619 for wearing "freshe flaming silks" on Sunday, and the wife of a collier was berated for wearing a "round bever hatt with a faire perle hatband, and a silken suite thereto correspondent."[25]

New England's Puritans were especially concerned about colonial fashions and passed sumptuary laws maintaining the order and perpetuating the class structure of the homeland they had left behind. The government of Massachusetts prohibited the wearing of any clothing trimmed with lace, silver and gold threads, or embroidery, it and tried to prevent women from making and selling lace in the colony. The 1634 law also proclaimed "that no person either man or woman shall make or buy any Slashed Clothes other than one Slash in each Sleeve and another in the Back. Also all Cut-works, embroideries, or Needlework Caps, Bands or Rails, are forbidden hereafter to be made and worn . . . also all gold or silver Girdles Hat bands, Belts, Ruffs, Beaver hats are prohibited to be bought and worn hereafter.[26]

Despite these laws, many women and men seized the freedom of the New World to question the status system of the Old. As they prospered, they wanted to wear clothing that reflected their growing wealth, but in doing so they confronted the established order of their society. Women who dressed above their station were viewed as especially threatening, for they not only challenged the social order but defied the authority of the men who made and enforced the colonies' sumptuary laws.

Puritan minister Roger Williams entered the debate over women's fashion in New England when he commanded the women in his Salem, Massachusetts, congregation to wear veils to church, symbolizing their submission to God, to him, and to their husbands. The women ignored him. Wisely, Williams never again presumed to tell his female congregants what they could and could not wear. In 1676, 36 Northampton women were fined for dressing too opulently. One of them, Hannah Lyman, was punished for "wearing silk in a fflonting manner, in an offensive way, not only before but when she stood Psentd. Not only in Ordinary but Extraordinary times."[27] It was probably Hannah's "fflonting manner" more than her silk gown that aggravated the town's male authorities. Although ministers and magistrates tried to impose their ideas of appropriate attire on colonial women, they met their match: "Little was done about it; for divers of the [church] elders' wives, etc., were in some measure partners in this general disorder." Perhaps with so little that was beautiful in their homes and in their lives, seventeenth-century women were reluctant to sacrifice the small luxuries—the silk neckerchief, the lace-trimmed hood, the embroidered petticoat—that enriched their attire. The portrait of Puritan Mistress Elizabeth Freake and her daughter Mary gives evidence of the beautiful clothing enjoyed by one New England matron (figure 9).[28]

Although wives of prosperous men dressed in a manner appropriate to their social class, most pious New England women eschewed wedding bands and the elaborate costumes fashionable in seventeenth-century England, wearing simply styled dresses made of durable fabrics. Puritan women and men wore black and white garb for Sunday meeting, but they also delighted in wearing vividly colored clothing. Their color pallet was limited only by the natural dyes then available for use. Although brown was perhaps the most common color, clothing of yellow, orange, red, green, purple, and blue was not unusual.[29]

Only women of the upper classes probably wore the heavily boned bodices, corsets, and wide skirts then fashionable in England. These garments inhibited a woman's freedom of movement, signifying that their wearer did not have to perform heavy labor or work in the fields. They also reflected her husband's ability to employ servants or slaves to do much of her domestic work. Thus, as colonial planters prospered, the clothing worn by their wives reflected changes in their social class.[30]

Figure 9. Mrs. Elizabeth Freake and Baby Mary, circa 1671–1674. Unknown artist. *Courtesy, Worcester Art Museum, Worcester, Massachusetts. Gift of Mr. and Mrs. Albert W. Rice.*

Wealthy women and those of the "middling sort" saved their finest clothing for special occasions. Many first-generation colonial women kept these seldom-worn gowns as reminders of their lives in England. On the frontier, the carefully stored jewel-toned petticoats and silk gowns trimmed with gold and silver lace were treasured. Passed on to favored daughters or female relatives, they afforded a glimpse of what the future might hold for them in the New World.

Dutch women brought the fashions of their homeland to North America. Madam Sarah Kemble Knight, herself English, observed during a business visit to New York in 1706: "The English go very fasheonable in their dress. But the Dutch, especially the middling sort, differ from our women, in their habitt go loose, were French muches wch are like a Capp and a head band in one, leaving their ears bare, which are sett out wth Jewells of a large size and many in number." This keen observer of fashion also noted that "their fingers [are] hoop't with Rings, some with large stones in them of many Coullers as were their pendants in their ears, which You should see very old women wear as well as Young." Dutch women, like their English counterparts, emulated the fashions of their homeland, maintaining a connection with the way of life and the land they had left behind (figure 10).[31]

Colonial mothers also dressed their young children as they had in England. Girls and boys alike wore front-opening robes decorated at the shoulders with ribbons, the legacy of leading strings once worn to guide or restrain them. When the child began to walk, the robe was shortened. Anne Bradstreet advised, "A prudent mother will not cloth her little childe with a long and cumbersome garment; she easily foresees what events it is like to produce, at the best but falls and bruises, or perhaps somewhat worse."[32] Boys and girls wore the same clothing until they were five or six years old. Then, little girls were attired in gowns like their mothers and boys wore breeches like their fathers. The 1670 portrait of David, Joanna, and Abigail Mason reflects the custom of dressing children in the manner of their parents (figure 11). Although they wore clothing like their elders', boys and girls were not necessarily viewed as adults. Rather, the change in their clothing marked the beginning of their transformation from child to adult.[33]

Figure 10. Dutch girl with red shoes. Hudson Valley artist, 1740. *Courtesy, Winterthur Museum, Winterthur, Delaware.*

Figure 11. The Mason children: David, Joanna, and Abigail, 1670. Attributed to the Freake-Gibbs painter. *Courtesy, The Fine Arts Museums of San Francisco. Gift of Mr. and Mrs. John D. Rockefeller 3rd, 1979.7.3.*

SEWING AND THE NEEDLE ARTS

Women were responsible for making their families' clothes and teaching their daughters to sew. Virtually all girls learned "plain sewing," which included the construction and hemming of simple garments and knitting. They were also taught basic cross-stitch techniques, for all household linens and clothing were "marked" with the owner's initials or a number. More elaborate forms of needlework—crewel, tambour, and canvas work, which was also known as needlepoint—were called fancy work. The ability to do fancy work indicated a woman's social rank, for only the middle and upper classes could afford to educate their daughters in this kind of sewing.[34]

Most girls were taught to sew by their mothers when they were very young. Mistress Samuel Sewall of Massachusetts taught five-year-old Elizabeth and seven-year-old Hannah how to ply their needles and asked her husband to order "white Fustian drawn, enough for curtins, wallen counterpaine for a bed, and half a duz. chairs, with four threeded green worsted to wirk it" for her daughters to sew.[35] Young girls practiced their stitches, as well as embroidery designs, and recorded them for future reference. These records were known as samplers. Samplers were testimony of a young woman's skill at needlework and served as her guide when she wished to replicate a stitch later on.

Seventeenth-century English samplers and those found in early America are similar, indicating that women brought the custom of making samplers with them to the colonies and passed down methods of stitchery to their daughters and granddaughters. The earliest samplers were long strips of narrow fabric, usually linen although sometimes wool, never intended for display. Rolled up and stored in a sewing box, they were taken out for study when needed. Embroidery stitches and designs formed bands across the fabric, and some samplers included strips of lace—cutwork and drawn work—as well. Unlike eighteenth-century samplers, which were ornamental as well as practical, those made in the seventeenth century contained no artwork, although some girls stitched the alphabet, numbers, and Bible verses to practice their "marking" skills (figure 12).[36]

Because textiles were valued in early America and inventoried as part of a family's estate, their preservation and care was an important part of women's work. Girls were taught how to mend fabrics; the ability to make an invisible repair was highly esteemed in a needlewoman. Some girls had darning samplers on which they practiced their mending skills. Cuts emulating tears—both straight, across the grain, and L-shaped—were made in the sampler. Girls then rewove the fabric with threads or yarn in a contrasting color so that they could replicate their stitches at a later time.[37]

Only the daughters of very wealthy colonists were taught needlepoint, one of the most expensive forms of needlework. Fine canvas stretched over a wooden frame served as the background for this stitchery, which used fine embroidery yarn. Finished canvases were used as tablecloths, seat covers for chairs, pockets, and fire screens. Crewel embroidery—designs worked on twill-woven fabric or linen using wool yarns—was more common than needlepoint because printed fabrics were rare and expensive in the colonies. The richly embroidered fabric, sometimes taking many years to complete, was often made into draperies to enclose the master bedstead. Displayed in the parlor and visible

Figure 12. Sampler, circa 1665–1670. Made by Mary Hollingsworth of Salem, Massachusetts. Unbleached linen worked in colored silks, mostly cross-stitch 25 × 8½ inches. *Courtesy Essex Institute, Salem, Massachusetts.*

to visiting neighbors and friends, these fabrics were a conspicuous example of their maker's industry and skill (figure 13). Needlepoint and crewel work were time-consuming, however, and most busy housewives, lacking the assistance of servants or slaves, did not have the time or money to devote to such purely ornamental work.[38]

WOMEN'S DOMESTIC DUTIES

Colonial women who performed the more practical skills of spinning and weaving capitalized on their abilities and traded their labor or the goods they produced for things they could not make themselves. New England women, confined indoors during the winter months, spent many hours spinning wool and flax into thread for the manufacture of cloth. Implements for carding wool and preparing flax, as well as the wheels and distaffs used in spinning, were common in their households. Few southern women, however, had the time to spin or weave during the seventeenth century and so purchased the cloth they needed. By the early eighteenth century some southern housewives had found time to spin, but most still took their yarn to weavers and paid them to make their cloth.[39]

Young women also learned the basics of cookery from their mothers. Even daughters of wealthy planters had to know how to grow, prepare, and serve foods if they were to teach and supervise the servants or slaves who performed the actual labor. Colonial women prepared foods they ate in the Old World, perhaps believing that by eating familiar foods, prepared in familiar ways, they could preserve and continue the civility they had left behind. Some varieties of wheat and other grains grown in England did not take to the climate and soil of North America. Although English settlers resisted adopting the foods of the Native Americans, they soon adopted corn as a staple in their diet.[40]

Colonial housewives adapted traditional English recipes to the new staple. Pounding corn, or grinding it in mills, they made a meal that replaced wheat flour in most homes. Roger Williams described one method for preparing it: "Nawsamp is a kind of meal pottage unparched. From this the English call their samp, which is the Indian corn beaten, boiled and eaten hot or cold with milk and butter, and is a diet exceedingly wholesome for English bodies."[41] South Carolina

Figure 13. Crewel on linen bedhangings, circa 1745. Made by Mary Bulman, wife of Dr. Alexander Bulman, in York, Maine. The verse on the valance piece is "Meditation in a Grave" by Isaac Watts, 1706. *Courtesy, The Old York Historical Society, York, Maine.*

settler Mary Stafford described her daily breakfast: "a dish you meet not with in England: it is Indian Corn ground upon a steel Mill and boiled stiff, and eaten with milk, it is called homony; that is the most plenty full food in the Country."[42] Housewives also made the Native American dish of "sukquattahhash," a mixture of corn cooked with beans, which they called succotash.

Rice was a South Carolina staple. Probably brought to the colony by slaves from the rice-producing regions of West Africa and grown to augment their own diets, it quickly became a profitable crop for their masters. Women were central to rice cultivation in Africa, and they probably imported it to the New World. They planted it in the spring by pressing a hole in the soil with their heel, dropping in the seed, and covering it with a movement of their foot. During the summer months, women and children working in gangs weeded, thinned, and transplanted the plants with hoes. In the fall, men and women harvested the crop, while the women threshed the grain by fanning it in the wind using large flat coiled baskets.[43]

Female slaves made baskets in South Carolina using techniques they brought with them from Senegambia. They handed down their skills from mother to daughter, using materials they found in the low country. Rolled sea grass provided the basis for the basket and palmetto leaves were cut and sewn, using a pierced bone as an awl or needle, to bind the coiled sea grass together. Pine needles provided variations in color and design. Made in many different sizes and shapes, sea-grass baskets were used for a variety of purposes by slaves and their masters throughout the century.[44]

The rice-fanning baskets used by South Carolina slave women resembled those made in Africa. These wide, circular baskets were nearly two feet across and only one inch deep, with a wide splayed edge to facilitate the fanning of rice (figure 14). The basket was held in front of the person performing the task, with a hand at either side. First the rice was "rayed," sliding it back and forth in the basket to loosen the kernels from the husks that encased them. Then, using a quick movement of the wrists, the rice was "fanned" into the air to separate the kernels from the chaff. The heavier kernels were shaken, or "winnowed," from the basket to the ground, and the wind blew away the chaff. In this manner, the rice was cleaned.[45]

In addition to transporting rice to the New World, African women probably brought benne seeds, also known as sesame seeds, to South

Figure 14. Sea grass rice-fanning basket. *Courtesy of The Charleston Museum. Charleston, South Carolina.*

Carolina. In West Africa, these seeds were thought to have magical properties and were used in fertility rituals. On the sea islands women sowed them in plots near the rice fields to bring good luck. They also carried to the Carolina low country the seeds for durra, or "guinea corn," watermelons, yams, gourds, okra, and cowpeas. African cooks used these fruits and vegetables in the meals they prepared for their English masters and mistresses, adding a distinctive flavor to the region's cuisine.

English women also brought seeds from the Old World to the New and shared them with their neighbors. In kitchen gardens adjacent to their homes, housewives grew the herbs, vegetables, and fruits they used to feed and care for their families. A visitor to Plymouth noted that the kitchen gardens were "enclosed behind and at the sides with clapboards, so that their houses and courtyards are arranged in very good order." One traveler to South Carolina observed that "[t]heir Gardens are supplied with such European Plants and Herbs as are necessary for the Kitchen, and they begin to be beautiful and adorned with such Flowers as to the Smell or Eye are pleasing or agreeable, viz.: the Rose, Tulip, Carnation, Lilly, etc." Many colonial housewives brought flower seeds and cuttings from England for their beauty and as a reminder of the homes and gardens they had left behind.[46] As in England,

> Good huswives in summer will save their own seeds,
> against the next year, as occasion needs:
> One seed for another, to make an exchange,
> with fellowly neighbourhood, seemeth not strange.[47]

By sharing seeds and plants brought from their mother country, women built bonds of friendship with other women in their community.

Friendships, sealed with a gift of flower or vegetable seeds, were extremely important to colonial women. Friends provided emotional support during trying times like childbirth or the death of a loved one. They made for someone to talk to in good times and bad and to turn to for advice about the care of a sick child or the trimmings for a new dress. Female friends affirmed values and shared dreams for the future, and they assisted each other in their work. "Change work" permitted women to provide for their families while working with their neighbors. They shared their work, helping each other complete a particularly arduous or time-consuming task, at soap-making time, while butchering, or when making preserves. Sometimes women spun and sewed together, recognizing that work goes faster and is more pleasant when the labor is shared.[48]

Female friendships also provided the basis for trading networks among women. In their kitchen gardens, some women tended fowl imported from England, bartering their eggs for products made by other women. Because not all families owned cows, a woman skilled in the dairy might trade butter and cheese for goods her friends made. In this way, the hidden, and often overlooked, barter network of women helped sustain their families in early America.[49] The absence of female friends was sorely felt by women who had to shoulder their domestic duties alone and to assist their husbands as well. Friendships affirmed the importance of women's work to themselves and to others and provided them with the support and encouragement they needed as they braved the New World frontier.

A familiar proverb captures the realities of women's lives and constant labor: "A man works from sun to sun, but a woman's work is never done." While much of women's work was performed on a daily or weekly basis, it had its seasonal cycles as well. Each day the colonial housewife cooked for her family, tried to keep her home clean—not an easy task—and cared for her children. Much of what she did, however, depended on the assistance of her husband. Theirs was a family enterprise. Starting and tending a fire in the hearth built by her husband and fueled by wood he chopped, the colonial housewife prepared the day's meal. She mixed her bread using flour ground by her husband from grains he raised on the farm and "sponge" (yeast starter saved from earlier bread making). She baked the bread in an oven built by her husband in the hearth or in the dooryard of her house. If she did not have an oven, she baked it in an iron pot on the hearth, its lid covered with coals.

The housewife fed the livestock and poultry, collected eggs, milked the cows, and weeded the kitchen garden each day. On a weekly or biweekly basis she laundered the family's clothing and linens. Using a large kettle filled with water hauled from a well or stream by her husband, she boiled the clothing using soap she made herself.[50] In autumn, women assisted their husbands with butchering and prepared the meat for salting, smoking, or drying. Tallow was collected and, when mixed with lye produced by her husband from hardwood ashes, was made into soap. In the winter, with time to spare, the housewife dipped or molded candles, following the advice of Thomas Tusser:

> Wife, make thine own candle,
> Spare penny to handle.
> Provide for thy tallow ere frost cometh in,
> And make thine own candle ere winter begin.[51]

Autumn was when apples were harvested and dried and made into apple butter and cider. Some skilled housewives also brewed beer from hops, herbs, malt, and yeast. In England, one observer remarked, "[brewing] is properly the work and care of a woman, for it is a housework. The man ought only to bring in and to provide the grain."[52] In the northern and middle colonies this pattern was repeated, and housewives made "small beer" for their families' consumption. Some women even practiced the trade commercially and others operated taverns. There is little evidence, however, that women were brewers in the southern colonies. Instead, colonists there drank homemade cider and metheglin, a beverage made of water and honey.

Carolina pioneer Mary Stafford complained to her English cousin about the unappetizing choice of beverages in her new home: "that which is the greater punishment of all to me is the drinking allmost allways water for we cannot afford wine, it is dear, and there no beer but what is made of treacle and that but now and then to be met with all."[53] Stafford was right to fear drinking water, for it was often contaminated. Those who were wealthy imported wines from Europe, rum from England's Caribbean colonies, tea, and brandies.[54]

Mothers welcomed the birth of daughters to assist them with their domestic chores. It was a mother's duty to teach her daughters the essential domestic skills needed to be good "huswives" and to manage their own households one day. A daughter might be taught to card wool as soon as she was able to walk, learning the first of many tasks necessary in the spinning of yarn. Or, she might be instructed how to churn butter or scald and scour the pans used in making cheese. When she was older, she looked after her brothers and sisters, freeing her mother to do work that was more time-consuming and profitable for the family. United in their domesticity, working at jobs segregated by gender, the bond between mothers and daughters was strong.

Mistress, Servant, Slave

Women accustomed to domestic servants in England felt their absence in North America because few single women came to New England as indentured servants. Mary Dudley begged her mother's assistance in finding a maid: "I still continue to be a troublesome suter to you, in the behalfe of a mayd . . . I desire the mayd that you provide me may be one that hath been used to all kinds of work and must refuse none. If she have skill in the dayrie I shall be the gladder." Margaret Winthrop came to her daughter's aid, but the maid proved to be a "great affliction" to her mistress. Mary Dudley reported: "at her first coming she carried herself dutifully as became a servant; but . . . she hath got such a head, and is growen soe insolent that her carriage towards us, especially myselfe, is unsufferable. If I bid her doe a thing shee will bid me to doe it myselfe, and she says how she can give content as well as any servant byt shee will not, and says if I love not quietness I was never so fitted in my life for shee would make me have enough of it."[55] Mary Dudley's maid, like other indentured servants, clearly understood her value and capitalized on it.

Many New England servants were children whom their parents placed in neighbors' homes. This custom was a modification of the apprenticeship system with which settlers were familiar in England. The Puritans may have relied on this practice for religious reasons as well. Fearing that their love for their children would interfere with discipline and training, they chose to relinquish this God-given responsibility to others. New England sons were probably "put out" more often than daughters. The Puritans considered the discovery of a boy's God-ordained "calling," his trade or career, important. Because they assumed that God's "calling" for girls was marriage and motherhood, and because mothers valued their daughters' domestic assistance, girls were less frequently placed with other families to learn household skills. Some poor families, however, put out their daughters to relieve themselves of their maintenance. Others sent daughters to live with families of higher social status, hoping they would learn domestic skills that would improve their marriage opportunities.[56] On 23 April 1688, Lawrence Hammon noted the arrival of a neighbor's daughter in his diary: "This day came into our family Elizabeth Nevenson, daughter of Mr. John Nevinson and Elizabeth his wife, who wilbe 13 yeares of age the 22d day of October next: The verbal Covenant betweene my wife and Mrs. Nevenson is, that she the said Elizabeth shall dwell with my wife as a servant six yeares, to be taught, instructed and provided for as shalbe meet, and that she shall not depart from our family during the said time without my wives consent."[57]

Whether children or adults, most servants and even African slaves lived with their masters and mistresses on intimate terms. Housed in small quarters, they commonly shared their meals with the family. In 1704 traveler Sarah Knight decried this practice. Connecticut servants and slaves, she said, "[g]enerally lived very well and comfortably in their famelies. But too Indulgent (especially ye farmers) to their slaves: sufering too great familiarity from them, permitting ym to sit at Table and eat with them, (as they say to save time), and into the dish goes the black hoof as freely as the white hand."[58] While servants and slaves often worked side by side with their mistresses and masters at home, in the fields or at a craft, proximity did not imply that they were the equals of their masters.[59]

The bigger the farm or plantation and the more specialized its product, the more narrowly defined was slave women's work; the smaller the farm and the more diversified its products, the more varied their responsibilities. On the small farms of New England, slave women's agricultural work was mixed with domestic labor, and they were often taught skills by their mistresses. On large plantations, women's field work was of primary importance, and this repetitive and monotonous labor seldom permitted them to learn any other skills.[60]

African women brought to New England as slaves supplemented the labor of English families and their servants during the seventeenth century. Many worked on farms where they served as maids, cooks, laundresses, and general house servants, assisting their mistresses at their tasks. Some worked in the dairy and manufactured butter and cheese. Others learned how to spin, weave, and sew, making cloth and clothing for use by their master's family or for sale. The region's economy meant that they often worked with and learned from their mistresses.

THE PURITANS AND WOMEN'S EDUCATION

In addition to training their daughters, servants, and slaves in domestic responsibilities, Puritan women educated their daughters and sons in religious matters and taught them to read. In 1642 the colony of Massachusetts passed a law requiring that all children be taught to read, and other New England colonies followed its lead. The Quaker colony of Pennsylvania was the only non-Puritan colony to mandate that all children, regardless of gender, be taught to read and write by the time they were 12 years old.

Girls and boys progressed from the hornbook to the primer, Psalter, Testament, and, finally, the Bible as they learned to read. Hornbooks— wooden paddles with the alphabet, a few lines containing an introduction to syllables, and the Lord's Prayer—were often used in dame schools, private schools for small children run by women, often widows, in their homes. Many children learned to read at these schools or at home before they entered regular schools. There they encountered books like the *New England Primer*, containing vocabulary and catechism. The Psalter—the Book of Psalms—was often used as the minimum standard of reading competency in the Puritan colonies, while the New and Old Testaments were the objective of reading education. Writing was taught separately from reading, and girls were less likely to know how to write than boys. The ministry, the law, and trade were professions requiring the ability to write, and because women were barred from them by custom, girls were typically excluded from writing instruction. The percentage of women able to write was much lower than that of men, and probably no more than a third were able to sign their names.[61]

Instead of learning to write, girls were taught to sew. Their tool was the needle rather than the pen; their medium thread rather than ink. New England poet Anne Bradstreet encountered criticism for her unusual pursuits and responded:

> I am obnoxious to each carping tongue
> Who says my hand a needle better fits,
> A Poets pen all scorn I should thus wrong
> For such despite they cast on female wits.[62]

With such hostility to female learning, it is not surprising that in the colonies, as in England, only exceptional women learned to write more than their own names.

While the Puritans in England and America believed that women should be educated in all domestic skills and in the tenets of their religion, they thought excessive education a dangerous thing. Did not women who devoted themselves to the study of theology or politics usurp the place of men and challenge the will of God? John Winthrop blamed intellectual pursuits for the insanity of Mistress Hopkins, the wife of Connecticut's governor: "Her husband, being very loving and tender of her, was loath to grieve her; but he saw his error, when it was too late. For if she had attended her household affairs, and such things as belong to women, and not gone out of her way and calling to meddle in such things as are proper for men, whose minds are stronger, etc., she had kept her wits, and might have improved them usefully and honorably in the place God had set her."[63] Women who "meddled in such things as are proper for men," like Anne Hutchinson and Anne Bradstreet, courted the censure of New England men and women alike. While Anne Hutchinson dared to challenge publicly the authority of Massachusetts's ministers and magistrates, Bradstreet subtly defied them as a poet.

ANNE BRADSTREET

Anne Bradstreet's poetry, with its use of domestic imagery, provides insight into one woman's life in seventeenth-century New England. Bradstreet was an exceptionally well-educated, pious woman who personified the Puritan ideal of the goodwife. She was a loving wife and mother and a God-fearing woman who was skilled in all of the domestic arts. But the poet and her poetry defied contemporary assumptions about women's intellectual capabilities. In a poem honoring Queen Elizabeth, she lamented the passing of an age when women's intellect was esteemed:

> Now say, have women worth? or have they
>   none?
> Or had they some, but with our Queen is't gone?
> Nay, masculines, you have thus taxed us long,
> Let such as say our sex is void of reason,
> Know 'tis slander now but once was treason.[64]

Anne Dudley Bradstreet was born in England in 1612 to Puritan Thomas Dudley, steward to the Earl of Lincoln, and Dorothy Dudley, "a gentlewoman whose Extract and Estate were Considerable." With her father's support and encouragement, she received an excellent education and had access to the earl's extensive library. She married Simon Bradstreet, the son of a nonconformist minister, when she was 16 years of age, and traveled with him and her parents to Massachusetts in 1630. There her father served as a magistrate, governor, deputy governor, assistant (a representative on the governor's council), and justice of the peace, while her husband held the offices of governor and deputy governor.

Anne Bradstreet gave birth to four sons and four daughters while residing first in the town of Ipswich, and later in Andover, Massachusetts. As she remarked, "I had eight birds hatcht in one nest, / Four Cocks there wer, and Hens the rest."[65] Devoted to her family, Bradstreet took refuge in her faith, her husband, and her poetry. Although she struggled privately with the tenets of her religion—for a time she even questioned the existence of God—she resolved her doubts through her writing.

A collection of Bradstreet's poetry was published in England in 1650 as *The Tenth Muse, lately sprung up in America,* the first volume of poetry produced by an American colonist. Although many of her early poems were derivative of the works of Philip Sidney and Guillaume du Bartas, it is Bradstreet's "private" poetry, written about her home and family, that distinguish her as an artist. In these poems, she revealed herself as a woman with a sense of humor who loved her family and derived pleasure from her domestic responsibilities. At the same time, her writing demonstrates the skillful wit of an intelligent woman, capable of defending her art. Amidst her many household duties and the rearing of eight children, Bradstreet found the time to write, leaving a legacy for her children and for posterity.

Bradstreet's relationship with her "Dear and loving Husband" was happy. Her poems describe their love as passionate and fulfilling:

> If ever two were one, then surely we;
> If ever man were lov'd by wife then thee;
> If ever wife was happy in a man,
> Compare with me ye women if you can.
> I prize thy love more than whole Mines of
>   gold,
> Or all the riches that the East doth hold.
> My love is such that Rivers cannot quench,
> Nor ought but love from thee, give
>   recompence.
> Thy love is such I can no way repay,
> The heavens reward thee manifold I pray.
> Then while we live, in love lets so persever,
> That when we live no more, we may live
>   ever.[66]

Bradstreet's poems to her husband reveal the devotion of a wife and husband and the rich emotional texture of one Puritan marriage.[67]

MARRIAGE

Marriage was the single most important event in a young woman's life in early America. Who she married defined her identity and her fate. Most women fortunate enough to have living parents consulted them before choosing a marriage partner, although during the seventeenth century parental mortality, especially in the southern colonies, often made this impossible. Because they saw family as central to the perpetuation of faith, Puritans and Quakers were particularly interested in the marriage relationship. Both groups sought to redefine the meaning of marriage as a way of promoting their religious beliefs.

Puritan ministers championed marriage, believing it was a God-sanctioned relationship. As the Reverend John Cotton remarked: "Women are Creatures without which there is no comfortable Living for man: it is true of them what is wont to be said of Governments, That bad ones are better than none: They are a sort of Blasphemers then who dispise and decry them, and call them a necessary Evil, for they are a necessary Good; such as it was not good that man should be without."[68]

The Puritans believed parents had a responsibility to assist children in selecting their mates, and most young women and men trusted their parents' wisdom in making their match. At the same time, parents were urged to be sensitive to the wants and desires of their children and not force them into marriages against their will. They acknowledged the importance of mutual affection in marriage relationships, although matches based solely on sexual attraction were discouraged.

Puritans and Quakers both placed a premium on piety as a qualification for marriage and encouraged their sons and daughters to marry within their religion. They believed a common faith united a couple and would be passed on to their children. In this way, they hoped that the religious beliefs so important to the first generation of colonists would be sustained from generation to generation.

As in England, marriage in the colonies was also influenced by economic factors. Parents were especially concerned that their daughters marry men who could support them and their children and urged their daughters to marry men of similar class and background. While they might marry men from better families than their own, they were discouraged from marrying men of lesser rank. Because women assumed the status and name of their husbands, marriage beneath them lowered their status. Marriage to a man with land, the prospect of inheriting land, or a skill was the goal of most seventeenth-century women.

Because of the high mortality in the southern colonies, parents had little influence over their children's choice of marriage partners. But they were concerned about the men their daughters chose to marry, probably because southern women married at a much earlier age than did men. Orphaned girls could inherit at the age of 16, and parents feared that ambitious men might exploit their young daughters. Their fears were well-founded. In Maryland, young women orphaned before their parents could contract a marriage for them had a higher rate of premarital pregnancy than those whose parents were living. Those whose mothers were alive but whose fathers had died also had a higher rate of bridal pregnancy. Clearly, fathers protected their daughters' virtue and property from exploitation by suitors.[69]

Colonists also brought Old World customs of courtship to the New World. Their rituals of courtship and marriage followed the familiar seasonal patterns found in most agricultural areas in England and on the continent. Men usually courted women during the winter, when farm work was less demanding. In the northern colonies, winter weather and shorter days meant couples had to court indoors, where there was little privacy. In a culture where beds were often shared with others in homes and inns, bundling, a custom brought to the colonies from England and Europe, was practiced. Fully clothed couples lay together in bed, where, surrounded by family members, they achieved some degree of privacy for themselves. That this custom sometimes led to premarital sexual activity can only have been expected.[70]

Civil and religious authorities in all the colonies discouraged premarital sex, but engaged couples who consummated their relationship were not censured as severely as those not engaged to marry. Plymouth magistrates developed a three-tiered classification system for the crime of "fornication": couples were prosecuted for having sexual intercourse "Without Contract," before a formal engagement; "If they be or will be married," but without having contracted themselves; and "After Contract," having declared their intention to wed. Punishment was most severe for those who had sex without any intention of marrying and least for those who were publicly espoused.

An Anglican minister visiting New York in 1695 was appalled by the colonists' toleration of premarital sex: "[t]hose who in earnest do intend to be married together in so much haste, that, commonly, enjoyment precedes the marriage, to which they seldom come till a great belly puts it so forward, that they must either submit to that, or to shame and disgrace which they avoid by marriage; ante-nuptial fornication, where that succeeds, being not looked upon as any scandal or sin at all."[71] Most couples were prosecuted for fornication only if a woman's pregnancy was discovered or if she gave birth less than nine months after her marriage.[72]

The Puritans brought many familiar marriage customs with them, regularizing them as they established their model society in the New World. In New England, couples who desired to marry announced their intention to do so at three public meetings in their town or printed their marriage plans and posted them on the meeting house for a period of two weeks. Because Puritans did not believe that marriage was a sacrament, all marriages in the region were civil ceremonies, conducted by magistrates rather than ministers. After 1686, however, as the faith and authority of the Puritans declined, ministers were permitted to conduct ceremonies in New England.

In the southern colonies, settlers replicated the marriage customs of their mother country. Couples were espoused and publicly announced their intention to marry, and weddings were conducted by a minister in a church, when possible. Frontier conditions and the scarcity of clergy during most of the century, however, often prevented the solemnization of marriage vows in church. Then, as was the custom in England, a union was recognized as valid if it "had been consummated in sexual union and preceded by a contract, either public or private, with witnesses or without, in the present tense or the future tense."[73] In Catholic Maryland, banns, announcements of a couples intention to marry, were not regularly published until after 1696, and the absence of Protestant clergy or justices of the peace there meant that many couples wed themselves.[74]

Once a couple married, their relationship had to be consummated to be legally valid. In the New England colonies where absolute divorce was permitted, failure to consummate the marriage was grounds for divorce.[75] Sexual intercourse was viewed as a natural and necessary component of any marriage relationship. While the Puritans warned against premarital and extramarital sexual relations, they believed a loving relationship was affirmed by sexual desire. Indeed, Puritan theologians exhorted husbands and wives to desire each other, their passion bonding them together as one. But desire was always to be moderate and subordinate to love of God. To place passion for husband or wife before God was idolatry, for it upset the order of creation.[76]

HUSBANDS AND WIVES

Most colonists assumed that the husband was the superior in marriage and that a wife must submit to his authority. Yet the Puritans believed that the relationship between husband and wife should also be loving. Samuel Willard advised husbands to wield their authority gently and temper it with love and concern, "as that his Wife may take delight in it and not account it a Slavery, but a Liberty and Priviledge; and the Wife ought to carry it so to her Husband, as he may take Content in her."[77]

While Anne Bradstreet's love for her husband bordered on idolatry, the relationship between John Winthrop and his wife in many ways embodied the model Puritan marriage. Margaret Tyndal became the wife of twice-widowed John Winthrop in April 1618. When they married, Winthrop was a 31-year-old father of four and she was a 27-year-old "spinster." Theirs was a long and happy union. They resided at his family home in Groton, Suffolk, England, where in 1619 she gave birth to a son, Stephen, and two years later, another son, Adam. The couple was often apart because of Winthrop's work. In his absence, Margaret managed the family's business affairs as well as her domestic responsibilities. Their letters reveal the nature of their marriage. Winthrop referred to his wife as "My Chiefe Joy in this World" and freely expressed his affection to her. Margaret's letters convey her piety and desire to please her husband. Addressing Winthrop as "my most sweet husband," she remarked, "I wish that I may be allwayes pleasinge to thee, and that those comforts we have in each other may be dayly increaced as far as they be pleasing to God. . . . I have many resons to make me love thee wheareof I will name two; first because thou lovest God, and secondly because that thou lovest me." Noting their correspondence kept her from her household duties, she signed her letter, "Your obedyent wife, Margaret Winthrop."[78]

John Winthrop tried to be a loving, yet authoritative husband. While he consulted Margaret about domestic matters, he made all the important family decisions. "A true wife accounts her subjection her honor and freedom," he believed, "and would not think her condition safe and free, but in her subjection to her husband's authority."[79] Doubtless it was his decision to migrate to New England, although Margaret offered her support and encouragement. He traveled to Massachusetts before her, feeling "as loath to leave my kinde wife behinde me as she wilbe to stay, but we must leave all in Gods good Providence." He wrote to her affectionately from the *Arabella* on 28 March 1630: "And now my sweet soul, I must once again take my last farewell of thee in Old England. It goeth very near to my heart to leave thee." Always careful to subordinate his love for Margaret to his love of God, he continued, "but I know to whom I have committed thee even to Him, who loves thee better than any husband can."[80]

Margaret joined her husband in Boston, Massachusetts, in November 1631. There, until her death in 1647, she tried to replicate the home and domestic comforts she had left behind. Because her husband was governor of Massachusetts for many years, her home was a meeting place for colonial leaders. She supervised a large household of English and Native American servants, tended her husbands' needs, and cared for her children and stepchildren. In many ways, Margaret Tyndal embodied the ideal Puritan goodwife: self-effacing, pious, loving, and kind.

CHILDBEARING AND CHILDREARING

In the seventeenth century, regardless of their race, religion, or class, women's anatomy shaped their destiny. They regarded bearing and rearing children as their principle purpose in life and their major contribution to their family and society. Because Native American culture revolved around kinship, Algonquin women's fertility was both honored and feared. A girl's coming of age with first menstruation was identified as an important moment in her life. Menstruating women were believed to possess dangerously great spiritual power that could deprive men of their strength or blight the crops. Therefore, virtually all tribes required the seclusion of women during their periods. While temporary banishment in menstrual huts outside the village may be viewed as ostracism from the tribe, it was also a time when women contemplated their nature and its importance in their community. Free from laboring for the tribe when they were in seclusion, it is possible they saw this as an opportunity to be alone and meditate, or share the company of other women.[81]

European men were struck by the apparent ease with which Native American women gave birth. A Jesuit missionary among the Hurons was amazed to find that "[e]ven the women with child are so strong that they give birth by themselves, and for the most part do not lie up [recuperate in bed]. I have seen some of them come in from the woods, laden with a big bundle of wood, and give birth to a child as soon as they arrive; then immediately they are on their feet at their ordinary employment."[82]

Roger Williams believed Narragansett women suffered less pain in childbirth than English women. This he attributed to "the hardness of their constitution, in which respect they beare their sorrowes the easier," and to their physical strength. He was also struck by their demeanor during childbirth. "Most of them count it a shame for a Woman in Travell to make complaint, and many of them are scarcely heard to groane," he noted. "I have often knowne in one Quarter of an houre a Woman merry in the House, and delivered and merry again: and within two dayes abroad, and after foure or five dayes at worke, &c."[83] While Williams's belief that Native American women felt less pain than English women was probably false, it is possible that they endorsed silent courage during childbirth as an example for their newborn infants.[84]

Many European men assumed that Native American women gave birth alone. While this is possible, it is more likely that laboring women were secluded from men, who were kept ignorant of the rituals of birth. In virtually all tribes, as in seventeenth-century England and the American colonies, older women served as mediators and facilitators of childbirth. Some women's agricultural skills extended into the realm of herbal medicine and the healing arts, and they were elevated to the position of shaman, or spiritual leader, in their tribes. Often these female shamans were skilled midwives who gave women spiritual and medicinal comfort during childbirth.[85]

Once they gave birth, the women of most Algonquin tribes nursed their infants for three or four years, much longer than their English counterparts. As they may also have practiced sexual abstinence during this time, they bore fewer children than English women in the colonies. Some observers noted that when Native American women became pregnant while nursing, they abruptly weaned their infants, believing that to continue nursing injured the infant and the unborn child.[86]

The lives of African slave women were also affected by their ability to bear and rear children. Once masters recognized that their initial investment in slaves increased through natural reproduction, they encouraged African women's fertility. The women themselves recognized the importance of their ability to bear children and sought as much control as possible over their reproductive lives. To prove their worth to their owners and forestall their sale from their home plantations, African women bore their first child earlier than their English counterparts. After this demonstration of their fertility, they usually delayed the birth of their next child. African women also learned that masters often reduced their workload while they were pregnant or nursing their children and gave them better rations as inducement to procreate.

On large plantations where their labor could be temporarily spared, pregnant and nursing women were sometimes put to work in female "trash gangs." These women weeded garden plots and performed light hoeing, tasks that did not place undue stress on their bodies. Adolescent girls often worked with these women, and it was probably in these work groups that girls learned about sex, childbirth, and survival within the constraints of slavery. Some masters, however, required pregnant slave women to work in their fields. These women probably had a higher rate of miscarriage and stillbirths and fewer children born to them than their English mistresses during the seventeenth century.[87]

The practice of long-term nursing carried out by many African women and their daughters was brought from their homeland. In this way they not only perpetuated African traditions but, to some degree, controlled the number of children they bore. Once slave women reached menopause and were no longer able to bear children, however, they were sent to the fields to do the work of men. When they grew too old for fieldwork, they were assigned to work in plantation trash gangs or to care for toddlers and young children whose mothers worked in the fields.

Like Native American and African women, English women in the American colonies found their lives were defined by pregnancy and childbirth. Pregnant usually within a year of marriage, most experienced the "travail" of pregnancy many times before giving birth to their last child around the age of 40, when menopause commenced. While they viewed pregnancy as a time to rest and eat properly and were treated by their husbands with greater care, women were still expected to perform their domestic duties. Women of simple means, without daughters, servants, or slaves to assist them, found that the necessity of their labor outweighed their desire to rest.[88]

Childbirth gave meaning to women's lives in early America. Those who found it difficult to conceive, or whose pregnancies ended in miscarriage or stillbirth, often despaired and viewed themselves as failures. Anne Bradstreet painfully recalled her early infertility: "It pleased God to keep me a long time without a child, which was a great grief to me, and cost mee many prayers and tears before I obtaind one, and after him gave mee many more."[89]

Childbirth was a dramatic moment in a woman's life. In childbirth she risked death to bring forth life. Giving birth placed her at center stage in the drama of life, temporarily usurping the position of men.

Although most rituals of childbirth in seventeenth-century America are shrouded in mystery, it is clear that women ruled over the birth process. There is no evidence that men were customarily present or assisted at births. Midwives were highly esteemed because they performed a valuable service to their communities. Although some acquired their position by bearing many children, others, who observed births and studied herbal medicine, apprenticed in the profession.[90]

Female friends and neighbors congregated at the expectant mother's home to offer comfort and support while the midwife supervised the birth and tended the laboring woman. The mother-to-be was responsible for providing her visitors with refreshments, and the early stages of a woman's labor had a party-like atmosphere about them. Relieved of their own domestic duties for the occasion, women enjoyed the opportunity to socialize with their neighbors and to pray together. Most had experienced childbirth themselves and offered their advice and assistance. Whether single, unmarried women were permitted to attend a lying-in is unclear, although a woman's daughters probably attended her.[91]

Herbal medicines eased women's discomfort in labor. Colonial women, like those in England and their Native American counterparts, grew herbs and distilled medicines to treat common family ailments. Many possessed recipe books containing instructions not only for preparing foods but also for making possetts, compresses, and medicines. Most probably stocked their pantries with substances understood to have healthful properties. Englishman Thomas Tusser recommended the following:

> Good huswives provide ere an sickness do come
> Of sundry good things in her house do have
>   some.
> Good aqua compisita, vinegar tart,
> Rosewater and treacle to comfort the heart.
> Conserve of the barberry, quinces and such,
> With sirops that easeth the sickly so much.
> Ask Medicus counsel ere medicine ye make,
> And honor that man for necessity's sake.[92]

Syrups made of betony and poppy juice, poultices made of eggs, and lubricants made of butter and lard aided the midwife in her work. Some believed that "The Livers and Galls of Eeles, dried slowly in an Oven, powdered, and given to the Quantity of a Walnut in White Wine, have kept Multitudes of Women, from dying in Hard Labour." Still, childbirth was "natural" in the seventeenth century, and women expected to experience pain.[93]

Women who were religious saw childbirth as a means of redemption from the curse of Eve. Cotton Mather believed that,

> The Truth is, That tho' the Hazards and Hardships undergone by Travailing Women be a considerable Article of the Curse, which the Transgression whereinto our Mother was Deceived has brought upon a Miserable World, yett our Great Redeemer has procured this Grace from God unto the Daughters of Zion, that the Curse is turned into a Blessing. The Approach of their Travails, putts them upon those Exercises of Piety, which render them truly Blessed ones; Blessed because their Transgression is forgiven; Blessed because they are Turned from their Iniquities.[94]

Some fortunate women received childbed linens from their mothers as part of their dowry when they married. Following the birth, the new mother's bed was dressed in these linens, often richly embroidered and trimmed with lace, and she received her visitors. If she did not survive childbirth, however, the linen became her shroud. Thus, childbed linen had both practical use and symbolic importance in the lives of seventeenth-century women.

Fear of death in childbirth, common among women of all races and classes, is reflected in the poetry of Anne Bradstreet. As she wrote for her husband:

> How soone, my Dear, death may my steps attend,
> How soon't may be thy Lot to lose thy friend . . .
> Look to my little babes my dear remains.
> And if thou love thy self, or loved'st me
> These O protect from step Dames injury.[95]

It was customary for mothers to breastfeed their children in early America. A nursing woman was welcome at the birth for she nursed the infant until the mother's milk began to flow. Colostrum, the first issue from the mother's breasts, was thought unhealthy for the infant to ingest. Although wealthy women in England hired wet nurses to feed their infants, most colonial women did not follow their lead and nursed their infants themselves. They took heed of Thomas Tusser's advice:

> Good Huswives take paine, and do count
> it good luck,
> To make their own brests their own child
> to give suk,
> Though wrauling and rocking be noysome
> so near,
> Yet lost by ill nursing is worser to hear.[96]

Puritan ministers deplored the use of wet nurses and believed that mothers who refused to breastfeed violated God's will. Cotton Mather commanded women to "Suckle your Infant your Selfe if you can; Be not such an Ostrich as to Decline it, merely because you would be One of the Careless Women, Living at Ease. Of such we read, They are Dead while they Live."[97] Only when a woman was ill or physically incapable of nursing was she thought justified in employing a wet nurse. The belief that an infant ingested the characteristics and temperament of the nurse through her breast milk precluded the use of African or Native American women as wet nurses during the century.[98]

Most women nursed their infants for 12 to 18 months during the seventeenth century. By breastfeeding their infants on demand, they experienced the temporary contraceptive effects of lactation and gave birth to children at roughly two-year intervals. While some women also abstained from intercourse while breastfeeding—they believed sexual activity tainted the milk and injured the nursing child—most probably resumed sexual relations with their husbands when their babies could eat other foods. Partially nursing, however, they became fertile once more. If they became pregnant while nursing, they immediately weaned their child. Like Native Americans, they thought the nursing baby deprived the unborn infant of nourishment and threatened both their lives.

Infant weaning was a traumatic event and a rite of passage for mother and child. Some women gradually weaned their babies, supplementing their diet with pap—a mixture of bread and milk or water—or other soft foods; others abruptly weaned them. Poor women, and probably many slaves, nursed longer than those who were prosperous for they had neither the time nor the means to prepare special foods for their babies. Instead, they probably breastfed until their children could eat the same food as the rest of the family.

Most English children were weaned when their first teeth began to appear. One early authority on childrearing warned mothers that "It is . . . safest, not to wean infants before they have all or most of their teeth, that they may have somewhat to trust in case of sickness; for they will take the nipple when all other nourishment is refused." Because children were thought especially vulnerable to illness when weaning, the process usually occurred during the healthier months of autumn or spring.[99]

The most common method used by mothers to wean their babies was to paint their breasts and nipples with a bitter mixture to discourage sucking. Anne Bradstreet revealed her own recipe for such a mixture: "Some children are hardly weaned: although the teat be rubbed with wormwood or mustard, they will either wipe it off or else suck down sweet and bitter together." Other mothers embarked on "weaning journeys," leaving their baby at home while they visited family and friends far from the child's cries, or placed the child in the home of friends until the process was complete.[100]

The experiences of two New England mothers illustrate how pregnancy, childbearing, and childrearing dominated women's lives. Mary Champney married Ebenezer Parkman, a Congregational minister, in 1724 when she was 24 years old. She gave birth to five children before her death in 1736. Her first child, Mary, was born 14 months after her marriage. Subsequent pregnancies resulted in the births of Ebenezer, Thomas, Lydia, and Lucy, at intervals of 23, 22, 26, and 36 months. Mary nursed her children for 10 to 20 months following their births.

After Mary's death from pregnancy complications, her husband married 21-year-old Hannah Breck. Hannah's first pregnancy ended in a miscarriage six months after her marriage. Within ten months, however, she gave birth to a daughter, Elizabeth, who died 17 days after she was born. Hannah quickly conceived and miscarried again 11 months after her daughter's death. Fourteen months later, however, she gave birth to a son, William. Following his birth, Hannah bore nine more children at intervals ranging from 23 to 35 months. She gave birth to her last child when she was 44 years old.

THE PURITAN GOODWIFE

While Mary Parkman's life was cut short by pregnancy, Hannah Parkman's was governed by maternity. A mother of ten and a stepmother of five children, Hannah's days were full. Although the Parkman family had servants, it was Hannah's job to supervise their activities and see their work was done. She was responsible for seeing that her family was well-fed and well-clothed and that her bustling house was kept clean. She relied on her daughters and stepdaughters to help care for the youngest children, preparing them for their future "calling" as wives and mothers. This Puritan goodwife also supervised her children's religious lessons while serving as her minister husband's helpmate and confidant.[101]

Anne Bradstreet's poem honoring her mother, Dorothy Dudley, reflects the qualities to which Hannah Parkman and other women like her aspired. Although they often fell short of this ideal, most strove to be

> A Worthy Matron of unspotted life,
> A loving Mother and obedient wife,
> A friendly Neighbor, pitiful to poor,
> Whom oft she fed, and clothed with her store;
> To Servants wisely aweful, but yet kind,
> And as they did, so they reward did find:

A true Instructor of her Family,
The which she ordered with dexterity.
The publick meetings ever did frequent,
and in her Closet constant hours she spent;
Religious in all her words and wayes,
Preparing still for death till end of dayes:
Of all her Children, Children, liv'd to see,
Then dying, left a blessed memory.[102]

Women's ability to bear and rear children dominated their lives in some colonies by the end of the seventeenth century. Earlier generations of women, and those who continued to live on the edge of civilization, struggled to bear children as they shouldered men's work and adjusted to alien environments. Subsequent generations focused more and more of their attention on motherhood and their domestic role. No longer required to perform the work of men, these women redirected their energies into fulfilling their "traditional" roles. They became preoccupied with bearing and rearing their children, reveling in tasks they believed only women could perform.[103]

DEPUTY HUSBANDS

In addition to caring for her children, the colonial housewife often helped her husband at his work. Acting as his "deputy," she frequently was well-versed in matters in her husband's domain. Although married women, "femes covert," had no legal right to make contracts in most colonies, wives were sometimes required to stand in for their absent husbands. A woman "in her husband's absence," one man remarked, "is wife and deputy-husband, which makes her double the files of her diligence. At his return he finds all things so well he wonders to see himself at home when he was abroad."[104] Thus, despite married women's legal limitations, there was some flexibility in gender roles. But while women might act for their husbands, it was rare for a husband to assume his wife's responsibilities, which society perceived as less important than his own.

The range of women's activities as deputy husbands and supporters of their families is evident in Henrietta Johnston's life. Born in England in 1674, the daughter of French Huguenot émigrés, Henrietta de Beau-lieu may have studied painting with English artist Thomas Forster. At the age of 20 she married Robert Dering and moved with him to Dublin, where she gave birth to two daughters. When her husband died, she married Anglican minister Gideon Johnston, a widower with two sons. While in Ireland, Johnston painted portraits of prominent residents who assisted her and her family. Then Rev. Johnston was appointed as the Bishop's Commissary in South Carolina and assigned to St. Philip's Church in Charles Town. The family traveled to the colony in the spring of 1708, where hardship awaited them. Rev. Johnston suffered from the "fluxes" and fevers endemic to the region and never again enjoyed good health. To his dismay, he discovered that the position at St. Philip's Church was already occupied, leaving the family without a home. With no income, the family was destitute. Rising to the occasion, Henrietta supported her family by painting portraits of Charles Town's gentry, many of whom were of Huguenot ancestry (figure 15).

Acknowledging his wife's contribution to the family's support, Rev. Johnston admitted, "were it not for the Assistance my wife gives me by drawing of Pictures (which can last but a little time in a place so ill peopled) I shou'd not have been able to live." By 1710, Henrietta had used up her art supplies. Her husband ruefully noted, "My wife who greatly helped me, by drawing pictures, has long ago made an end of her materials." Fortunately, friends in Ireland sent her pastel crayons, enabling her to create some of the loveliest portraits in Charles Town.

Henrietta Johnston also acted as her husband's deputy while he fought for his position at St. Philip's Church. In 1711, she departed for London carrying reports, letters, and petitions to Anglican authorities from him and his supporters in the colony. Off the coast of Virginia pirates captured her ship, which was presumed lost. Plucky Henrietta eventually reached London, secured her husband's appointment, and returned to Charles Town in 1712. After her husband's death by drowning in 1716, she continued to paint portraits, even traveling to New York for a time. Henrietta eventually returned to Charles Town and supported her family as an artist until her death in 1726.[105]

Like Henrietta Johnston, other women championed their husbands' interests, and their own, in the economic and political disruptions known as Bacon's Rebellion. Led by Nathaniel Bacon in 1675, this event began as a campaign against Virginia's Native Americans but

Figure 15. Pastel of Mrs. Samuel Prioleau, 1715. (Mary Magdalen Gendron) Crayon on paper, 12 × 9 inches. Artist: Henrietta Johnston. *Collection of the Museum of Early Southern Decorative Arts, Winston-Salem, North Carolina.*

eventually embroiled the entire colony in civil war. Bacon orchestrated a short-lived coup against the colony's aging governor, William Berkeley, and women were public supporters of both men. Frances Culpeper Berkeley, the governor's ambitious and aristocratic wife, was a chief protagonist in the conflict. She greatly influenced her husband's political appointments and defended him against those who challenged his authority. She voyaged to England and petitioned Charles II to intervene on her husband's behalf. The king responded by sending investigators and troops to bring peace to the colony. In defending her husband, "Lady Berkeley," as her detractors called her, was defending her own position in the colony. Other wives of Berkeley loyalists were held hostage in Jamestown and found themselves used as human shields on its battlements when Bacon and his supporters seized the capital.

Nathaniel Bacon also had female supporters who believed he represented the economic and political interests of their husbands and fathers and, by inference, themselves. Many served as "news wives," mobilizing public opinion against the governor's policies. Some, like Mrs. Hanyland, traveled throughout the colony encouraging rebellion, while others, like Mrs. Cheezman, urged their husbands to support Bacon's cause. Firebrand Sarah Drummond, wife of one of the rebellion's leaders, even defied imperial authority. "I fear the power of England," she boasted, "no more than a broken straw." She urged the rebels to consider independence from England, believing, "We shall do well enough."[106]

The "news wives" of Bacon's Rebellion identified men's interests as their own and actively participated in the public sphere of colonial politics as their husbands' surrogates. Although they lacked the legal right to voice their opinions in the political arena, they would not be silenced. They seized the opportunity to influence events, confirming their "oneness" with their husbands and affirming the values of their time.

Mrs. John Davenport, the wife of Rev. John Davenport, also transcended the role of "deputy husband" when she assumed responsibility for the financial affairs of Connecticut's Governor John Winthrop, Jr., in addition to those of her family. With her husband's consent and support, Davenport conducted business in the governor's name, trading corn for beaver skins and wampum. It was she who decided when Winthrop was to plant his corn and how much his crop was worth; it was she who rejected some skins as unfit for trade. As Rev. Davidson explained to the governor: "My wife desireth to add that she received for you of Mr. Goodenhouse 30s worth of beaver & 4s in wampum. She purposeth to send your beaver to the Baye when the best time is, to sell it for your advantage and afterwards to give you an account what it comes to . . . Sister Hobbadge has paid my wife in part of her debt to you a bushel of winter wheat."[107]

SHOPKEEPERS, TRADERS, AND ARTISANS

As the English colonies flourished, towns grew as centers of commerce and trade. Craftsmen prospered as demand increased for the goods they produced. Most artisans and craftsmen worked out of their homes, literally living above their shop. Many wives assisted their husbands while performing their household work. Although some husbands encouraged their wives' involvement in business matters, others did not. And, while some women welcomed the opportunity to enter men's domain of commerce and trade, others saw it as an additional responsibility in a life already full of duties and obligations.

Some urban women capitalized on their skills with the needle to augment their fathers' and husbands' wages. Itinerant seamstresses were often employed by wealthy women to make their family's clothes. Female mantua makers and lace makers frequently advertised their artistry in urban newspapers, while other women specialized in laundering, starching, and dyeing fine articles of clothing. Mary Stafford struggled to "earn an honest living" in Charles Town, South Carolina. She told her English cousin that she had "undertook to clear starch[,] dress heads & make linen which I continue still to doe." Later Stafford took in boarders. Without funds to purchase a slave, she leased one, instead, and hired a female indentured servant. With their assistance she took in more lodgers and saved enough to purchase a male slave.[108]

Inn keeping and tavern keeping were a profitable extension of women's domestic responsibilities, and many widows whose legacy from their husbands included their home opened their doors to travelers and boarders. Sarah Knight visited a number of inns operated by women, not all of whom were exemplary hostesses or good housekeepers. At an inn at Saybrook Ferry she encountered the "Landlady . . . with her hair about her ears, and hands at full pay, scratching. Shee told us shee had some mutton wch shee would broil for us, wch I was glad to hear: But I supose forgot to wash her scratchers; in a little time she brot it in, but it being pikled and my guid said it smelt strong of head sauce. We left it, and paid sixpence apiece for our Dinners, which was only smell."[109]

It was not unusual for a widow to continue her husband's business as a merchant or shopkeeper. Many continued their husbands' work as soap and tallow chandlers, millers and brewers, bakers and butchers. More unusual were widows who carried on their husbands' rope-making, cutlery, and blacksmithing businesses.[110] So many widows assumed their husbands' shops in the city of New York that they met and submitted a letter to editor John Peter Zenger, who published it in the *New York Journal* in early 1733. In their letter the women declared: "We are House keepers, Pay our Taxes, carry on Trade, and most of us are she Merchants, and as we in some measure contribute to the Support of Government, we ought to be Intituled to some of the Sweets of it." They resented that they were not "invited to Dine at Court" and believed their exclusion from such "men only" gatherings gave their male competitors an unfair advantage in business. Unfortunately, the widows' complaint was deemed frivolous and never seriously addressed.[111]

A number of widows operated printing businesses in the colonies. William Nuthead established a press at St. Mary's City, Maryland, in 1686, and his wife, Dinah, inherited it upon his death in 1695. She moved the press to Annapolis when the capitol was relocated there, and, although she could not write, Dinah secured the government's printing contract, signing the agreement with her mark. It is likely that she managed the business and employed a journeyman printer to operate the press. The shop was her husband's legacy to their sons, and she kept it in trust for them. More unusual was Benjamin Franklin's sister-in-law, Anne Franklin, who in 1735 inherited her husband's press in Newport, Rhode Island. There, with the assistance of her daughters, she operated a printing business, securing the Rhode Island government's contract. Anne's shop printed pamphlets, forms, and an edition of the colony's laws.[112]

Martha Smith helped her husband with his whaling business, accompanying him on voyages where she observed crews rendering the whales' blubber for valuable oil. When her husband died, he entrusted her with the business until their sons came of age. Not one to wait ashore while her fleet sailed the Atlantic, Martha Smith commanded her own ship. In the ship's log of 16 January 1707, she recorded, "My company killed a yearling whale made 27 barrels." On 4 February, "Indian Harry with his boat struck a whale and called for my boat to help him," she noted. "I had but a third which was 4 barrels." One suspects this lively widow enjoyed sailing the high seas while safeguarding her sons' legacy.[113]

Widows like Martha Smith made Cotton Mather uneasy. He commended wives who assisted their husbands—"While her Husband was alive she still acted as a deputy Husband, for the maintaining of all good Orders in the House, when he was out of the Way"—but was critical of widows who presumed to run their husbands' businesses— "And now her Husband is deceas'd, she thinks that upon the Setting of the Sun, the Moon is to govern."[114] Clearly, Mather felt threatened by women who disrupted God's order by usurping the authority of men.

Tragically, the ranks of widows who had to support themselves and their families were swelled by warfare. War disrupted life in New England and affected the lives of women throughout the colonies. Between 1689 and 1713 as many as one-fifth of all Massachusetts men fought in King William's War and Queen Anne's War, colonial counterparts to European dynastic struggles. One-quarter of them lost their lives in battle with the French and their Native American allies at Port Royal, Montreal, and Quebec.[115]

Although some men became rich provisioning armies, women and children suffered as their menfolk died in battle. Soldiers tended to be young men who died before accumulating estates large enough to support their widows and minor children. Often destitute, with no means of supporting themselves or their children, their widows searched for work in urban centers, where many became financial burdens in the postwar years. Widows made up 14.3 percent of Boston's population from 1689 to 1699, and were 16 percent of the population in 1725. The city was "full of widows and orphans, and many of them helpless creatures."[116]

Ironically, the migration of war widows to Boston and other urban centers increased educational opportunities for their daughters. Some widows supported themselves by opening dame schools. Proximity to these schools meant that many more girls had access to learning, while economic necessity motivated them to seek a better education. Men's attitudes about educating women also changed as governments faced the escalating cost of providing for poor unskilled women and their daughters. Women's education was less problematic than their destitution. As a result, the quality of girls' education slowly improved and their literacy, measured by their ability to sign their names on wills, increased in urban centers.[117]

* * *

The colonial woman took pride in her home and family and tried to perform her domestic responsibilities as she had in England. She was her husband's companion, a "consort," offering him solace and encouragement as he faced the challenges of building a future for his family in the New World. His partner, or helpmeet, her labor complemented his, and she often assisted him at his work. Her most important responsibility was to bear children, and her life was measured by cycles of pregnancy, childbirth, breastfeeding, and weaning. She taught her daughters the domestic skills they needed to manage homes of their own. She tried to be a good neighbor and hoped to have female neighbors on whom she could rely in times of joy and sorrow. Their friendship sustained her as she faced the perils of childbirth and widowhood. Together these women found security and purpose in their traditional roles as wives and mothers in the New World.

African and Native American women also tried to keep alive the rich cultural traditions of their peoples in the face of enslavement and conquest. African women transported agricultural skills and cultural practices from their homeland and passed them on to their children whenever possible. Native American women held on to familiar customs and traditions as they faced a world of change. Although devalued and disparaged by English women and men who saw them as savages, Native American women were integral to the survival of their people. Gatherers, traders, farmers, and mothers, they contributed to tribal economies and were the foundation of tribal societies, even when their way of life was threatened and their people destroyed by disease and warfare.

Life on the American frontier also required that women, regardless of their race and class, adapt and change if they were to survive. Many English women learned to till the soil and perform work that was the responsibility of men in their homeland. Others handled their husbands' business affairs, assuming responsibility for making decisions in their absence. Widowed by disease and warfare, they managed estates and served as guardians for their children. African women, often isolated from others of their race on remote farms and plantations, also performed work unfamiliar to them and were forced to adapt to the horrors of slavery.

Most women reluctantly sacrificed their assumptions about men's and women's proper roles. While English women looked forward to the day when their daughters or granddaughters might resume their traditional, domestic role, African and Native American women were deprived of that hope by their enslavement and destruction. Many women, however, found new strength in their ability to adapt and change and meet the challenges of the New World.

CHAPTER FOUR

Women's Rights and the Law

She was alone.

The mourners had finally left, and the children were crying, tired and hungry after a long, solemn day. She must look after them and comfort them, but who would comfort her?

As she sat before the hearth and gazed into the glowing embers, she thought of how her family had been shattered by the events of the past few days. Their lives changed forever when the tree her husband was felling suddenly twisted, catching him in its branches as it crashed to the ground. He died in the field, his blood watering the land he tended with such care.

They buried him today in the churchyard. The preacher and her neighbors offered words of condolence. But what good were their kind words when she was all alone? She had no one to guide and protect her, or help her care for their three small children. He had not counted on dying young.

He had so many plans for their future—mortgaging their farm, buying much of what they owned on credit, counting on next year's crops to pay their debts. She never asked about their finances; men took care of such things. When she was a girl, her father had provided for her. And when she wed, her father gave her marriage portion to her husband to do with as he wished. As a married woman, she had no property of her own. This was how it always was and how it should be, she thought.

But she had not realized how deeply in debt they were—debts that had to be *honored before she was granted her "widow's third." Would there be anything left for her and the children? Who would look out for them now that her husband was gone?*

As she gazed into the dying fire, the sound of the children's weeping stirred her from her troubled thoughts. She rose to comfort them.

This young widow was confronting some of the legal limitations many women faced in seventeenth-century America. Her experience shows how laws constructed to protect men's authority within the family and their control of private property often placed women in a dependent position, jeopardizing their economic well-being and, sometimes, even their lives. The legal position of English women in the American colonies was not, however, uniform or static. It differed from colony to colony and changed over time, reflecting the distinctive experiences and shifts in the values of the colonists. Yet the overriding concern in the establishment of women's legal position in all the colonies was the same: to protect and promote not the interests of women but of the patriarchal, patrilineal English family. Although some women initially enjoyed more rights and freedoms than their counterparts in England and in other colonies, this proved only temporary. By the end of the century, their rights had been subordinated to those of their fathers, husbands, and sons.

Law is a form of social control; laws influence people's behavior and reflect their ideals. Most colonists hoped to transplant English culture and institutions to the New World, and the laws they established clarified their beliefs and defined their collective values. Their laws guided them as they confronted the challenges of the wilderness, providing them with benchmarks against which to measure their own behavior and with tools to enforce community ideals. At the same time, changes in the laws, and in the rigor with which they were enforced, reflected changes in community values. Because most colonists believed that the patriarchal family was the very foundation of English civilization, the legal systems they crafted preserved the sanctity of the male-headed family and safeguarded the private property that sustained it. Consequently, the legal position of women in the colonies promoted these ends.

The Common Law and Women

Women's legal status in English North America was derived from England's common law. The common law seldom recognized the existence of the single woman, the *feme sole*, except as someone about to be married. Her rights were subsumed under those of her father or nearest male relative, and when she married she legally became "one" with her husband.[1] "By marriage, the husband and wife are one person in law," remarked eighteenth-century legal commentator William Blackstone. "[t]he very being or legal existence of the woman is suspended during the marriage, . . . and consolidated into that of the husband; under whose wing, protection, and cover, she performs every thing; and is therefore called in our law . . . a feme-covert . . . and her condition during her marriage is called her coverture."[2] Under the common law, a married woman was legally and economically dependent on her husband: she could not make contracts, buy and sell property, manage their estate, or serve as guardian of their children. Because all her personal possessions became her husband's when they married, she did not even own her clothing or her jewelry.

The English custom of "dower" compensated wives for their total dependence on their husbands. Dower ensured women legal protection and financial provision in a society that prevented them from supporting themselves. A widow's dower right entitled her to use one-third of her husband's real property until her death. She could use the proceeds from this property to support herself but was barred from selling it unless it was absolutely necessary. Although a man could will his wife more than her "widow's third," he could neither leave her less nor sell or mortgage property that might risk her dower.[3] In England a widow's dower was granted before creditors could make claims on the estate, and, if there were no creditors, the remaining two-thirds of the estate was divided among the surviving children. Custom decreed that the eldest son receive a double portion, while the remaining sons and daughters received equal portions. If there were no sons, the estate was divided equally among the daughters. And, if all children were minors at the time of their father's death, his widow, or a court-appointed guardian, managed their inheritance until they came of age. When his widow died, her "third" was divided among the surviving children.[4]

English daughters seldom enjoyed their inheritance, for, like their mothers, they did not actually own property. Instead, it was usually held in trust for them as a marriage portion—their "dowry"—until they wed. At a time when economics played a major role in matchmaking, a young woman's marriage prospects increased with the size of her dowry. Although she retained legal title to this property when she married, her husband controlled it, and it became their children's property when he died. If she died without children, it returned to her family.

While most husbands responsibly managed their estates, not all acted in the best interest of their wives. Consequently, laws had to be crafted to protect women from exploitation by the men on whom they depended. This protective legislation was necessary in a legal system constructed to promote patriarchy. These protective laws barred husbands from selling or mortgaging their wives' property without their wives' permission, and wives were questioned privately to confirm their consent. Trusts secured a married woman's property from her husband or his creditors, and marriage settlements permitted women to have estates free from their husbands' control. These laws safeguarded vulnerable women from their husbands' financial mismanagement.

Although English lawmakers acknowledged that some women needed protection from their husbands, they feared that a man's estates, inherited by his widow, might be lost to another man if she remarried. Instead of strengthening married women's right to own and manage property, they increased men's authority to dispose of property beyond the grave. To prevent other men from acquiring their estates by marrying their widows, some men terminated their widows' property rights if they remarried. Clearly, at least in this instance, English women's rights were subject to men's desire to control their estates even after death.[5]

In early America, women's legal status also reflected men's goals and ideals. Although women enjoyed more rights in some colonies than in England, they did so because it served men's ends—to promote patriarchal families and preserve the private property that sustained such families. Because of the high mortality rate among men in the southern colonies, for example, single and married women in the region temporarily exercised more legal rights than women in England or New England. But this regional difference had diminished by the end of the century. As southern men lived longer and their families grew, and as plantation slavery developed in the region, men reasserted their power and authority at women's expense.[6]

MARITAL UNITY AND WOMEN'S RIGHTS

Religious reformers and dissenters who voyaged to North America especially modified English women's legal rights to promote their conception of the "ideal" family in the New World. New England Puritans believed that husband and wife to be "yoak-fellows in mutuall familiaritie, not in equall authoritie." William Gouge explained that "If therefore he will one thing, and she another, she may not thinke to have an equall right and power. She must give place and yeeld."[7] Believing in the God-ordained authority of husbands, the region's lawmakers granted men even greater responsibility for family property, including the property their wives inherited or earned, than lawmakers elsewhere. Unlike their English counterparts, who created legal provisions to defend women from the harshness of patriarchy, New England Puritans believed obedient, dutiful wives did not need legal protection from their husbands. They thought that laws guarding a wife's property from her husband undermined marital unity and fostered family discord. Consequently, they prohibited marriage settlements and most other kinds of protective legislation that they believed sanctioned married women's economic independence.[8]

The stability of New England's patriarchal, patrilineal families and the longevity of the region's men meant that women in the Puritan colonies remained legally subordinate to men. Men lived long enough to name adult sons or even grandsons executors of their estates, easing the transfer of property from one generation of men to the next. Although New England men sometimes willed property to their widows, they usually granted control of it to their sons, instructing them to look out for their mothers' needs. In this way, the region's men orchestrated family obligations and influenced the relationships of mothers and sons long after death. If a New England man died young or without a will, however, the courts often gave his widow control of his estate, especially if she was young and poor and had small children. His estate was intended as her dowry. It assisted her in finding a new husband who could manage her late husband's estate and support her and her children. In this manner, too, the region's courts promoted the creation and perpetuation of male-headed families in the region.[9]

Although New England's Puritans barred married women from owning property separately from their husbands because it violated their belief in the unity of marriage, they allowed the creation of jointures.

A jointure was "a contract between husband and wife, often made as a part of a marriage settlement, designating what property the woman would receive if her husband died before her." A jointure created before the marriage preempted a woman's dower rights; if it was executed after marriage, the widow could choose between the jointure or dower. As Puritan lawmakers saw it, jointures protected rather than empowered women and did not challenge married women's dependence on their husbands.[10]

Pennsylvania's Quaker lawmakers also placed family unity before women's rights. Like the Puritans, they believed a dutiful wife needed no protection from her husband. And, because they did not think loving husbands would coerce their wives' consent to the sale or mortgaging of property, they discarded the custom of privately examining wives about such transactions. Believing, too, that responsible husbands never jeopardized their wives' dower through indebtedness, they awarded widows dower only after debts were paid from estates. As a result, widows made indigent by their husbands' insolvency had to rely on their children, relatives, or the community.[11]

There were few legal protections for married women's property rights in the New England colonies or in Pennsylvania. Although most English colonists thought wives should submit to their husbands, only Puritan and Quaker lawmakers made women's submission to men the basis for laws regarding their property rights. In these colonies, when English married women's property rights were at odds with the lawmakers' ideal notion of marriage, the ideal won. Lawmakers in Quaker Pennsylvania and in Puritan New England failed to acknowledge or address the problems faced by some married women until the eighteenth century. Thus, women in these colonies paid the price for their founders' belief in the fiction of marital unity.[12]

MORTALITY AND WOMEN'S RIGHTS

In contrast to the founders of the Puritan and Quaker colonies, southern men sometimes protected and expanded women's legal rights beyond those granted them in England. They did so, however, not because they believed women were men's equal or capable of managing estates but because they, too, wished to expedite the transfer of property from one generation of men to the next. In other words, they used different means to achieve the same end.

Southern colonists also valued the patriarchal family but were forced to confront a bitter reality. Unlike their Puritan and Quaker counterparts, they did not have the luxury of legislating marital unity. The harsh environment of the South in the seventeenth century virtually demanded that women be permitted to own and control property. Men's high mortality rate meant that many women were widowed. Nor could men count on their sons to support their mothers in old age, for the child mortality rate, too, was high in the region. They had little choice but to expand women's right to own and control property in order to safeguard their estates and secure their children's inheritance.[13] But men in the Chesapeake region also acknowledged women's importance in settling the region and for a time even entrusted them with the estates they helped build. More than half of the region's men who wrote wills during the seventeenth century named their wives as sole executors, and most left their entire estates to their widows, especially if they had no heirs. While some men named male overseers to manage their children's inheritance, the majority trusted their widows to look out for their daughters and sons.[14]

Widows quickly remarried in the Chesapeake. Women's scarcity during the seventeenth century practically guaranteed them proposals of marriage, and the difficulty of surviving on their own demanded that they find new mates. Remarriage, however, brought its share of problems for women, for it gave their new husbands legal right to their property. To guard their interests and those of their children, some women drew up premarital agreements in which their new husbands gave up control of their stepchildren's inheritance and their wives' estates.[15]

During the seventeenth century, when land was cheap and plentiful in the Chesapeake colonies, men often broke with English custom and endowed their daughters with land and slaves in addition to the customary cash and personal property. Late in the century, however, land became more valuable in the region. Fathers then developed the custom of willing land to their sons and slaves to their daughters. Although this practice kept land in the family, sons often did not have enough slaves to work the lands they inherited. Thus, arranged marriages pairing men and women, land and slaves, became common among elite families in the Chesapeake.[16]

By the end of the century, as the Chesapeake population stabilized, women's rights to own and control property diminished. Men and women lived longer and had larger families. More men saw their children grow to adulthood and marry, and did not need to appoint their widows executors of their estates or guardians of minor children. Instead, they relied on their eldest sons or other male relatives to perform these duties. Men also restricted their widows' settlements, cutting them off if they remarried. Widows became less desirable as marriage partners. Their greater age, their lack of property, and the growing number of young women in the region meant that fewer widows remarried by the eighteenth century. With adult children to care for them, it was thought that women no longer needed to own or control property, and they were relegated to an even more dependent position.[17]

THE RIGHT TO MAKE CONTRACTS

Married women were also barred from making contracts in most colonies, but necessity demanded that they be permitted to do so. England's common law decreed that a married woman could not make a contract, the reason being that since she owned nothing, nothing could be seized for restitution if she violated a contract. Her labor could not be seized by the courts and she could not be imprisoned because her husband, an innocent party, would be deprived of her labor. A married woman was also prohibited from contracting with her husband because, as Blackstone observed, "A man cannot grant any thing to his wife, or enter into covenant with her for the grant would be to suppose her separate existence; and to covenant with her, would be only to covenant with himself."[18] Despite these obstacles, women throughout the colonies did contract with their husbands or acted as their husbands' agents. The wife who acted for her husband usually possessed a document from him authorizing her to conduct business in his name. This departure from English law and custom was tolerated by lawmakers throughout the colonies because it facilitated the development of colonial economies and suited men's ends. Even in Puritan New England men defended this practice as evidence of the economic interdependence— the marital unity—of husbands and wives.

A seventeenth-century Maryland case illustrates how one married woman made contracts and sued others in that colony's courts. Walter Pakes's wife, a healer, agreed to cure John Trussel's servant for 100 pounds of tobacco. Trussel, however, refused to pay Mistress Pakes for her services, and she was forced to sue for payment. In court, Trussel challenged her right as a married woman to make a contract. In self-defense she presented a letter of attorney drawn up by her husband authorizing her "to doe any business whatsoever." She won her case and collected payment from Trussel for her services.[19]

Other women represented their husbands in Maryland's courts on a regular basis. Mistress Anne Hammond possessed a letter from her husband, John, authorizing her to "act, doe, Say, Implead, buy sell, order & dispose of" anything belonging to him, "in as full and ample power as may or can be Exprest, and as if my Selfe were personally present." Other women appeared in court without such documents because their community understood they represented their husbands' interests. But in 1658, perhaps fearing that the colony's men would completely abdicate their legal responsibilities to women, the governor and council of Maryland passed a law forbidding men from authorizing their wives to act as their agents in court and requiring that they appoint men instead.[20]

Virginians were less alarmed by wives acting as their husbands' agents. John Bland, a prosperous London merchant who owned land in the colony, named his wife, Sarah, his "true and lawful attorney" and sent her there to manage his properties in 1678. Soon after her arrival, Sarah presented her power of attorney to the judge at the Court of Charles City County. She then sold her husband's lands and sued those who were in his debt. When John Bland died in 1680, he named his wife as coexecutor of his estate with a London agent, Thomas Povey. Sarah Bland continued to conduct legal actions as a *feme sole* in the colony for Povey. Her activities were tolerated because she acted in her husband's stead, as a "deputy husband." In this manner, she affirmed the unity of her marriage and assuaged the concerns of those reluctant to permit women the legal rights to act in their own behalf.[21]

Many women served as their husbands' deputies in court and in business, but it was unusual for a woman to act as an "attorney in fact" for someone who was not a family member. Consider Rebecca Heathersall, who in 1682 represented the absent Anthony Hall in a Virginia court. In his letter of attorney, Hall identified Heathersall as "my trusty and well-beloved friend" and authorized her to "recover and receive of all and every such person and persons which are indebted to me" and to conduct his business affairs in his stead. Heathersall was remarkable in acting as the agent of a man who was not her husband. In most cases, women were tolerated in colonial courts only when they acted in behalf of male relatives. In this way, their presence in court could be justified as affirming the unity of marriage and confirming the patriarchal ideal of the family.[22]

MARGARET BRENT

Even more exceptional than Heathersall, however, was Maryland's Margaret Brent, the most famous of all women "attorneys in fact" in seventeenth-century America. Brent, her two brothers, Giles and Fulke, and her sister, Mary, emigrated to the colony in 1638. There she and Mary became independent landowners, importing servants, acquiring headrights, and managing their own plantations. Margaret Brent never married and used her *feme sole* rights to make contracts, conduct business, and prosecute debtors. From 1642 until 1650 her name appears 134 times in Maryland's court records, and most cases were decided in her favor. Her reputation prompted family and friends to ask her to represent them in the colony's courts, and Governor Leonard Calvert frequently consulted her on personal and political matters.

When Governor Calvert died in 1647, Margaret Brent was named the executor of his estate. She received permission from the court to manage his affairs and bring suits against those in his debt. Calvert's death left Maryland without a representative of the colony's proprietor, Lord Baltimore, and so the court appointed Brent his attorney as well. During her tenure as Calvert's executor and Baltimore's attorney, a suit was brought against Lord Baltimore by soldiers from Virginia. Calvert, as the proprietor's representative, had called them to Maryland to suppress a local rebellion in 1646 but never paid them for their services. Because the governor's estate was not large enough to reimburse them, Brent sold some of Lord Baltimore's cattle to settle their claim. When Baltimore objected, the Maryland assembly defended her, declaring "the Colony was safer in her hands than any man's in the Province." They rebuked Lord Baltimore, commenting, "she rather deserves favor and thanks from your Honour for her so much concerning for the public safety."[23]

On 21 January 1647, Margaret Brent petitioned the Maryland Assembly for the right to vote so that she might better handle Calvert's business affairs. The minutes of the assembly recorded this first request for the right to vote by an English woman in colonial America: "Came Mrs. Margarett Brent and requested to have vote in the howse for herselfe and voyce also for that att the last Court 3d: Jan: it was ordered that the said Mrs Brent was to be looked upon and received as his Lordships Attorney. The Governor denyed that the sd Mrs Brent should have any vote in the howse."[24] In vain, Brent appealed this decision. Soon afterward, perhaps because of her actions, she and her family fell into disfavor with Lord Baltimore and eventually moved to Virginia.

Few women were as audacious as Margaret Brent in requesting the right to vote. In early America, all women and the majority of men were prohibited by custom and law from participating in colonial government. In most colonies, property qualifications restricted political power to the few, and in some colonies, at least for a time, church membership requirements also limited access to public office. This was a culture of deference, not democracy, in which men deferred to their economic and social betters in the belief that what was good for their superiors would benefit them as well. This was also a culture that assumed that men ruled. Men represented the interests of their families in the marketplace and in the meetinghouse, and lawmakers could not comprehend that women might have interests separate from those of their fathers and husbands. The assumption that all women were members of male-headed families precluded their direct, active participation in government, regardless of their wealth or standing in the community.

FEMES SOLE

Because Margaret and Mary Brent were adult single women, however, they conducted business, made contracts, and bought and sold property as *femes sole*. Some colonies also permitted married women to own and operate businesses, but only with their husbands' consent. These women made contracts, sued, and were sued in courts of law, as if they were single women—*femes sole*. Their husbands were usually not held liable for their actions, especially if the women were well-known in their communities as businesswomen. But unless a husband explicitly gave his wife permission to keep the proceeds of her labor, all she earned was his to do with as he pleased. Thus, these women depended on their husbands' goodwill to enjoy the fruits of their own labor.

Mary Venderdonck, the daughter of Anglican minister Francis Doughtie, was a *feme sole* "physician" with a lucrative practice in Maryland. She claimed that the colony's former governor had hired her to treat three of his servants and failed to pay her. Perhaps he believed she would not take him to court to collect her fee, but in 1661 Mary successfully sued him for 1,200 pounds of tobacco. After her marriage to Hugh O'Neale, Mary continued her medical practice and sued William Heard for defamation after he spread a rumor that she had poisoned a patient. She won this case, too. Heard was ordered to apologize to her publicly and pay her 400 pounds of "good sound merchantable leaf tob[acco]" in damages.[25]

Despite their desire to protect and promote the patriarchal family in North America, colonial men discovered that the restrictions they had placed on married women's economic activities could be costly to their communities. Consequently, lawmakers granted some married women the legal rights traditionally permitted single women in English society. In Pennsylvania, for example, women whose husbands had deserted them or had been absent for a long period of time were eventually allowed to act as *femes sole* without their husbands' consent. Other married women wishing to conduct business required their husbands' permission to do so. Pennsylvania's lawmakers learned that permitting deserted wives to work was far better, and much less expensive, than having them become a burden on the community. Legislators in other colonies passed special laws known as empowering acts. These acts enabled indigent married women to assume *feme sole* status. They permitted them to sell property, discharge debts, and gain access to their inheritance so that they and their families would not become public charges.[26] Although these laws enabled women to escape the legal restraints placed on them by marriage, their passage was motivated less out of a sense of injustice than economic necessity. In this manner, the colonial lawmakers' ideal of marital unity gave way to practical considerations.

The case of Susannah Cooper reflects the economic motive behind the private empowering acts passed by the Virginia House of Burgesses. In 1744, Cooper petitioned the House of Burgesses for passage of an act permitting her to conduct business in her own behalf. She had wed Isles Cooper in 1717 and brought a sizable estate to her marriage. Within three years, however, her husband spent most of her dowry, contracted immense debts, and deserted her. He later entered two bigamous marriages and fathered a number of illegitimate children. Adding insult to injury, what was left of Susannah Cooper's estate was seized by creditors to pay his debts. For 20 long years she relied on friends and neighbors for her maintenance. Finally, through her own hard work, she accumulated a small estate and purchased a few slaves. As a married woman under coverture, however, she was legally prohibited from making contracts and selling or willing her property; her estranged husband still had legal title to all that she earned. To protect her property she asked the Virginia House of Burgesses to declare her a *feme sole*. Her request was granted on the condition that she, in turn, renounce all claims to her husband's estate. This she did willingly.[27]

By the end of the seventeenth century, colonial lawmakers were grappling with the restrictions placed on married women. The realities of marriage proved that the unity of husbands and wives was a fiction. If married women were forced to live on their own, then the law must accommodate them. If not, their community would have to support them. By the end of the century lawmakers in virtually all the colonies, with the exception of Puritan Massachusetts and Connecticut, addressed these concerns by expanding the rights of *feme sole* traders, giving women a greater voice in the sale of property and even permitting married women to have separate estates.[28] This liberalization of married women's property rights was necessary because during the seventeenth century, in all but the colonies founded by Puritans, divorce was prohibited.

DIVORCE

Two kinds of divorce were recognized by English law. Absolute divorce—*Divortium a vinculo matrimonii*—gave the couple the right to remarry. Instituted to protect nobles from adulterous wives and ensure the legitimacy of their heirs, an absolute divorce required a private act of Parliament. Absolute divorces were extremely rare and granted only when a marriage was judged to be null from the beginning. Thus, adultery by the wife, bigamy, sexual incapacity, and marriage with a blood relation were grounds for such a divorce. Once the divorce was granted, all children born to the union were declared illegitimate. Although both parties granted an absolute divorce could remarry, an adulterous wife was barred from marrying her lover. The second kind of divorce recognized in English law did not permit the couple to remarry. Separations from bed and board—*Divortium a mensa et thoro*—were usually granted in cases of adultery, cruelty, or desertion. Unless the woman was identified as the guilty party, she was granted support and her children remained legitimate.[29]

In Virginia, New York, Maryland, and South Carolina, lawmakers prohibited absolute divorce. They recognized, however, that not all marriages were happy and permitted couples to separate, often ordering husbands to support their wives and children. When Margaret Taylor complained before a Virginia court in 1699 that her husband was "so cross and cruel" she was unable to live with him, she requested a separation and asked the court for maintenance. Her request to live "secure from danger" was granted. The court then ordered her husband to supply her with furniture and clothing and pay her either 1,200 pounds of tobacco or £6 a year. Like Taylor, Margaret Macnamara complained of her husband's brutal treatment to a Maryland court in 1707. On proof of his cruelty, Thomas Macnamara was ordered to give Margaret her clothing and pay £15 annually for her support.

The amount of support colonial courts awarded separated women was influenced by their social status and the size of their dowries. In 1676–78, when Maryland residents Robert and Elizabeth Leshley declared that they could not live together, Elizabeth requested an allowance proportional to the estate she had brought to the marriage. Robert complied with her request. Sometimes, however, traditional inheritance rights were honored and the estranged wife received one-third to one-half of her husband's estate.[30] Then as now, however, many men refused to pay support to their estranged wives and many separated women found themselves in an untenable situation. Unable to remarry, they were also unable to support themselves. They were trapped in a legal limbo created by laws restricting their rights as married women and prohibitions against absolute divorce. Consequently, men granted some married women the right to control property and permitted them to function as *feme sole* traders. They did so not because they believed women deserved these rights but because they wanted to save themselves and their communities the cost of maintaining indigent women. Granting women these rights served men's ends.[31]

Unhappily married New England women had little incentive to separate from their husbands. Unlike women in other colonies, they could not function as *femes sole* once they separated; the ideal of marital unity that informed the region's laws did not permit them this freedom. And, although the courts routinely awarded them support, their husbands often refused to pay it. A separated woman's status was, therefore, ambiguous: she could not remarry or support herself, nor could she depend on her husband's support. Only absolute divorce freed New England women to act in their own behalf.[32]

Because New England Puritans believed that marriage was a civil contract, not a sacrament, they permitted absolute divorce. Strong advocates of family life and marriage, Puritan reformers believed a divorce was better than a bad marriage; divorce ended flawed relationships and preserved the theoretical unity of marriage. Clearly, many Puritan marriages were less than harmonious and not all women and men exemplified the ideals prescribed by the region's founding fathers. William Whately acknowledged this when he cynically remarked that "marriage proveth to many, just as the stocks to the drunkard; into which when his head was warme with wine and Ale, he put his foot laughingly and with merriment: but a little after (having slept out his wine and cooled his head with a nap) he longs as much to get it out againe. Hence it is that divers houses are none other but even very fencing schools, wherein the two sexes seem to have met together for nothing but to try masteries."[33] New England divorce petitions reveal that the Puritans' ideal of marital unity was for some couples, indeed, a myth.

The majority of New England divorce petitions were filed by women who claimed their husbands failed to perform their responsibilities as household heads. Wives most often accused their husbands of desertion, "continued absence without a word," adultery, and bigamy. They also cited impotence, failure to provide, cruelty or violence, incest, and heresy. Most women who charged their husbands with more than one offense understood that their chances of securing a divorce improved if their husband violated the Puritan ideal of the family patriarch. Thus, their divorce petitions reaffirmed their culture's assumptions about men's and women's roles.[34]

With greater freedom of movement and access to funds than women, more men deserted their wives and families than endured the scrutiny and humiliation of divorce proceedings. But the Puritans believed that a man's desertion violated God's order and left a household without a head. Because they thought women were morally weaker than men, they saw deserted women as vulnerable to temptation. A man's desertion also placed the financial burden of his family on the larger community, for women without husbands often had to depend on the assistance of others. While most New England courts ordered deserting husbands to return to their wives and put up collateral so that their families would not become public charges, they were often ignored. Consequently, desertion was the most frequently cited cause of divorce in Puritan New England.[35]

While many married men came to the colonies ahead of their families to prepare the way for them, others probably came to escape unhappy marriages, never intending to send for their wives and children. Because the Puritans believed that lengthy separations violated God's will, the Massachusetts General Court tried to prevent them:

> Whereas divers persons both men and woemen living within this Jurisdiction whose Wives, and Husbands are in England, or elsewhere, by means wherof they live under greet temptations heer, and some of them committing lewdnes and filthines heer among us, others make love to woemen, and attempt Marriage, and some have attained it; and some of them live under suspicion of uncleannes, and all to the great dishonor of God, reproach of Religion, Commonwealthe and Churches, it is therfore ordered by this Court and Authoritie therof (for the prevention of all such future evils) That all such married persons as aforesaid shall repair to their said relations by the first opportunitie of shipping upon the pain, or penaltie of twenty pounds.[36]

Despite this edict, some New England men remarried without divorcing their first wives. Bigamy was easy to conceal because communication with the Old World was uncertain and prior marriages could be kept secret. Nonetheless, the first divorce in Massachusetts was awarded on the grounds of bigamy. In 1639, Mrs. Luxford petitioned for divorce claiming her husband, James Luxford, had another wife. Her request was granted, and Luxford's estate was seized by the court to support her and their children. Her husband was fined £100, sentenced "to be set in the stocks upon the market day after the lecture," and banished to England for his offense. Men guilty of bigamy were ordered to leave the colonies so that their presence would not corrupt others.[37]

THE SEXUAL DOUBLE STANDARD

Adultery violated the sexual exclusivity of the marital covenant and provided grounds for divorce in Puritan New England.[38] In fact, until the 1670s, New England law prescribed the death penalty for any man found guilty of adultery with an engaged or married woman. Such laws were more symbolic than practical, however, and by the end of the century guilty parties were whipped, branded, or fined, depending on the nature of their offense. Although adultery was thought a serious offense whether committed by husband or wife, a sexual double standard was evident in its prosecution. An unfaithful husband was punished severely only if he committed adultery with the wife, or the betrothed, of another man. This was thought more serious than a relationship with an unmarried woman because a liaison with someone else's wife violated another marriage covenant and challenged that man's control of his wife. If a married man seduced a single woman, he was usually charged with committing fornication, a lesser offense.[39]

A married woman's infidelity was always treated as adultery, for in giving herself to another man, whether married or single, she betrayed her vow to her husband and threatened the unity of the family. Puritan William Gouge explained why a wife's adultery was a greater crime than her husband's: "[m]ore inconueniences may follow vpon the womans default than vpon the mans," he said, "as greater infamy before men, worse disturbance of the family, more mistaking of legitimate, or illegitimate children, with the like."[40]

In the plantation South, a sexual double standard also prevailed. There, too, a wife's adultery was perceived as a threat to her husband's authority and to the legitimacy of his heirs. Southern men also demanded their wives' fidelity to ensure the racial purity of their children. Their own sexual exploitation of African women was tacitly condoned. Planters' wives understood that such behavior was inadequate grounds for separation from their husbands and bitterly learned they had little choice but to suffer their husbands' infidelities. A woman who wanted a separation soon learned that her request was more likely to be granted if she accused her husband of cruelty or abuse and denied if she accused him of adultery or sexual misconduct. As a result, southern women rarely sought separations on the grounds of their husbands' adultery alone.

Even in the southern colonies, however, men were reluctant to charge their wives with infidelity publicly. Such was the case of Maryland resident Robert Taylor whose wife, Mary, had an affair with Virginia planter George Catchmey. In December 1652 she bore Catchmey's son. When Mary begged Robert to forgive her, he cried, "O! thou wicked base women how can I forgive thee, I cannot forgive thee, the Law will take hold of thee." Yet Taylor and Catchmey privately resolved their differences: Catchmey paid Taylor a sum of tobacco and Taylor agreed to raise Catchmey's son as his own. In this way, Robert Taylor avoided the public humiliation of admitting his wife's infidelity in court and being called cuckold by his friends and neighbors.[41]

DOMESTIC VIOLENCE

Excessive cruelty constituted grounds for divorce in Puritan New England, but Massachusetts and Plymouth were the only colonies to outlaw the physical abuse of women by their husbands. Lawmakers there believed that domestic violence not only threatened the ability of the family to carry out its responsibilities but violated God's will. The Massachusetts Body of Liberties of 1641 attempted to protect women from "bodily correction or stripes by her husband, unlesse it be [given] in his owne defence upon her assault."[42]

Religious leader Cotton Mather preached against domestic violence: "A man [who] Beat his Wife was as bad as any Sacriledge," he thundered, "And such a Rascal were better buried alive, than show his Head among his Neighbours any more."[43] While he proclaimed that men who beat their wives into submission revealed their own weakness, he believed a woman who beat her husband was "a shame to her profession of Christianity." An abusive wife "dishonors God and provokes the glorious God, tramples his Authority under her feet; she not only affronts her Husband," he declared, "but also God her Maker, Lawgiver and Judge."[44]

Even in Massachusetts and Plymouth, however, preserving the family took precedence over punishing the abuser. At least one abusive Plymouth couple was counseled to "apply themselves to such waies as might make for the recovering of peace and love betwixt them."[45] Moreover, the battered wife was often suspected of provoking her husband's abuse by nagging or disobedience. During the domestic violence trial of Lemuel Phelps, Mrs. Phelps confessed that she "transgressed the Rules and Duties of a Wife towards her husband in some of my past conduct in assuming too much authority over him and controlling him in civil and religious matters." She promised to reform. Women suing for divorce on grounds of excessive abuse had to demonstrate that they were dutiful wives and had not provoked their husbands. Thus, while the Puritans legislated against wife abuse, they helped its victims only if they proved themselves blameless in the eyes of their community.[46]

Although Puritan lawmakers charged neighbors with reporting marital abuse when they witnessed it, not all men welcomed interference into their private affairs. John Barrett, accused of abusing his wife, defiantly demanded of the court "What hath any man to do with it, have not I power to Correct my owne wife?" He defended his behavior, citing the Puritan's ideal of the patriarchal family and exploiting its ambiguities to justify his actions. And both Thomas and Susan Dutton denied their neighbors' accusations that he abused her when he was presented for the crime in Woburn, Massachusetts, in 1661. Many women probably denied they were battered or submitted to abuse in silence, fearful of additional violence if they charged their husbands publicly and reluctant to be the subject of scandalous tongues. A Salem woman poignantly expressed the humiliation felt by many battered wives then and now when she testified that she "was rather willing to groane under it thaen to make a publique discovery of his wicked and brutish carriage to me."[47]

Although more men were prosecuted for spousal abuse than women, women who abused their husbands were more severely punished than men who battered their wives. While abusive women were whipped, guilty husbands were fined for their crime. Even the fines women paid were greater than those levied against men, and twice as many men as women, proportionately, were simply admonished for their crime. It was believed that the woman who beat her husband not only violated his authority over her but defied the God-ordained hierarchy that was the basis for all society and government. In fighting back, she challenged the belief that women were, indeed, physically weaker than men.[48]

A sexual double standard was also apparent in rape trials in New England and elsewhere. Because rape was defined as having "carnal knowledge of any woman above the age of ten years against her will and of a woman child under the age of 10 years with or against her will," some New England courts differentiated between the assault of married and single women.[49] Rape of a betrothed or married woman was viewed as a crime against the estate of her fiancè or husband rather than the woman herself, and was punishable by death.[50] Although convicted rapists of single women were also subject to the death penalty, most courts were reluctant to sentence men to death for their crime, ordering them severely whipped or publicly humiliated instead.[51] Marital rape was not a crime in colonial America, "for by their mutual matrimonial consent and contract his wife hath given up herself in this kind to her husband, which she cannot retract."[52] Consequently, women seeking divorces in New England could not charge their husbands with this kind of abuse.

The Thrall Divorce Case

The problems one unhappily married Connecticut woman encountered demonstrate why, despite their legal right to do so, few women sued for divorce in seventeenth-century New England. Hannah Thrall left her husband, William Thrall, on 12 May 1732 after three and a half years of marriage. The couple often quarreled, and when William beat her, Hannah fled to her parents' house in Windsor, leaving her seven-year-old daughter, Charity, behind. Her husband denied that they had fought or that he had abused his wife. Instead, he claimed that Hannah left him because she did not wish to live in the same house as his mother. While Hannah could have sued for divorce on the grounds of her husband's cruelty, she probably realized that unless she proved William's abuse was life threatening she had little chance of ending her marriage. She may also have feared being accused of desertion by her husband, jeopardizing her dower rights in William's estate.

After Hannah left him, William Thrall, standing before a committee of his church, charged her with violating the seventh, eighth, and ninth commandments—of adultery, theft of services by desertion, and slander. He hoped the committee would command his wife to return home to him or find her guilty of adultery. If they found her guilty of adultery, he could immediately divorce her. If not, he must wait three years before he could charge her with desertion. William badly miscalculated. His church found him to blame for the couple's marital problems, pronouncing "that if a man by hard usage and cruel treatment drive his wife away from him . . . he is to be esteemed the Desertor." William then had to wait three years to divorce his wife for desertion.

As the Thralls waited to divorce, Hannah feared her husband and her mother-in-law were ill-treating her daughter, Charity. Two years after she fled her home, Hannah returned to rescue her daughter. Because the couple was still married and Hannah was legally "one" with her husband, William could not sue her for Charity's return. Instead, he sued Hannah's father for the loss of Charity's domestic labor. Although William won this case, he was awarded only one shilling in compensation by the court, which clearly disapproved of his actions. Charity was permitted to live with her mother.

Finally, in 1735, William Thrall sued Hannah for divorce, charging her with desertion and claiming that she had failed to perform her domestic duties as his wife. "Who can live with such a woman?" he asked the court. William's mother also testified against her daughter-in-law. Obviously there was tension between the two women, for other witnesses reported that Hannah "declared She was a Going away from her Husband, and She would not live with him Except said William would gett his Mother out of the House or goe and Live in another House." William also charged Hannah with adultery, knowing that if she was found guilty of desertion or adultery she would be deprived of her right to dower in his estate.

Despite William Thrall's claims, in May 1737 the court decided there were insufficient grounds for granting a divorce. By this time, William was himself vulnerable to accusations of adultery, having fathered a child with a neighbor's daughter. Although he petitioned for divorce again in 1738, he died before his case came to trial. In his will, William Thrall left Hannah only ten shillings, a sum far less than she was entitled to receive. Hannah, of course, claimed her "widow's third" instead of his bequest and was free of her husband at last. Hannah

Thrall's ordeal reveals the problems that many women endured rather than end their marriages in colonial courts.[53]

WOMEN AND CRIME

While few New England women actually petitioned for divorce, more did so between 1656 and 1664 than at any other time during the seventeenth century. During these years an influx of Quakers, including women preachers, seriously challenged the authority of Puritan leaders. Some New England women, emboldened both by the Quakers' theology and their challenge to male authority, petitioned for divorce during this eight-year period.[54] The women's self-assertion threatened the very fabric of Puritan society, fundamentally challenging the hierarchy of the family, the church, and the state. Whether more women actually engaged in disruptive behavior or greater numbers were tried and punished for their actions, a veritable "female crime wave" swept New England as authorities focused their energies on policing women offenders.[55] Women were accused of criminal activities at nearly twice the rate of men, and especially of crimes that violated the sexual norms of their society.[56]

Crime was "gendered" in early America, reflecting the cultural values of the settlers. The crimes identified almost exclusively with women were bastardy, adultery, fornication, infanticide, and witchcraft. These crimes involved women's sexuality and symbolized their rejection of the gender order prescribed by their society. In the years immediately following the Quaker "invasion" of New England, more women were tried and found guilty of these crimes than ever before. In fact, by the end of this period, well over half of all female offenders were charged with fornication, a significant increase over the preceding years.[57] This backlash reflected the sexual tensions inherent in Puritan culture. Women were also prosecuted for speaking openly against ministers and magistrates, interrupting church services, and dressing in a provocative manner. Cotton Mather made clear the sexual challenge underlying women's misbehavior when he reproved them for "promiscuous" dancing:

> Because the daughters of Zion are haughty,
> and walk with outstretched necks,
> glancing wantonly with their eyes,

Mincing along as they go,
tinkling with their feet;
The Lord will smite with a scab
the heads of the daughters of Zion,
and the Lord will lay bare their private parts.[58]

Men blamed women for the disorder that plagued the region and vigorously prosecuted "unruly" women who violated their society's norms.

A double standard also influenced the kinds of punishment meted out to women offenders, with the harshest, most humiliating punishments reserved for women who committed "sexual" crimes. Women were publicly whipped for many such offenses, while men were fined instead. Because married women had no property of their own, their husbands would have had to pay their fines. And single or widowed women who had property might have been made destitute by fines. Whipping ensured that guilty women "paid" for their crimes themselves. Stripped to the waist and tied to a whipping post, they were punished before an audience of men and women, their neighbors and friends. The women's public humiliation and degradation served as a warning to others who might emulate them. Male offenders, in contrast, enjoyed the relative privacy of paying fines for the same offenses.[59]

Many women served as witnesses in the prosecution of other women and testified as friends, neighbors, and gossips in colonial trials. In doing so, they often affirmed the dominant gender roles of their culture. Midwives, too, were called to examine women charged with infanticide and to identify fathers in illegitimate births, for it was thought that women questioned in the last stages of labor could not lie about the fathers of their children. In witchcraft trials, female juries inspected the bodies of accused women for "witches' teats," evidence of their covenant with the Devil. Most women took these responsibilities seriously and saw themselves as upholders and enforcers of community morality. But some challenged the double standards of magistrates more concerned with prosecuting women than men for the same sexual offenses. These women testified in behalf of accused women or requested clemency for them, expressing understanding of even those women who pled guilty to committing serious crimes.[60]

Women and Witchcraft

The backlash against New England women "criminals" in the late seventeenth century culminated in the Salem witchcraft trials. Witchcraft was a capital offense in the law codes drawn up in all the colonies. Although it was perceived as a crime against God, it was considered a crime against the state, and witchcraft trials took place in civil courts. In the colonies, as in Europe, witchcraft was a crime identified with middle-aged and married women. Of the 344 people accused of witchcraft in New England during the seventeenth century, nearly 80 percent were women. Most accused women were 40 years of age or older, although only 18 percent were more than 60 years old. Nearly three-quarters of those women accused of witchcraft before the Salem outbreak were women. Around half of the men accused of witchcraft were suspect by virtue of their relationship to accused women.[61]

Witchcraft accusations were often preceded by years of gossip about a woman's character and behavior. As long as she had a male family member to defend her name in a court of law, such gossip could be deflected before it culminated in accusations of witchcraft. Some men sued their daughters' or wives' accusers for slander or defamation of character to protect them from further charges. Turning the tables— taking the offensive—men shielded their womenfolk from attack. Once a woman's male protector died, she was defenseless against her neighbors' gossip. Single, widowed, divorced, or deserted women without the direct protection of a male relative were especially vulnerable to witchcraft accusation. Although some women sued their accusers for slander themselves, this was risky; if the accuser's case appeared credible, the accused further jeopardized her position. Although a woman might win her slander suit, her reputation usually suffered. By taking action against her accuser, she had to be aggressive and assertive, defying the Puritan ideal of the submissive goodwife.[62]

Women accused of witchcraft in New England came from all levels of society, but most were of the "middling sort." Although the courts tended to dismiss allegations against wealthy women from prominent families, poorer women did not fare so well. They were disproportionately represented among those convicted of witchcraft in colonial New England. Another factor that made some women especially vulnerable to witchcraft accusation in New England was the Puritans' inheritance laws, designed to keep property in men's hands, and the restrictions they placed on women's property rights. Women who were their parents' sole heir, had no sons of their own, or were childless stood to inherit and control more property than many men in the region. In a culture where property meant power, these women were especially threatening. They were looked on with suspicion by their neighbors and accused of using occult powers to acquire their wealth. These inheriting women were especially conspicuous during the last quarter of the seventeenth century, when the longevity of the region's men threatened young men's prospects for the future.[63]

As men's life expectancy increased and available farm land in the region declined, the age when sons received their inheritance rose. Young men delayed marrying until they could acquire land to support families of their own. Dependent on their fathers and unable to control their own lives, they resented women with property and saw themselves as impotent victims of a system that benefited women at their expense. Not surprisingly, young men were among the principle accusers of propertied women tried for witchcraft in colonial New England.[64]

Katherine Harrison was one such propertied victim of witchcraft accusation. The wife of wealthy Wethersfield, Connecticut, landowner John Harrison, Katherine was well-known in her community as a healer but was also whispered about by those neighbors who feared her skills. When Katherine was widowed in 1666, her devoted husband bequeathed her and their daughters his entire estate of £929. Rather than remarry, Katherine chose to rear her daughters and manage the estate herself, inspiring jealousy and resentment in the community. In the years following her husband's death, her properties were vandalized, her livestock was injured, and her crops were destroyed, yet the court did not act on her complaints.

Her neighbors, Michael and Ann Griswold, spread malicious rumors about her, accusing her of witchcraft. When she defended herself against them, they sued her for slander and won. Katherine was fined £40 and ordered to admit the error of her remarks publicly. While she confessed her faults, she refused to pay the fine. In her petition to the court, Katherine portrayed herself as "a female, a weaker vessell, subject to passion" in deference to the goodwife ideal, but challenged the court's legal right to levy such a fine. And she angrily accused Michael Griswold of having designs on her estate. She clearly believed that the motive behind Griswold's malicious gossip was acquisition of her lands. Fearful that her inheritance might be the cause of her demise, she placed it in trust for her daughters under the oversight of two men and left the colony before she could be prosecuted for witchcraft. Other women with less foresight were not so lucky.[65]

WOMEN'S RIGHTS IN NEW NETHERLAND

The legal restrictions single and married women faced in England's American colonies can be better understood in contrast with the rights enjoyed by women in the colony of New Netherland (later to become New York), founded by the Dutch in 1624 in the region between England's colonies of Virginia and Plymouth. The Roman-Dutch law there recognized women as individuals and granted them many of the same legal rights, responsibilities, and privileges as men. When New Netherland was conquered by England in 1664, however, women lost these rights and were subject to English law. In New Netherland, as in the Netherlands, unmarried women had the same legal rights as men. The Netherlands was a seafaring nation, and many men were absent from their homes and businesses for long periods of time. To ensure the survival of the economy, lawmakers gave married and single women the right to own and control property. Acknowledging this fundamental equality of women and men, Dutch fathers equally endowed their sons and daughters.[66]

Dutch women also had the right to choose their legal status when they married. Women could enter a *manus* or *usus* marriage. In a *manus* marriage, the woman accepted her husband's authority over her and she became legally dependent on him. Like the *feme covert* in English law, she was under her husband's guardianship and had no legal identity. He represented her, and she could not make contracts without his permission. Her property became "community property," managed by her husband, when she married. If either spouse died, this community property was divided in half: half for the surviving spouse and the rest divided among the couple's heirs.

In a *usus* marriage, however, the woman retained all the rights of a single woman and her husband had no power over her. Like the English *feme sole*, she owned property, engaged in business transactions without her husband's permission, and could sue and be sued in a court of law. She could even retain her surname when she married. This kind of marriage enabled women to contribute to the commercial development of the colony. New Netherland women in *usus* marriages owned land, operated shops, bought and sold staple foods, traded furs, and engaged in the manufacture and sale of spirits. Others were even active in shipbuilding and international trade.[67]

When the English conquered New Netherland in 1664 and renamed it New York, they assured the Dutch that all contracts made under Dutch law were binding and that Dutch inheritance practices would continue. But the English were unfamiliar with women's legal position in the colony. Despite women's protests, their rights were rescinded, and they were forced into dependence on male relatives. During the first four decades of English rule, the number of women in New York operating as traders and business proprietors sharply declined, and they appeared less frequently in court as plaintiffs and as defendants. The number of women who inherited real property also markedly decreased, as did the number of women who made wills jointly with their husbands. By 1690, in a move emblematic of women's legal subordination to men, women of Dutch heritage began to adopt their husbands' last names when they married.[68]

Trader Margaret Hardenbroeck experienced firsthand the decline in women's rights as English law supplanted Roman-Dutch law in New York. Born in the Netherlands, the only daughter of a prosperous trader, she migrated to New Netherland with her parents and her two brothers in 1659. Initially, Hardenbroeck served as her cousin Wolter Valck's agent in New Amsterdam and appeared in court in his behalf. Later, she represented other Dutch merchants while she established herself as a successful trader in her own right.

On 10 October 1659 Hardenbroeck married the prominent New Amsterdam merchant and trader Pieter Rudolphus DeVries. When DeVries died in 1661, she was left a wealthy widow. The mother of an infant daughter, she managed her own trading enterprises as well as those of her late husband. Hardenbroeck was frequently in court as she sorted out her husband's business affairs. She manipulated the court system to delay payment of her husband's creditors, assuring herself of capital to invest in trade.

Hardenbroeck's second husband, Frederick Philipsen was a New Amsterdam carpenter and trader. Before their marriage, the couple drew up a contract indicating that theirs would be a *usus* marriage. Hardenbroeck retained legal rights to her own property and to the estate she and her daughter had inherited from DeVries. This enabled her to continue her business, make contracts, sue, and be sued in the colony's courts of law. After their marriage, Philipsen and Hardenbroeck engaged in trade as individuals and as business partners. Sometimes her husband granted her power of attorney to act in his behalf, and she occasionally granted him power of attorney to act for her. Theirs was one of the most successful trading partnerships in North America.

But the English conquest of New Netherland required that Margaret Hardenbroeck change her methods of doing business. As the couple adjusted to English rule, Frederick Philipsen anglicized his name to Philips and swore an oath of allegiance to Great Britain. Hardenbroeck did not, for the English government assumed that her husband acted for her. She began to play a less visible role in her trading company's activities and was no longer welcome in court. Her husband now represented her interests in legal matters.

Despite this change in her legal status, however, Hardenbroeck continued to act independently as a trader. The couple's trading network grew to include the West Indies, where they established a home on the English island colony of Barbados. Their business empire involved trade in tobacco, grain, lumber, and meat as well as rum, sugar, and slaves. The couple also heavily speculated in New York land. Although Hardenbroeck was barred from purchasing property under English law, her husband bought lands for her. In this manner, the couple manipulated the law so that she could conduct business in the colony. By the time of her death in 1691, Margaret Hardenbroeck was the wealthiest woman in New York. But during her life she had sadly watched the erosion of her rights under English rule.[69]

The Dutch, like the English, constructed their legal system to promote economic development and the transfer of property from one generation to the next. Given the nature of their economy, many Dutch men relied on their wives and daughters to act in their stead. The legal position enjoyed by women in New Netherland was informed by this custom and facilitated this end. As a result, Dutch colonists viewed the family differently from their English counterparts. They saw the family not as a patriarchal institution but as a parental institution; they vested power in both husband and wife rather than in the husband and his male heirs.[70] Consequently, for many years after England's conquest of New Netherland, Dutch men circumvented the English common law distribution of their estates and protected the legal rights of their wives and daughters. Through their wills they granted their widows the rights customary under the old Roman-Dutch law and divided their estates equally between their sons and daughters, resisting the English custom of primogeniture.[71]

But by 1730, Dutch inheritance traditions declined, and many men of Dutch ancestry adopted English inheritance practices. Fewer Dutch men named their widows sole executors of their estates, appointing male friends and relatives or their sons as executors in addition to, or instead of, their wives. They also restricted their wives' property rights as widows; widows no longer received half of the marital estate upon their spouses' death, and only a few were given any of their husbands' real estate if they remarried. Children could claim their inheritance, or a portion of it, before their mothers' deaths, although men who died without children continued to name their wives as their principal heirs. Rather than bequeath lands to both their daughters and sons, men granted all their lands to their sons and willed their daughters cash or movable goods. Still, unlike their English counterparts who favored sons over daughters, they remained faithful to ethnic traditions and endowed their sons and daughters equally.[72]

These changes in women's property rights and in inheritance patterns marked changes in attitudes about family life and authority in New York and in England's other North American colonies over the course of the seventeenth century. In the increasingly competitive and individualistic world of the eighteenth century, men promoted the well-being and success of their sons at the expense of their wives and widows. They "protected" their daughters by creating jointures and trusts, even as they limited women's ability to control their own fate. Ironically, the more stable the colonial family, the more restricted were women's rights under the law. The stability that led to the rise of the affectionate family meant a decline in the legal rights of colonial American women and perhaps a decline in the perception of women's abilities as well. In 1710 the New York assembly adopted a statute classifying married women together with minors and those "not of Sound mind," all of whom were not thought capable of acting responsibly on their own.[73]

* * *

Women's legal position throughout England's North American colonies during the seventeenth century was conditional on men's goals and needs. In colonies founded by men with orthodox religious principles, women's rights were subordinated to men's ideal of the family; where commerce and trade were the basis for settlement, men temporarily extended rights to women to secure their own economic ends. In all the colonies, demographic factors—sex ratios, women's fertility, and men's mortality rates—also affected women's legal position. In colonies where men's mortality rate was unusually high, husbands had to rely on their wives to manage their estates and act as guardians of their children. Consequently, they extended married women the right to control property until the children were able to do so themselves. In colonies with stable, patriarchal families, men limited married women's right to own and control property, and they ensured their control of estates even after death through trusts, jointures, and restrictions on their widows' dower rights. Thus, changes in married women's legal position during the seventeenth century mirrored changes in their value to men as conveyors of property from one generation to another.[74]

Was the seventeenth century a golden age for women's rights in the American colonies, as some historians have asserted?[75] If the position of some English and most Dutch women in the seventeenth century is compared with that of most women in the eighteenth century, it appears that lawmakers in a few colonies during the earlier century were more liberal regarding women legal rights. But these rights came at a high price—men's high mortality and social instability. Ill-equipped to handle the legal responsibilities placed on their shoulders, most English women probably saw the expansion of their rights as a burden, not a welcome change. The speed with which most widows remarried in the Chesapeake region, for example, indicates how many seventeenth-century women viewed their new legal position: they willingly gave up their rights and responsibilities to their new husbands and resumed their subordinate, dependent position.

The transfer of laws regarding marriage and women's property rights from England to the American colonies demonstrates the continuity in women's lives from the Old World to the New. The ability to replicate, enforce, and even improve on the laws of their Mother Country was a measure of the colonists' success in "civilizing" their new home. At the same time, changes in women's legal position over time, and the differences in women's rights from colony to colony, reflected English men's beliefs about the relative importance of women, and the families they helped create, in the formation of colonial societies and economies. Ironically, the very stability and order provided by women in England's

North American colonies limited their legal rights, but most colonial women did not mourn the restrictions placed on them. More women probably found the loss of some legal rights and responsibilities a small price for the comfort and protection they believed their legal dependence afforded them. Relying on their husbands and their fathers, many women found security for themselves and their children in a strange New World.

CHAPTER FIVE

Women and Religion

The candle's flame flickered in the chill draft that seeped beneath the door and rattled the window in its frame. As cold winter winds buffeted the clapboard house, the girls crowded around the table before the hearth. The candle's light illuminated a goblet filled with swirling liquid. As they watched with rapt attention, mysterious shapes formed in the cloudy mixture.

Egg whites and water. That's what Tituba said. And she should know. Wasn't she a wise woman? Didn't she make charms and potions from the herbs she brought from her exotic tropical island home? And the stories she told—of evil spirits lurking in the darkness, eager to steal their souls away! Of witches, wizards, and voodoo!

They asked her to look into their futures and tell their fortunes. Who would they would marry? What would be their fate? As daughters and granddaughters of faithful Puritans they knew they should not ask such questions. They learned that God predetermined their destiny. He, alone, knew what the future had in store for them. They were hopeless to control it. They must resign themselves to His will and hold fast to their faith. Yet their faith gave them no answers to the questions that worried them. The ministers who thundered sermons at Sunday service were so remote, so frightening. How could they, mere girls, bother them with their silly questions?

Still, they needed to know. Would their families' fortunes grow or diminish? Would there be money for their dowries? Would they marry well? To kind, *handsome men who would support them and their children in comfort? Or would they be spinsters all their lives? Must they live in other people's homes, at their bidding, forever dependent on the kindness and charity of others?*

The Bible gave them no answers to these questions, their ministers did not comfort them. Their faith no longer sustained them in the face of their fears. And so they sought out Tituba. With her guidance, they made their own crystal from a goblet, egg whites, and water, and peered into its depths to discover their fates.

As the winter wind shrieked and howled outside, the girls nervously huddled together over the flickering flame and peered into the depths of the swirling liquid.

They gasped!

What did they see?

Death.

These young girls of Salem, Massachusetts, who gathered in the Reverend Samuel Parris's home in the winter of 1691–92, wanted to know what the future held for them. Their Christian training failed to provide them with the comfort and reassurance that had sustained their New England ancestors. Instead, they turned to magic, to witchcraft, to answer their questions and divine their fate. Yet these young women, whose actions precipitated the witchcraft hysteria at Salem, were the product of an evolving religious culture in New England in which women played an important role. Just as Puritan women had helped establish God's "cittee upon a hill" in Massachusetts, they were instrumental in sounding its death knell by the end of the seventeenth century. And, as agents of change, they helped usher in a new era of religious enthusiasm, "the Great Awakening," in eighteenth-century America.

The faith of colonial women sustained them during trying times and offered them spiritual comfort in the rapidly changing world of seventeenth-century America. While little is known about how Native American and African women's religious beliefs were affected by colonization and enslavement, English women helped spread their beliefs throughout England's New World colonies, and especially in Puritan New England. As "visible saints" in the region's churches, women's piety inspired others. Some "vessels of the supernatural" preached the word of God, while others were martyred for their faith.

The New World's challenges also tried women's faith. While their beliefs empowered many of them to act, they restrained others. And although their religious beliefs gave them with a sense of security in a strange and often intimidating environment, they also contributed to the oppression and persecution of others. Some women sought comfort beyond the boundaries of conventional religions; others crossed the fragile boundary between religion and folk magic and practiced witchcraft. But their quest for reassurance, for answers to their questions, prompted change—spiritual rebirth—throughout the colonies by the eighteenth century.

PURITANISM AND WOMEN

The Protestant Reformation provided a new understanding of women's natures and roles throughout Europe and England. Theologians promoted marriage as an honorable estate and invested the affectionate family with spiritual importance. The Puritans, especially, celebrated conjugal love and sexual fidelity as emblems of Christian devotion. Women, "necessary" companions to men, were called by God to love their husbands and to bear their children. But despite the Puritans' idealization of loving marriages and their belief in the spiritual equality of women and men, they advocated a hierarchy within the family. The wife was subordinate to the husband; she must submit to him and obey him in all things. This, they believed, was God's holy order.

Although some women felt confined by these beliefs, many more were avid supporters of Puritan reforms. Why did they endorse a theology that prescribed their submission to men? Because the Puritans also recognized and honored key qualities identified with women—self-sacrifice, humility, and submission to divine authority. Women's inferior position within the Puritan's patriarchal order mirrored humankind's powerlessness in God's eyes; women's piety was the model for all to emulate. Moreover, women's submission to both God and men was not the consequence of weakness. It demanded controlled and conscious effort on their part, required self-sacrifice and self-restraint, and was an active, not passive, form of worship. Suffering, too, was viewed as a particularly feminine mode of devotion. Puritan theology also provided women with behavioral models to embody or abhor: the temptress Eve, the evil witch, the shrewish virago, and the virtuous

"Daughter of Zion." As dedicated and devout wives and mothers, Puritan women saw opportunities for redemption, status, and authority in their society, and eagerly embraced the spiritual dimensions of the Puritan goodwife ideal.[1]

THE MODEL "GOODWIFE"

Puritan poet Anne Bradstreet exemplified this model of female piety esteemed by her culture. Anne experienced God's grace most during times of personal trial—her own illnesses, pregnancies, the sickness of a child, the death of a beloved parent. Stricken in her youth with smallpox, she recalled, "When I was in my affliction, I besought the Lord, and confessed my Pride and Vanity and he was entreated of me, and again restored me."[2] After her marriage to Simon Bradstreet, Anne was barren for many years. She saw her childlessness as a trial by God. But when she became pregnant and bore eight healthy children, she rejoiced in God's grace. Anne's God was not a cruel deity but a stern, loving one. "He hath never suffered me long to sit loose from Him, but by one affliction or other hath made me look home, and search what was amiss," she recalled. "I have no sooner felt my heart out of order, but I have expected correction for it, which most commonly hath been upon my own person in sickness, weakness, pains."[3]

Anne's marriage to Simon Bradstreet was also a living embodiment of God's grace. The loving union between husband and wife exemplified Christ's relationship with His devoted, yet unworthy, followers. The erotic nature of Anne's poetry reveals the sensuality of her faith; her submission to her husband paralleled her submission to God's will. She described herself as the bride of Christ and reveled in His love.

Still, Anne had religious doubts throughout her life and never enjoyed the certainty of her salvation. As she rather wistfully observed: "I have often been perplexed that I have not found that constant Joy in my Pilgrimage and refreshing which I supposed most of the servants of God have: although he hath not left me altogether without the wittnes of his holy spirit, who hath oft given mee his word and sett to his Seal that is shall bee well with me. . . . Yet I have many Times sinkings and droopings, and not enjoyed that felicity that sometimes I have done."

Throughout her life she questioned the veracity of Scriptures and even doubted the existence of God. Having witnessed no miracles, she reminded herself that God was all around her—in the miracles of "the Heaven and the Earth, the order of all things." She wondered if there was one "true" religion—"why may not the Popish Religion bee the right? They have the same God, the same Christ, the same word: they only enterprett it one way, wee another." Her sense of despair kept sleep at bay:

> By night when others
>   soundly slept,
> And had at once both ease
>   and Rest,
> My waking eyes were open
>   kept,
> and so to lie I found it best.[4]

Despite her doubts and sleepless nights, perhaps, indeed, because of them, Anne's faith endured: "But when I have been in darknes and seen no light, yet have I desired to stay my self upon the Lord."[5] No passive faith, hers was hard earned and cherished all the more.

Anne Bradstreet's thoughtful artistry also illustrates how Puritan women expanded on their religiously prescribed roles as goodwife and mother to achieve a degree of freedom and influence within their culture. Rather than subverting the qualities of humility, modesty, and pious self-deprecation, highly valued in Puritan women, Anne used them to disarm her reader. For example, she used domestic language and imagery to equate God's love of humankind with a mother's love of her children: "Some children are hardly weaned although the teat be rub'd wth wormwood or mustard, they wil either wipe it off, or else suck down sweet and bitter together so is it wth some Christians, let god imbitter all the sweets of this life, that so they might feed upon more substantiall food."[6] This meditation demonstrates how she, and perhaps many other women, saw God: as an all-powerful, yet loving, maternal being. Likening God's authority with a mother's, she feminizes God while she elevates the role of the goodwife. Thus, in embracing the conventions of her time, Anne Bradstreet crafted both a new poetic mode of expression and an approachable deity.

Throughout the colonies, but especially in New England, women like Anne Bradstreet encouraged the spread of religious beliefs and the creation of new congregations, contributing their time, energy, and property to religious institutions.[7] When Jesuit missionaries in Maryland eulogized a Catholic matron, they might well have been describing a pious Puritan goodwife or a Quaker woman: "She was given to much prayer, and most anxious for the salvation of her neighbors—a perfect example of right management as well in her self as in her domestic concerns—she was fond of our society while living, and a benefactor to it when dying—of blessed memory with all, for her notable examples, especially of charity to the sick, as well as of other virtues."[8]

CHURCH MEMBERSHIP

Women of all faiths depended on the spiritual comfort and sense of community that religious institutions provided. Church attendance was one public activity that was socially sanctioned for women in early America. Yet when their husbands claimed new lands at the frontier's edge, many found themselves living in isolation, far from the local church or meetinghouse and the company of other women. These "out-living" women, hampered by the care of small children and unable to walk long distances to worship, especially during New England winters, implored their husbands to build new churches so they might attend services and visit with neighbors and friends. Urging their husbands to found new congregations, these women reinforced the religious and social ties that bound early American communities together.[9]

Membership in New England's churches was based on personal salvation, not gender, race, marital status, or social position. Women qualified for admission to the region's congregations and, like their male counterparts, were rigorously examined to discover whether they were among God's chosen. Those seeking membership told their "tales of grace" to church committees or, privately, to their ministers. The candidate was asked detailed questions about her past behavior and required to describe her conversion experience. But some modest Puritan women found public testimony an ordeal. The Reverend John Cotton supported his wife's request for a private examination. Public examination "was against the apostle's [St. Paul's] rule," he argued, "and not fit for women's modesty." Thomas Hooker concurred, commenting that "we find it by experience, the feebleness in some, their shamefac'd modesty and melanchollick fearsomenesse is such, that they are not able to expresse themselves in the face of a Congregation." Consequently, many women were privately examined about their faith.[10] One critic of the Puritans remarked: "here is required such confessions, and professions, both in private and publique, both by men and women, before they be admitted, that three parts of the people of the Country remaine out of the Church."[11]

Women's "tales of grace" shared a common language and structure. Most candidates for church membership recalled when their sinful natures were revealed to them—the first stage in the conversion process. Some even remembered a specific moment when they became aware of their corruption and resolved to submit to God's will. Others confessed they initially ignored this warning, often for many years. All, however, eventually confronted their sinfulness, battling their fear of damnation until God blessed them with faith. In preparation for their own salvation, these "Saints" still struggled against the demons of the flesh and worldly distractions. But the conviction of their salvation sustained them.[12]

Citing St. Paul's injunction—"Let your women keep silent in the churches: for it is not permitted unto them to speak"—women members were barred from signing the church covenant and prohibited from publicly participating in its government.[13] Although women could only concur with men's decisions, most probably saw their submission to men's will as an act of humility, a further expression of their piety. Despite this exclusion, women indirectly, privately, subtly influenced church affairs. By the end of the century, women were a majority of the members in New England's churches and unfortunate was the minister who did not recognize this fact. Through networks of friends and neighbors, women monitored, gossiped about, and passed judgment on their ministers. Conflicts developed between many ministers, selfish of their authority, and the influential, older women in their congregations. And young ministers who behaved improperly or treated women "Saints" with contempt often found themselves without a position. Indirectly—through their husbands, brothers, and fathers—women church members could make or break a minister's career.[14]

Nonconformist Women

New England women were also devout followers and avid members of radical nonconformist Protestant sects. These sects emphasized women's receptivity to God's word and exaggerated the importance of submission to God's will. Some even permitted women to preach and assume leadership roles. No doubt many women welcomed the power and authority they derived from such responsibilities. Puritan ministers, however, were alarmed by women's attraction to the "heretical" ideas of the Antinomians, Anabaptists, Gortonists, and Quakers. Cotton Mather claimed women were attracted to these sects because the " 'weaker sex' is more easily gained by the devil."[15]

Devout women in Salem, Massachusetts, distinguished themselves as followers of New England's first religious rebel, Roger Williams. Williams advocated the separation of church and state, and angered religious and civil leaders alike. When he asserted the right of each individual to worship according to his or her own conscience, he was forced to leave Massachusetts. But before his exile, many of Williams's most devoted supporters were women. They were drawn to him because he believed all churchgoers—regardless of gender—must humble themselves before God. Meekness and humility were qualities identified with women, and by demanding them from all his congregants Williams elevated women as exemplars of piety.

Some women probably viewed Williams's defiance of both church and state as a vehicle for their own freedom from masculine authority. They may have been inspired by his support for liberty of conscience, recognizing that this was the key to both intellectual and spiritual freedom. For although Williams believed women were incapable of governing or interpreting the word of God, he held out to them the promise of authority over their own lives. Thus, Margery Reeves and maidservant Margery Holliman refused to worship with the Salem congregation, adopting Williams's claim that it was not a "True Church." But Williams's female supporters could do little more than protest his expulsion from the colony in 1636. Williams did not inspire women's rebellion against their subordinate role in Puritan society, but he did sow seeds of discontent among the powerless in Massachusetts. This discontent fueled the Antinomian Controversy, which racked the colony from 1636 until 1638.

Calvinists in England and New England argued among themselves about the importance of good works and grace in preparing men and women for salvation. Most New England ministers believed that good works alone were not enough to secure salvation; only God could save men and women from damnation. John Cotton warned his congregation against being duped by the appearance of goodness in people and admonished them to submit to God's will and accept His saving Grace. But this was cold comfort for men and women who longed to know their fate. Hungry for some indication of their own salvation, many sought comfort in a new strain of religious thought called Antinomianism, or Familism, by the ministers who opposed it.

Antinomians also emphasized the inability of individuals, regardless of gender, to achieve salvation on their own. They, too, espoused a "covenant of grace" and argued that only by submitting completely to God's will could women and men be saved. But unlike the orthodox ministers of New England, who said that no one could ever be certain of salvation or damnation, Antinomians believed in God's personal revelation of one's fate. How did you know if you were saved? they asked. God spoke to you directly. And, once saved, they proclaimed, you were no longer bound by moral or scriptural law. You no longer needed to heed the words of ministers or magistrates. Instead, you would be guided by the voice of God within. This was a dangerous theology.

New England's ministers and magistrates, their authority threatened, were alarmed. The hierarchy on which all Puritan society was constructed was imperiled, they declared. Malcontents would use personal revelation to justify revolution. Congregations would turn on their ministers, and citizens on their governors. But, perhaps most important, they feared that women, empowered by the Holy Spirit within them, would challenge the authority of men. Anne Hutchinson embodied all their worst fears.

ANNE HUTCHINSON

Born in Alford, England, in 1591, Anne Marbury was the daughter of a nonconformist minister who provided his intellectually gifted daughter with an excellent education. When she was 21, Anne married William Hutchinson, a successful merchant, and together they had 15 children.

She became a follower of nonconformist minister John Cotton and convinced her husband to follow him to Massachusetts in 1634. There she served the women of Boston and neighboring towns as a nurse and midwife. They, in turn, sought her out for spiritual comfort and religious counsel. Soon she was holding biweekly meetings in her home, attended by both women and men, at which she shared her Antinomian views. In interpreting the word of God, Anne ran afoul of the colony's ministers.

In the meetings at her home, Anne Hutchinson challenged the authority of many of the colony's ministers and questioned whether they were, indeed, "saved." She charged many of them with teaching a covenant of works and even walked out on a sermon by Boston pastor John Wilson to protest his interpretation of Scripture. Consequently, in 1636 she was called before a convocation of ministers alarmed by the growing number of men and women attending meetings at her home. When Hutchinson criticized her inquisitors' theology, they charged her with stepping beyond the God-ordained boundaries of women's sphere and usurping the role of men.

At her November 1637 examination by both ministers and magistrates, Hutchinson was indicted for holding meetings within her home, "a thing not tolerable or comely in the sight of God nor fitting for your sex." John Winthrop accused her of disobeying her "parents," the colony's magistrates, and usurping their authority. Finally, the Reverend Hugh Peter summarized her "crimes": "you have stept out of your place, *you have rather bine a Husband than a Wife and a preacher than a Hearer; and a Magistrate than a Subject.*"[16]

In her spirited rebuttal, Hutchinson defended her right to instruct women in religious matters. She quoted from Scripture that "the elder women should instruct the younger."[17] John Winthrop challenged her interpretation of this citation, arguing that older women should instruct young women to perform their domestic roles and love their husbands. They were not to teach other women, or men, about God. This, he asserted, violated St. Paul's injunction for women to keep silent in churches. Women, Winthrop thundered, could speak in church only when confessing their sins or singing hymns.[18]

Perhaps Anne Hutchinson's greatest threat to the Puritan community lay not in her theology but in her example. This strong, assertive, and articulate woman was confident in her own beliefs. She provided other New England women with an example of what they might become, a living alternative to the submissive goodwife prescribed by Puritan men: a role model and teacher, a woman who challenged the authority of the colony's men in the name of God. Although the colony's ministers and magistrates tried to catch her in some theological error, she deftly defended her beliefs and put them on the defensive. She proved herself their intellectual equal, if not their superior, and publicly challenged their authority.

Just when it appeared that Anne had triumphed over her inquisitors, she gave them the evidence they needed to convict her. God would punish the men who presumed to judge her, she proclaimed. "I know that for this you goe about to doe to me, God will ruine you and your posterity, and this whole State." When asked how she knew this, she replied, "By an immediate revelation."[19] Her claim that God spoke directly to her sealed her fate. This was heresy and a threat to the very order of Puritan New England. She was excommunicated from the Boston church and banished from the colony.

Anne Hutchinson's excommunication trial demonstrates the depth of her religious convictions, even as the ministers who questioned her revealed their own fears about women. John Cotton, her former mentor and supporter, chastised Anne: "I have often feared the higth of your Spirit and being puft up with your owne parts." He also predicted that her challenging spirit would lead her to question her husband's authority and, eventually, to adultery. Cotton clearly betrayed his anxiety that women's intellectual and spiritual freedom would inevitably lead to their sexual liberation. And women's sexual liberation, he feared, would destroy all that men held sacred. By labeling Hutchinson a "sexual deviant," Cotton tried to contain the threat she posed to the colony and men's authority and divert attention from the very real threat of her beliefs. He warned the women of Boston "to looke to your selves and to take heed that you recaeve nothinge for Truth which hath not the stamp of the Word of God." Anne's former mentor revealed his contempt for her and for all women when he explained "for you see she [Hutchinson] is but a Woman and many unsound and dayngerous principles are held by her."[20]

Although Anne Hutchinson spoke to a deep-seated need in their souls, most of her female followers had neither the courage nor the strength to stand up to the colony's male leaders. Although some men spoke in her defense, they were ridiculed for listening to a "mere woman" or accused of using her to further their own ambitions. Thus,

Anne's battle with New England's religious and political authorities ended. In April 1638, she, together with members of her family and a small band of supporters, fled Massachusetts for Rhode Island. Later, she and her husband moved to Long Island, then under Dutch rule, where they hoped to live free from persecution. There, tragically, Anne, her family, and most of her followers were killed in a raid by Native Americans in 1643.[21]

UNRULY WOMEN

Some of Anne Hutchinson's followers remained in Massachusetts and continued to challenge the colony's religious and civil authorities, and they, too, were punished. Phillipa Hammond, who stated publicly "that Mrs. Hutchinson neyther deserved the Censure which was putt upon her in the Church, nor in the Commonweal," was excommunicated by the Boston church in 1639. Mistress Anne Hibbens, another Hutchinson supporter, was excommunicated in 1641 for failing to be properly submissive.[22]

The wife of a Massachusetts assistant, Anne Hibbens attracted the authorities' attention when she accused a joiner of overcharging her for work she hired him to do at her home. She refused to accept the judgment of a board of arbitration composed of 10 joiners, claiming the board conspired to set prices, and asked that a new board be convened to rule on her case. The elders of Boston's First Church admonished her "great pride of spirit" and accused her of making "a wisp of her husband." She was charged with "usurping authority over him whom God hath made her head and husband, and in taking the power and authority which God hath given to him out of his hands . . . as if she were able to manage it better than her husband, which is a plain breach of the rule of Christ."[23] When she refused to accept their judgment, they excommunicated her. But they could not silence her, and she continued to speak out against the arbitrary rule of Boston's ministers and magistrates.

Then, shortly after her husband's death in 1654, Anne Hibbens's tale took a tragic turn. Her neighbors charged her with practicing witchcraft. How else could she know that they were gossiping about her? Although a jury found her innocent, the magistrates refused their verdict. Finally, the General Court of Massachusetts heard her case on appeal and proclaimed her guilty. Although minister John Norton desperately fought for Anne's release, he failed, and she was executed in 1656. As Norton bitterly reflected, Anne Hibbens was "hanged for a witch, only for having more wit than her neighbors."[24]

Like Anne Hutchinson and Mistress Hibbens, Lady Deborah Moody also ran afoul of Massachusetts ministers and magistrates. But she had the economic means to escape their wrath. Lady Moody came to New England in 1639 and settled on 400 acres near Lynn, Massachusetts. There she came into conflict with church leaders. Lady Moody was an Anabaptist and an Antinomian: she opposed infant baptism and believed in personal revelation. Consequently, in 1642 she was brought before the Essex County court and told that she must repent or risk banishment from the colony. Although there were few Anabaptists in Massachusetts, ministers and magistrates were concerned about the threat Lady Moody—a wealthy, well-born woman—posed to their authority. But before the General Court expelled all Anabaptists in 1644, Lady Moody and a group of followers departed for Dutch-controlled Long Island. There she established an Anabaptist community at Gravesend. A wealthy and powerful woman in her own right, Lady Moody defied the limits permitted women in Puritan New England.[25]

Were these "unruly" women early feminists? Were they aware of their culture's sexual inequalities and motivated to eliminate them? Certainly some of them chafed at the patriarchal, authoritarian nature of their world and felt constrained by their subordinate place within it. Some of them acted out their frustration by challenging their husbands within their homes; others undermined the authority of ministers in their churches. But was their rebellion a means to an end, or simply an end in itself? Did they desire to change the society in which they lived or its beliefs about women? Were they simply spirited women? Or were they spiritual women, compelled by a desire to live in accordance with their religious beliefs, transcending the boundaries of gender and class? It is little wonder to us today that many of them were drawn, consciously and unconsciously, to faiths that honored the "feminine" characteristics of humility and submission or that directly empowered them by divine revelation—or that they were punished for their beliefs by the church and state they hoped to change. Neither is it surprising that many New England women found hope in the message brought to them by missionaries of the Society of Friends, also known as Quakers.

THE SOCIETY OF FRIENDS

Like other Protestants reformers, the Society of Friends strove to restore the simplicity of Christian worship and return to the "primitive church." But, unlike the Puritans, they denied the sanctity of ordination, baptism, formal prayer, and the Lord's Supper, and believed Bible study alone did not make an individual a worthy religious leader. Instead, they relied on the "Inner Light," the in-dwelling spirit of God, to guide them in religious matters. Their meetings were characterized by silent meditation, interrupted only when a individual felt moved by the Holy Spirit to speak. The Quakers advocated complete liberty of conscience. Because they took Christ's admonition to love one another seriously, they were pacifists. They refused to bow before any man and adopted a plain language, using the familiar "thee" and "thou" instead of formal titles to address others, regardless of their social rank. And, most important, they believed that all women and men were equal in the eyes of God.[26]

George Fox, the founder of the Society of Friends, defended his belief in the equality of women and men, citing St. Paul's letter to the Galatians 3:28: "There is neither Jew nor Grecian: there is neither bond nor free: there is neither male nor female: for you are all one in Christ Jesus." Fox preached to his followers: "If the power of God and the Seed spoke in man or woman, it was Christ."[27] Thus, the Quakers constructed a new role for women that combined women's spiritual authority with their maternal nature, emphasizing women's spiritual equality even as it reinforced their biological difference from men.[28]

George Fox argued that the spiritual regeneration of conversion freed women from the curse of Eve. Before the Fall, Adam and Eve were equals in the Garden of Eden. After the Fall, men ruled over their wives. But, Fox argued, once women received the Word of God, the Inner Light, they were restored to equality with men. Empowered by Fox's teachings and emboldened by the presence of Christ within them, women were liberated from their traditionally prescribed roles and welcomed in the lay ministry of his society.[29] "Encourage all the women that are convinced, and minds virtue, and loves the truth, and walks in it, that they may come up into God's service," Fox implored, "that they may too be serviceable in their generation, and in the Creation."[30]

Heeding their Inner Light did not liberate Quaker women completely from the world in which they lived. Because they rejected women's traditional behavior in church, they were often subject to attack. They spoke spontaneously when the Holy Spirit inspired them, defying the idea that prayer, led by ministers, should be controlled, rational, and orderly. Although they claimed their words were inspired by God, others saw them as agents of Satan and accused them of witchcraft.[31]

One eloquent Quaker woman who paid the ultimate price for her beliefs was Mary Dyer. She emigrated to Boston with her husband, William, and joined the Reverend John Wilson's church. Soon after her arrival in the colony, she began to attend Anne Hutchinson's meetings and was "notoriously infected with Mrs. Hutchinson's errors." She, her husband, and their six children followed Hutchinson into exile and settled in Newport, Rhode Island. There William served in the local government and was appointed attorney general of the colony. In 1652, while in England with her husband on business, Mary joined the Society of Friends. When she returned to Boston in 1657 she was immediately imprisoned for preaching the word of God. This zealous woman was described by a Dutch admirer as "a person of no mean extract and parentage, of an estate pretty plentiful, of a comely stature and countenance, of a piercing knowledge in many things, of a wonderful sweet and pleasant discourse, so fit for great affairs, that she wanted [that is, lacked] nothing that was manly, except only the name and the sex."[32]

Mary Dyer, like Anne Hutchinson, believed God spoke directly to her, and this frightened the ministers and magistrates of Massachusetts. Unlike Hutchinson, however, Mary courted persecution by publicly challenging the laws barring Quakers from the colony. Whipped for her "unruly" behavior, she was twice banished from the colony, only to return in defiance of the law. In October 1659, she was sentenced to be hanged with Quakers Marmaduke Stevenson and William Robinson. In response to her son's petition, her life was spared as she stood on the scaffold awaiting execution. She was banished once more but returned a year later and was again arrested, tried, found guilty, and sentenced to death. William Dyer begged the governor and his council to pardon his wife: "I only say that yor selves have been & are or may bee husbands to wife or wives, so am I yet to one most dearely beloved: oh no not deprive me of her, but I pray give her me once agen & I shall bee so much obleiged for ever."[33] Dyer's heartfelt pleas fell on deaf ears. On 1 June 1660, Mary Dyer was executed.[34]

Angered by the execution of Dyer and other Quakers in Massachusetts, King Charles II ordered the colony to implement a policy of religious toleration. Ironically, Puritan ministers and magistrates soon discovered that ignoring the Quakers diminished their appeal.[35] Deprived of the opportunity to become martyrs for their faith, Quaker women reverted to more subdued, traditional roles. Their religious energy found a new outlet in the Quaker women's meetings.

Initially, there was great opposition to the idea of separate women's meetings from Quaker men and women alike. Some argued that men should not share authority with women. Others objected that separation of the sexes promoted women's inequality. In an open letter to all Quakers, written in 1678, Mary Penington tried to assuage these anxieties. She argued that women's meetings reflected women's "natural capacities"; they complimented rather than usurped the authority of men. She asserted that women were by nature better skilled at looking after the poor, the sick, and domestic matters. "Our place in ye creation is to bring forth & nurse up, to keep things orderly, sweet & clean in a family, . . . & to provide things necessary for food & raimt," she explained, "to whch or imploymt in ye Church of God appears to bring forth & nurture, to cleanse out wt is unsavoury & unclean, & cast out evill doers out of the house of God to preserve & keep wholesom & orderly things in this house." Equating women's meetings with keeping house and linking women's role within the Society of Friends to their role as wives and mothers, Penington tried to smooth the ruffled feathers of Quaker men.[36]

The first monthly women's meeting in North America was held in New Jersey in 1681. It was created "for the better management of the discipline and other affairs of the church more proper to be inspected by their sex." Women's meetings supervised the conduct of women within the religious community, reviewed and approved petitions for marriage, assisted the poor, and upheld the standards of family life expected of their faith. Their rulings were seldom questioned by the men. Yet, even as these meetings complimented and affirmed the spiritual equality of women and men, they reinforced women's traditional, "domestic" role in colonial society.[37]

WOMEN AND RELIGION IN THE SOUTHERN COLONIES

The stability of life in New England was envied by women who settled in the southern colonies. There the scarcity of women, their isolation on remote plantations, the preoccupation of men with economic survival, and the high mortality rate prevented women from having much of an impact on religious life. Some Catholic women migrated to Maryland, and Quaker and Moravian women established homes in the region, but most southern women were Anglican. Although they lacked the religious zeal of their northern sisters, they participated in church services and were responsible for sustaining religious institutions in the colonies. Less literate than their Puritan peers, few left testimony of their religious beliefs, but doubtless their faith sustained them as they confronted life and death in their New World homes.[38]

The development of a slave economy introduced to the southern colonies people with dramatically different religious beliefs. African women's experience was shaped by the cultural legacy they brought with them as well as by the beliefs of the colonists who enslaved them. The majority of slaves brought to North America came from the coast of West Africa. There they had a rich religious heritage in which women played important roles and participated in sacred rituals. Many slaves imported from the northernmost regions of West Africa were Muslims, followers of the prophet Mohammed, while those from the interior and the south had highly developed tribal religions. Regardless of their origins, religion shaped all facets of African peoples' secular lives: religious laws regulated sexuality and marriage, prescribed the responsibilities of women and men, defined the rituals of childbirth, and shaped the rearing of children. Although their religious beliefs varied, there were many practices common to all. In many West African religions, women were priestesses and performed important religious ceremonies. But many of these rituals, especially those involving African women, appeared bizarre, even sinful to European explorers and traders. The English justified their enslavement of Africans on the grounds that Africans were not Christians and did not deserve the same respect or treatment as those baptized in a Christian church.[39]

In seventeenth-century Virginia, the distinction between servant and slave was initially based on both race and religion. There an English servant was referred to as a "Christian servant," while Africans were referred to as "Negro servants," implying that they were not Christian.

Some masters barred their slaves from church services and refused them Christian baptism, believing that if their slaves became Christians they must free them. Although later colonists justified enslaving Africans to convert them, the first generation of slave holders saw the religious conversion of their slaves as a threat to ownership.

Some southern planters, however, encouraged their slaves to attend religious services, and it is likely that some African women welcomed the opportunity to participate in Christian services. Many slaves came to English North America through Spain's Caribbean colonies, where they were converted by their Catholic owners. Spanish colonists in the New World had no qualms about converting their African slaves because they did not believe baptism demanded emancipation. Consequently, many African women imported as slaves to the southern colonies had Spanish Christian names. An African woman named Isabella was on board the first ship bearing "Negro servants" to Virginia in 1619. She later married a shipmate named Anthony, and five years later parish records list "Anthony, negro, Isabell, a negro, and William, her child, baptized." Although it is unclear whether the entire family or only William was baptized, this is the first recorded baptism of a child of African ancestry in North America.[40]

Religion played an important role in securing the freedom of at least one African-American woman in early Virginia. Elizabeth Key, the illegitimate daughter of Thomas Key and a slave, was born around 1630. When she was five or six she was bound to Humphrey Higginson and, later, to John Mottrom. When Mottrom died in 1655, attorney William Greensted sued for Elizabeth's freedom, claiming that because she was the daughter of a free man she was free. Greensted also convincingly argued that because Elizabeth was a baptized Christian she could not be a slave. Consequently, the jury found Elizabeth Key a free woman. But, the Mottrom estate appealed this decision and the colony's General Court, fearful of establishing a precedent, ruled that Elizabeth was a slave. Greensted appealed their ruling to the House of Burgesses, and a special committee was formed to review Elizabeth's case. It was remanded for retrial, and her freedom was affirmed. Soon after, Attorney Greensted's motive in tenaciously pursuing Elizabeth's freedom was revealed when the couple married.[41]

Elizabeth Key's court case demonstrates how religion played a part in defining Africans' status in early Virginia. Elizabeth's Christian baptism conferred on her a status higher than that of a slave. She possessed a Christian first name and used her father's last name, although her parents were not wed. She claimed she was free because her father was free, and she used the English custom of patrilineage to affirm her status. Elizabeth's pursuit of freedom in a court of law indicates that the lines between slavehood and freedom were still unclear in early Virginia. Her subsequent marriage to Greensted reveals that the demand for wives in seventeenth-century Virginia overrode English cultural taboos against racial mixture, for miscegenation was not yet prohibited by law in the colony. Perhaps this couple's happy ending proves that love triumphed over all.

Elizabeth Key's lawsuit revealed the loopholes in Virginia's laws regarding slaves and servants, and lawmakers scrambled to close them. Recognizing that many Africans slaves had been baptized or were practicing Christians, the Virginia House of Burgesses passed laws to ensure that these women, men, and their children would remain slaves. In 1662 a statute defined the children of slave women as slaves, regardless of their mother's religious faith, and another law asserted that the baptism of a slave did not guarantee her or his freedom. These laws were copied in other English colonies as more African slaves were imported to North America.

African women embraced Christianity more readily than their male counterparts, perhaps because they hoped conversion would ensure better treatment for them and their children. The first African woman was admitted to church membership in Massachusetts in 1641 after demonstrating her "true godliness" for many years. Other African women, both slave and free, were baptized, became church members, and brought their children to their adopted churches for baptism.

In 1701 the Society for the Propagation of the Gospel in Foreign Parts sent missionaries to the colonies to educate and convert African slaves despite opposition from slave owners who resented any outside interference that might threaten their control over them. These missionaries noticed West African customs among the slaves whose souls they tended, including activities they labeled "immoral." They observed a high rate of prenuptial pregnancy among slave women and noted that some women had many "husbands" during their lifetimes. The missionaries urged the passage of legislation to "regularize" slave marriages and curb the "immorality" of slave women.

Most members of the Society of Friends in the southern colonies accepted the presence of slavery in their midst. Although they espoused the spiritual equality of men and women, regardless of race, their dependence on slave labor muted the inclination to free their slaves. Instead, they advocated their conversion and encouraged slaves' attendance at Quaker meetings. African women were especially attracted to the Quaker faith because of its emphasis on the "inner light" of divine revelation and the absence of a white male ministry. But some colonial authorities feared that slaves, empowered by the message of their spiritual equality, might rebel against their masters, and they instituted legislation barring slaves from attending Quaker meetings. In doing so, they acknowledged the important role religious beliefs played in the lives of the slaves.[42]

The Feminization of New England Congregations

By the end of the seventeenth century, the American colonies had grown and changed. As immigration from the British Isles, Europe, and Africa transformed the ethnic and racial composition of the colonies, population growth brought a demand for land and, inevitably, warfare with Native Americans. England's changing policies regarding colonial administration tested the colonists' resolve and brought uncertainty to their lives. Preoccupied with secular concerns, the faith and religious devotion of New England's Puritans waned.

Although men continued to govern, attend, and financially support their community churches, their religious fervor diminished with each passing generation. Years removed from the persecution experienced by their parents and grandparents, the intensity of their faith declined. They devoted less attention to their immortal souls and more to their lands and businesses. Fewer men qualified or applied for church membership. And once church membership was no longer required for voting or holding public office, a secular incentive for "joining" a church was lost. By the end of the century, women were the majority of members in most New England churches.[43]

The feminization of New England's congregations alarmed ministers, who saw their own importance and influence diminish with the decline in male membership. To revitalize and remasculinize their congregations, they instituted the "half-way covenant" in 1662. This new policy for church membership allowed children and grandchildren of "Saints" to be baptized and have their children baptized, thus granting them "half-way" membership in the church covenant. Half-way members, however, were barred from the Lord's Supper until they became full-fledged members of the church. By 1677, even this barrier to full church membership fell, and, in an effort to bring the children, grandchildren, and great-grandchildren of the original "Saints" back to church, communion was opened to all. But the half-way covenant failed to rejuvenate men's church membership or to revitalize their faith, and women continued to dominate church membership rolls.[44]

MARY ROWLANDSON

The wife of one Puritan minister from Lancaster, Massachusetts, exemplified the ideal of female piety during this trying period in New England history. A captive in the war with Native Americans that wracked the region, she embodied courage and a rugged piety that inspired women and men alike. Mary White Rowlandson was the daughter of first-generation Puritans who helped found the frontier community of Lancaster in the 1630s. In 1656, Mary wed the town's first minister, Joseph Rowlandson, and gave birth to four children, three of whom survived infancy. In 1675, several tribes, united under the leadership of Wampanoag chief Metacomet, known to the English as King Philip, attacked frontier settlements. On 20 February 1676, Mary Rowlandson and her six-year-old daughter Sarah were seized by Narragansett Natives during an attack on Lancaster. The injured goodwife and nearly two dozen others were marched into the wilderness. She despaired: "All was gone, my Husband gone (at least separated from me . . . and to my grief, the indians told me they would kill him as he came homeward), my Children gone, my relatives and Friends gone, our House . . . and home and all our comforts, within and without, all was gone (except my life) and [I] knew not but at the moment that might go too."[45]

The hostages walked westward for several days until they reached a Narragansett village where Mary and Sarah were sold to a chief and his three wives. Sarah soon died of her wounds, while her mother, separated from the other English captives, was frightened and alone. But rather than passively awaiting her fate, Mary took matters into her own capable hands. An accomplished seamstress, she made clothes for her mistress Weetamoo and Metacomet's son and traded her handwork for additional food.

Mary's captivity sorely tried her faith. She turned to prayer and asked God to "show me a sign for good, and if it were his blessed will, some sign of hope and relief." She was angered that God allowed "heathens" to live when her family and friends had been brutally killed. She struggled to understand why she had been captured and enslaved. "But what can I say?" she wondered, "God seemed to leave his People to themselves, and order all things for his own holy ends." She eventually came to believe that her ordeal was a test of her faith. Submitting to God's will, she embodied the proper religious posture of the Puritan goodwife. Yet she did not meekly await rescue. She urged her master to redeem her and negotiated her own release. After a captivity of 83 days, she was finally reunited with her husband in Boston.

Mary Rowlandson's captivity narrative, published in 1682, is an archetype of female piety in Puritan New England. Mary interpreted her captivity as God's trial of her faith. She did what she had to do to survive and attributed her "redemption" to God's will. Her religion provided her with the language to understand her ordeal. The lesson she learned was that "when God calls a Person to any thing, and through never so many difficulties, yet he is fully able to carry them through and make them see, and say they have been gainers thereby. . . . That we must rely upon God himself, and our whole dependence must be upon him." Mary's narrative combined the ideal of Christian resignation with resourceful adaptation. This hardy Puritan goodwife was a model worthy of emulation by both women and men during trying times in New England.[46]

THE SALEM WITCHCRAFT TRIALS

Wars with Native Americans, the Antinomian and Quaker Controversies, the Restoration of Charles II, and the Glorious Revolution challenged the Puritan's mission in New England. By the end of the century the values that united the original colonists had changed. The earliest years of settlement were characterized by a sense of community and cooperation—values that enabled the first generation of settlers to survive the wilderness and create God's "citee upon a hill." But economic success soon supplanted concerns about salvation, individualism emerged as the avenue for advancement, and competition replaced cooperation as the way to achieve success. The early social hierarchy based on church membership and service to the community gave way to a new one based on wealth and generated by self-interest. These changes had unfortunate consequences. Frustrated ministers preached powerful sermons, "Jeremiads," claiming that God was displeased with the people of New England and was punishing them.[47] As people's sense of guilt, coupled with feelings of resentment and jealousy, grew, they looked for someone on whom to blame their problems. Satan, they claimed, was in their midst, bringing God's wrath down upon them. And who were Satan's handmaidens? Witches![48]

The witchcraft hysteria that swept New England and culminated in the trials at Salem, Massachusetts, in 1692 was a sad expression of women's involvement in the region's religious life. As both accusers and the accused, women gave voice to the beliefs of their day. Their powerlessness and despair were emblematic of deeper anxieties that infected the entire culture and fueled the witchcraft craze. And they were its principle victims.

Despite the religious orthodoxy of New England, many colonists—even "Saints"—believed in magic. Religious belief supposes a supernatural authority that may be influenced only through prayer. Magic, on the other hand, permits one to harness supernatural forces for his or her own ends. But the boundaries between what a culture defines as religion and magic are fragile and blurred. Although Puritan theologians tried to purge the Anglican Church of its "magical" symbols and eliminate forever the belief in magic, they failed. Despite their claims that religious and magical traditions were antithetical, the common people refused to surrender "folk" beliefs—the charms, spells, superstitions, and traditions—that gave them a sense of control over their lives. A pregnant woman, for example, might earnestly pray to God for a safe delivery, yet consult the village "wise woman" for a charm to ensure her good health or to discover the sex of her unborn child. Even the most learned Puritan men blamed unusual natural phenomena on ghosts and specters or saw them as portents of things to come. Plagues of locusts, comets, earth tremors, and mighty storms were signs that in both the visible and the invisible world God was at war with Satan. Although some ministers warned women and men that they were helpless to control their fate, even they protected themselves and their families with magic.[49]

"White magic," the use of the occult to achieve positive ends, was relatively common in seventeenth-century America and viewed by most colonists as harmless. Potions and charms used to divine the future, ward off spells, and cure physical ailments, bore close resemblance to the medicines—homemade cordials, liquors, and poultices—made by women to remedy their families' ills. Virtually every New England town also had a "wise woman" known for her ability to treat the sick or her skill as a midwife. Some of them probably crossed the tenuous boundary between medicine and the occult. Orthodox ministers believed that even "healing witches" were empowered by Satan and opposed the practice of white magic as well as black. As one English witch-hunter warned: "For this must always be remembered . . . that by witches we understand not only those which kill and torment, but all Diviners, Charmers, Jugglers, all Wizards, commonly called wise men and wise women . . . and in the same number we reckon all good Witches, which do no hurt byt good, which do not spoil and destroy, but save and deliver. . . . It were a thousand times better for the land if all Witches, but especially the blessing Witch, might suffer death."[50]

Many women accused of witchcraft in the colonies prior to the Salem outbreak were healers or midwives. In Virginia in 1626 Goodwife Joan Wright, a midwife, was called to deliver the child of Gieles Allington. The superstitious Mrs. Allington discovered that Wright was left-handed and feared this would harm her child. She implored her husband to find another midwife, and Wright left the Allington house "very much discontented." Following her delivery, when Mrs. Allington suffered an abscessed breast, and her infant son sickened and died, she accused Wright of having cursed them. Although others testified that Goodwife Wright had practiced magic in England, the case against her was weak and she was never brought to trial. Perhaps the fledgling colony valued Wright's skills as a midwife too much to risk losing her, for she continued to tend Virginia's women at their births.[51] In Massachusetts, John Winthrop recalled the 1641 banishment of Jane Hawkins, a midwife and follower of Anne Hutchinson: "The midwife . . . went out of the jurisdiction; and indeed it was time for her to be gone, for it was known, that she used to give young women oil of mandrakes and other stuff to cause conception; and she grew into great suspicion to be a witch, for it was credibly reported, that, when she gave any medicines (for she practised physic), she would ask the party, if she did believe, she could help her, etc."[52]

Since maternity was the focus of most women's lives, women whose childbearing experience was "exceptional" were also regarded with suspicion. Anne Hutchinson and Rebecca Nurse of Salem, Massachusetts, had remarkable success in the bearing and rearing of children and were suspected of practicing witchcraft to ensure their good fortune. Women plagued by miscarriage or the death of a child were also viewed with trepidation by their neighbors; those accused of practicing witchcraft were twice as likely as their peers to be childless. Thus, women suspected of somehow interfering with birth and death, especially those recognized as nurses or midwives, were vulnerable to witchcraft accusation.[53] Many accused women were from the lower classes, but more from the middle and upper classes were "cried out" as the century progressed. The disintegration of the value system that bound Puritan communities together and the restructuring of the social hierarchy contributed to this change in who was "blamed" for the region's problems.[54]

The Salem Village witchcraft trials of 1692 marked the climax of witchcraft belief in colonial New England.[55] Late in the winter of 1691, a group of young girls met secretly in the Salem Village home of the Reverend Samuel Parris. Among them were Parris's daughter Elizabeth and his niece Abigail Williams. The girls wished to know who they would marry and "what trade their sweethearts should be of." To divine their fate, they created a primitive crystal ball from egg whites and a glass of water. But when their magic crystal revealed images of coffins, they were frightened. These daughters of Puritans knew that what they had done was wrong.

Early in 1692 young Elizabeth Parris and her cousin Abigail fell ill with "odd postures," "distempers," and "fits." When the physician could not diagnose their disturbing behavior, he attributed it to witchcraft. And as rumors of the girls' affliction spread throughout the village, other girls involved in their fortune-telling exhibited strange behavior, too. Finally, on 29 February 1692, warrants were issued for three Salem Village women whom the girls claimed had bewitched them.

Had events at Salem followed the pattern of earlier witchcraft accusations, the incident would most likely have ended with the imprisonment and trial of these three women. But the circumstances of Salem Village distinguished this outbreak from others. Deep-seated divisions in the community—embodied by the Putnam and Porter families—reflected the very different values battling for primacy in late seventeenth-century New England. This conflict fueled the outbreak of witchcraft at Salem.

John Putnam and John Porter came to Salem during the 1640s. Both prospered as farmers, but a half-century later the fortunes of their descendants diverged. The Putnams continued to farm the rocky lands around Salem, but watched helplessly as their wealth and political influence declined. The Porters diversified, participated in trade with surrounding communities, and prospered. The corporate values espoused by the earliest Puritan settlers, and embodied by the Putnams, gave way to the competition and individualism of a new, commercial age, represented by the Porters; while the Putnams held fast to the old, the Porters embraced the new. The Putnams fought hard to retain their influence in the Salem Village church—the traditional heart of their community. They championed the selection of the Reverend Samuel Parris in the face of the Porters' opposition. Thus, beneath the surface of Salem Village life, an intense battle raged between two families—two value systems—for the future of New England.

Within this family conflict, the experiences of Ann Carr Putnam and her daughter Ann Putnam illustrate how women's powerlessness and dependence fed the hysteria at Salem. The daughter of George Carr, one of the wealthiest men in Salisbury, Massachusetts, Ann Carr married Thomas Putnam, Jr., in 1678. The young couple had every reason to expect their fortunes would increase. But when George Carr died, he willed the bulk of his estate to his widow and his sons; Ann received only a modest cash settlement, much to her husband's disappointment. Thomas Putnam's widowed father remarried a younger woman and fathered a son, Joseph. When Putnam died in 1686, he left the best part of his estate to his widow and Joseph, naming them joint executors. Thomas challenged the wills of his father and his father-in-law to no avail. He was further angered when Joseph married into the Porter family, taking with him the wealth he inherited from their father. As Thomas witnessed his wealth and influence decline through no fault of his own, he felt powerless to control his fate. He attributed his bad fortune to witchcraft.[56]

Ann Carr Putnam was embittered by the actions of her father and helpless to assuage her husband's anger. She witnessed her family's decline with a sense of frustration, outrage, and jealousy, but as a dutiful goodwife was prohibited from expressing these emotions. At the same time, she harbored a sense of guilt: she was a disappointment to her husband, who had married her in hopes of advancing himself. Following their marriage, Ann gave birth to four sons and six daughters, including her namesake, Ann. While sons were an asset to a farming family, daughters were a liability, especially in an era of declining opportunity. Because a girl's future as a wife depended on the size of her dowry, it is little wonder that young Ann was among the girls divining their fates at the Reverend Parris's house. Most of Salem's "afflicted girls," like young Ann Putnam, were actually young single women over the age of 16. Many had lost one or more of their parents in the Indian wars that plagued New England's frontier and had been taken in by relatives. Few of these penniless young women had any real hope of marrying. Anxious about their futures, yet powerless to control them, they sought answers from a crystal ball.[57]

The outrageous behavior of Salem's afflicted girls and women immediately thrust them into the public eye. Ordinarily, they would have been punished severely for their actions, but these were extraordinary times in Salem. Important men examined them and concluded that they were possessed. When asked who afflicted them, the girls were slow to identify their tormenters. When pressed, however, they named three women: Tituba, a West Indian slave owned by the Reverend Parris, Sarah Good, and Sarah Osborne. All were arrested and imprisoned in Boston to await trial.[58]

THE ACCUSED

Tituba was an outsider. A native of Barbados, possibly of both African and West Indian ancestry, she was probably exposed to Native American and African religions on this Caribbean island. Although she came to Salem as the Reverend Parris's slave, it is unlikely that she was a baptized Christian. Whether Tituba practiced what the English colonists called witchcraft or merely worshipped her God or gods as she saw fit, she was an easy target for accusation in Salem.[59]

Imprisoned with Mary Black, another slave accused during the witchcraft hysteria, Tituba testified that in Barbados she learned how to discover a witch and prevent bewitchment. And she admitted making a cake of meal and the afflicted girls' urine "to find out the Witch," an age-old method used by English folk to ward off enchantment.[60] She argued that she was not a witch, although "her Master did beat her and otherways abuse her to make her confess and accuse (such as he call'd) her Sister-Witches." A slave in a free society, a person of color in a white society, a woman in a society dominated by men, Tituba fulfilled the expectations of her masters by confessing. But, in doing so, she saved her life.[61]

Sarah Good's life was filled with misfortune. The daughter of a wealthy man, Sarah married beneath herself, a penniless indentured servant. When he died, Sarah was held liable for his debts and had to sell her dowry lands. Her second husband, a weaver, was unable to support her. They lost their home and depended on the charity of Salem's residents to survive. A bitter, angry woman, Sarah Good grudgingly accepted assistance for herself and her young daughter, Dorcas. Those who helped her criticized her resentful attitude and feared her muttered curses. Even her husband feared her wrath, testifying at her trial that he was "afraid that she was a witch or would be one very quickly."[62] Pregnant at the time of her arrest, Sarah Good reminded all women of their vulnerability: a bad marriage could propel a woman from wealth to poverty. In Sarah, they saw their own worst fears come to life.

Sarah Price Osborne was neither poor nor an outsider. A long-time Salem resident, she was the wife of a successful village farmer. When her husband died, he left his considerable property to her in trust for their two sons. But village gossips had much to talk about when Sarah married her young Irish indentured servant, Alexander Osbourne, and tried to break her first husband's will. In trying to secure title to her sons' inheritance, Sarah violated the ideal of the selfless goodwife who placed her children's welfare before her own. She also challenged the colony's laws regarding inheritance. Her behavior attracted the censure of both women and men, who saw her as a threat to their own values and well-being. Goody (short for Goodwife) Osborne died of natural causes on 10 May 1692 while imprisoned in Boston.[63]

Tituba, Sarah Good, and Sarah Osborne were women the afflicted girls knew made Salem's adults uncomfortable. Tituba's confession prompted the afflicted girls' inquisitors to ask if there were other witches in the community. At first they named no others, but then young Ann Putnam accused Martha Corey of witchcraft.

Goodwife Corey laughed when told she was accused of witchcraft. She pointed out that she was a "Gosple-woman"—a church member—and claimed there were no witches in New England. But her accusation marked a major change in whom the girls of Salem "cried out" as witches. The circle of the accused expanded to include married women of property and standing in the community, church members, and even men. Instead of targeting those who violated the norms of their society, the girls "cried out" those whose who embodied the very qualities they were reared to respect and emulate. Martha Corey, a "Gosple-woman," epitomized the ideal Puritan goodwife.[64]

The afflicted girls then named the elderly Rebecca Nurse and middle-aged Elizabeth Procter, both from wealthy families, as their tormenters. Goody Nurse was the daughter of a suspected witch, and her sisters—Mary Easty and Sarah Cloyse—were also accused, tried, and found guilty of witchcraft at Salem. Little Dorcas Good, Sarah Good's daughter, was also accused of witchcraft and confessed, while Elizabeth Procter was the granddaughter of an accused witch. Many who had survived earlier suspicions of witchcraft—Bridget Bishop, Susanna Martin, and Dorcas Hoar—lost their lives at Salem, and even male relatives of the accused were vulnerable. Elizabeth Procter's husband, John, was the first man named at Salem. Giles Corey, Martha's husband, was also accused of witchcraft and died while being tortured to exact a plea.

Of the nearly 200 people accused of witchcraft in the Salem outbreak, 75 percent were women.[65] That so many men were accused probably reflects the underlying political tensions within the community. It is also possible that the afflicted girls, emboldened by community support, directly challenged men's authority by accusing them, as well as their wives, mothers, and daughters, of witchcraft.

GUILTY OR INNOCENT?

By the summer of 1692, the circle of witchcraft accusation widened to include men and women whose "quality . . . did bespeak better things" and whose "blameless and holy lives before did testify for them." Among those accused were Governor William Phips's wife, Lady Mary Phips, and the wife of the Reverend John Hale. When one of the most respected ministers in the colony, the Reverend Samuel Willard, was named, the ministers and magistrates decided to halt the trials. But before the trials ended in October 1692, at least fifty people accused of witchcraft in Salem and surrounding towns had confessed. The majority of confessed witches were women. The authorities' decision to spare those who admitted their guilt probably prompted some of these confessions, for those who did not confess and were found guilty were executed by hanging.

It is possible that some women who confessed their guilt were intimidated by male magistrates. Schooled all their lives to be submissive to men, to defer to their judgment and authority, some women may have confessed to the crime of witchcraft despite their innocence. Margaret Jacobs wrote to her father from the Salem jail: "The reason of my Confinement is this, I having, through the Magistrates Threatnings, and my own Vile and Wretched Heart, confessed several things contrary to my Conscience and Knowledg . . . I was forced to confess the truth of all before the Magistrates, who would not believe me [until I confessed]."[66] Many accused women were subjected to pretrial examinations lasting several hours, and their examiners took turns questioning them until they confessed.[67]

That so many Salem women confessed to witchcraft—whether guilty or not—reflects a crisis in their religious beliefs. If their confessions were sincere and they truly were witches, their faith clearly failed them. Living in a culture that emphasized the powerlessness of women in the face of God and men, they turned to witchcraft to acquire some control over their lives. But, if they were not witches, their confessions were motivated solely by self-preservation. And, unlike the pagan Tituba, a Puritan goodwife understood she compromised her salvation by lying. If she confessed to a crime she did not commit, merely to save her life, she placed herself before her God and violated the tenets of her faith. Thus, a "Gosple-woman" like Martha Corey would rather die than risk God's wrath. Whether guilty or not, a confession of witchcraft signified a failure of a Puritan woman's faith.

The events in Salem in 1692 marked a turning point in women's religious lives in Puritan New England. The afflicted girls' beliefs and fears led them to accuse others in their community of witchcraft. Ministers, magistrates, and townspeople initially encouraged their actions to revitalize religious faith and restore traditional values in their community. Yet even as the afflicted girls reinforced the subordinate position of women in Puritan society through their accusation of other women, they rebelled against the gender norms of their community. When their accusations reached beyond those suspected by their community of sinful, inappropriate behavior, they threatened the very foundations of Puritan patriarchy. The ministers and magistrates had to restrain them to preserve their authority in the community. The tables were turned and the bewitched were now suspected of being possessed by the Devil. Once doubts were raised about the veracity of their allegations, the afflicted girls were restrained. They were discredited and their sex was vilified.

The Puritans' distrust of women was reinforced by the Salem Village witchcraft trials. Women and men alike blamed the outbreak on women's failure to submit to men. Like Eve in the Garden of Eden, the afflicted girls sought knowledge about their future, violating the norms of their society and the will of God. Women who confessed their "guilt" as witches also affirmed the belief that women were especially vulnerable to Satan's lures. Their confessions strengthened their culture's suspicions about women and justified their continued subordination in New England. Women who proclaimed their innocence at Salem and met their deaths on the gallows were also victims of women's powerlessness in Puritan society. Their execution was emblematic of women's vulnerability in patriarchal Puritan New England. That women were chief among both the accusers and the accused at Salem, demonstrates how deeply Puritans' ideas about women's sinful nature were imbedded in the minds of all. Frustration, resentment, fear, and self-loathing led the afflicted girls to turn on other women, the most vulnerable in their society, and blame them for their own powerlessness. Thus, female accusers and the accused, alike, were victims at Salem.

Puritan minister Cotton Mather helped shape the course of the Salem trials. In 1692 Mather completed *Wonders of the Invisible World*, in which he explained his belief in witchcraft and defended the Salem trials. Mather argued that women, the daughters of Eve, were more vulnerable to evil than men and that Satan seduced them into undermining the Puritan's Christian commonwealth. Proud, contentious, and jealous women, he claimed, were potential witches. Not content with their lot, these "unnatural" women aspired to supremacy over others—a supremacy that could be achieved only through an alliance with Satan.

Mather's witches were women who failed to submit to men. Dangerous threats to the well-being of church and state, they deserved execution.

VIRTUOUS WOMEN

Salem's witchcraft trials rent the very fabric of life in Puritan New England by bringing into question the virtue of the region's women. Thus, it became necessary for ministers to construct a new model of Christian behavior for women to embody. In *Ornaments for the Daughters of Zion*, also published in 1692, Cotton Mather created a new archetype of Christian womanhood for Puritan women to emulate, the opposite of the evil woman/witch described in *Wonders of the Invisible World*. Even as he reinforced men's authority over women, Mather sought to appease women's sense of powerlessness, which fueled the Salem trials.

Ornaments for the Daughters of Zion was written explicitly for women, for Mather acknowledged that they were a majority of the members in most New England churches. He admitted, "Tho' both *Sexes*, be thro the Marvellous Providence of our God Born into the World, in pretty Aequal Numbers, yet, in the Female, there seem to be the Larger Numbers of them that are *Born Again*, and brought into the Kingdom of God."[68] He recognized that women's discontent and frustration helped fuel the witchcraft outbreak and strove to elevate women in their own eyes and in the eyes of men. Mather disparaged men who refused to write for women, remarking to his female readers that "the Actions of even the meanest Milk-maid or Cook-maid, when done in the fear of God, are in the Account of God more noble Things than the Victories of a Cesar! Thus do I set before you, the Way for you to be enabled; and thus ennobled, many of you already are."[69]

Mather urged women to emulate the "Daughters of Zion," the heroic women of the Bible. He evoked the qualities of Solomon's mother, Bathsheba, as the model of a virtuous woman: a loving wife, a skilled worker, and a thrifty housewife who "looketh well to the ways of her household and eateth not the bread of idleness"; she saw that her husband and family were well-clothed and fed, assisted the needy, and spoke with wisdom and kindness. Finally, and most important, the virtuous woman "feareth the Lord." In fulfilling these obligations to her husband, family, friends, and God, she proved her worth.[70]

In *Ornaments for the Daughters of Zion,* Mather constructed a new archetype for Puritan women. He affirmed their importance, commended their virtues, and encouraged them to be helpmates to their husbands. He acknowledged their intellectual capabilities and urged them to read the Bible, citing especially gifted women whose dedication to God was demonstrated through studying Scripture. By acknowledging them, Mather hoped to harness women's energies and channel them in what he deemed acceptable ways. But at the same time he urged all women to subordinate their needs to those of their husbands and families.

Mather's "virtuous woman" served as a crucial link between the two value systems emerging in seventeenth-century New England. She could assist in the preservation of the older, communal values brought to North America by Puritan ancestors, while her husband embraced the new values of individualism and competition: women's place was in the home with their families, men's place was the much larger world of commerce and trade. Together, men and women could preserve the old while embracing the new. Thus, Mather believed, women had a special role to play in the future of New England.[71]

Many women welcomed the elevated model of Christian womanhood constructed by Mather, for it prescribed a secure place for them in a rapidly changing world. It assigned spiritual importance to familiar domestic duties and reassured them of their own worth. If their own interests had to be subordinate to those of men and if their husbands were still their masters, at least they could take refuge in knowing that they performed their duties in accordance with God's will.

Hannah Dunston of Haverhill, Massachusetts, became the living embodiment of Cotton Mather's new Christian woman. Carried off by Native Americans during an attack on her home only five days after giving birth, Dunston, together with another woman and a young man, killed her captors and returned home with their scalps. This deed made Hannah Dunston's name a byword in New England, and Cotton Mather quickly seized her example to serve his ends. In a sermon preached shortly after her return to Haverhill, Mather found biblical precedent for Hannah's violent behavior in the story of Jael, who welcomed her enemy into her household and killed him while he slept, saving her people. Likening Hannah to Jael, Mather elevated her to heroic status, even though she denied her culture's assumption that women were physically weaker than men. In doing so, Mather honored a strong, assertive woman, yet carefully presented her actions in terms that did not challenge the authority of Puritan men. He claimed her behavior was ordained by God and that she acted selflessly for the salvation of the English colonists. But it is also possible that Mather saw in Hannah a real danger to the patriarchal society of New England. That women were capable of violence against men who subordinated them against their will was too horrifying to acknowledge. It evoked the specter of the malevolent woman only recently put to rest with the conclusion of the Salem witchcraft trials. Thus, Mather "tamed" Hannah by translating her experience into a socially acceptable model of Puritan womanhood. He defused the threat of her violence against the men who held her in captivity.[72]

Perhaps more disturbing to Cotton Mather than Hannah Dunston's violence, however, was Eunice Williams's rejection of her culture and religion. Early one snowy, cold morning in February 1704, this seven-year-old daughter of Deerfield minister John Williams was taken captive with her parents and five siblings by raiding Mohawks. Along with others from their town, they were marched northward to Quebec. Although Eunice's father was released and returned to Boston after two and a half years of captivity, Eunice stayed with the Mohawk family that adopted her. She forgot her native tongue, married a Mohawk brave, adopted his Roman Catholic faith, and bore his children. She chose not to return to her family, even when given the opportunity for "redemption." What was to be made of this daughter of the Puritans who repudiated her culture for another? Did she find greater freedoms, a happier life, a more supportive faith among her adopted people than among her own kind? Eunice Williams's decision to remain with her "savage" captors was more deeply disturbing than Hannah Dunston's violence, for it brought into question all that the New England Puritans believed and what they thought they had accomplished in North America.[73]

The eighteenth century witnessed the continued feminization of religion as men turned to economic pursuits and left women to claim the church as their own. Recognizing this, and concerned about maintaining their dwindling authority, ministers addressed what they perceived as the needs of their female congregants. They praised women for their piety and eulogized their saintly qualities in sermons and prescriptive literature. In their sermons they began to replace the image of God, the vengeful patriarch, with the gentler image of Christ, his loving son, to appeal to women's sensibilities. They began to use the metaphor of marriage, an institution with which all women were familiar, to illustrate the experience of regeneration: As women served their husbands, so were they to serve Christ, their bridegroom; as their husbands cared for them, Christ would fulfill all their spiritual needs.[74]

Despite the fact that women were the majority of church members, ministers were loath to empower them with greater public authority. Instead, women were encouraged to pray together in "private circles" within their homes. Not until the Great Awakening, a period of intense religious fervor that swept through England's American colonies during the first half of the eighteenth century, was women's spirituality publicly acknowledged and their religious experience made the model of conversion for both men and women.

Sarah Pierrepont, the daughter of New Haven, Connecticut, minister James Pierrepont, embodied the spiritual qualities of the soul "awakened" to Christ. In a tribute written by her future husband, the Reverend Jonathan Edwards, the 13-year-old girl was described as having "a wonderful sweetness, calmness and universal benevolence of mind." Edwards observed that "She will sometimes go about from place to place, singing sweetly; and seems to be always full of joy and pleasure; and no one knows for what. She loves to be alone, walking in the fields, and groves, and seems to have some one invisible always conversing with her." Sarah's faith in her salvation was intense. She was certain she would "be raised up out of the world and caught up into heaven." There she would dwell with [god], and "be ravished with his love and delight forever."

Sarah Pierrepont was Edwards's paradigm of faith and belief. He later described her religious affections as being so great that her "soul dwelt on high, and was lost in God, and seemed almost to leave the body." Although he aspired to emulate her, he never knew God with the same intensity as she. Nor did he ever experience the "exceeding sweet delight," her certainty of salvation, that was the joy of her life. Yet she was his ideal of God's chosen, a true "Saint." Hers was the example of spiritual "awakening" he used again and again in the sermons he preached throughout New England. Thus, Sarah became the model of Christian faith for countless women and men in eighteenth-century America.[75]

* * *

Religion played a major role in the lives of the women and men who migrated to England's North American colonies in the seventeenth century. It was also important to the Native American women they encountered here and the African women they enslaved. English theologians influenced colonial beliefs about women's nature and their proper roles in society. These beliefs justified women's subordinate status in the family, the church, and the state and were crucial to the patriarchal, authoritarian family the colonists hoped to transplant in America. They also influenced the way English women and men responded to Native Americans and shaped the evolution of African slavery in the American colonies.

While most colonial English women found security and comfort in preserving the beliefs and practices of their religion as they struggled to survive on the seventeenth-century American frontier, others drew on their faith for the strength to challenge women's subordinate role in the family, the church, and the state. Religion supplied colonists with the language in which to express their anxieties about their enemies and their future in the New World, as well as about women's roles. When women became the majority in most New England congregations by the eighteenth century, they challenged the spiritual and secular authority of men. This tension between the sexes climaxed in the witchcraft hysteria at Salem, Massachusetts. Women accused of witchcraft were blamed for the social, economic, and political disorder that plagued the region; they became scapegoats for people reluctant to embrace change. By the early eighteenth century, a new model of womanhood had to be constructed by theologians to encompass women's experience in the colonies. Striving to embody these new ideals, English women found purpose and meaning in their lives.

AFTERWORD

There was a wind over England, and it blew.
(Have you heard the news of Virginia?)
A west wind blowing, the wind of a western star,
To gather men's lives like pollen and cast them forth,
Blowing in hedge and highway and seaport town,
Whirling dead leaf and living, but always blowing,
A salt wind, a sea wind, a wind from the world's end,
From the coasts that have new, wild names, from the huge unknown.
——Stephen Vincent Benét, *Western Star*

The wind of change that blew over England carrying word of the newfound land, Virginia, touched women's lives, too. It caressed the faces of the English huswife in her kitchen garden and the servant girl in London-town. It carried them across the wide oceans from England to the American frontier, where they confronted hardships and challenges they could not even imagine. Struggling to survive in this strange new land, they took refuge in memories of the homes and families they had left behind. They lived, toiled, and died not for themselves but for their children, leaving a legacy of faith and hope for a better tomorrow.

The wind of change blew along the coast of West Africa. Through the slave-trading forts that faced the crashing sea and up the rivers that fed the rich, rice fields where dark skinned women sang as they planted their crops, their skirts

196

raised high above the water. Neither could these women imagine the changes that the west wind brought, or the pain and misery that they, and their children, would face in the harsh New World across the sea. But they, too, would seek comfort in their memories of Africa, in re-creating the world they lost when they were stolen from their homes and families. Their survival and endurance was their greatest legacy.

The wind of change whispered through the long houses of North America and ruffled the leaves of the corn plants ripening in the golden summer sun. It cooled the brows of the Native American women tending the "three sisters" that fed their people. As they joyfully prepared for their harvest festival, how could they know this gentle breeze was a portent of things to come? That it would bring shiploads of men and women across the sea and a legacy of disease, death, and destruction? They, too, faced a future they could not imagine. They, too, would remember their lives as they once were before the winds of change began to blow. They, too, would fight to survive and preserve their heritage in this "new" land that had long been their home.

These women of early America—English, African, Native American—all confronted the wind of change that swept through their lives and altered them forever. How they accommodated the rigors of settlement, the inhumanity of enslavement, and the conquest of their continent are testimony to the strength they derived from their roles as women in their respective cultures. Their courage in the face of the New World's challenges is remarkable.

Did these women see the North American frontier as a "paradise," or view this era as a "golden age," as later historians surmised? It is doubtful that they or their daughters and granddaughters would have painted their lives in such rosy hues. Certainly Native American and African women would scorn the notion that seventeenth-century America was a paradise for them or their people. And while some English women did enjoy greater "freedoms" in the New World than in the Old, most would likely have traded those rights, and their attendant responsibilities, for the security of a loving household and the survival of their children. If these women did not embrace the adventure of the frontier or expand opportunities for themselves and their daughters, but instead perpetuated the conventions of their day, who are we to judge them? We must view their lives not by our standards but by theirs. Only in this way may we even begin to understand how they survived and endured in the New World of seventeenth-century America.[1]

NOTES

Preface

1. The "golden age" theory was first asserted by Elisabeth Anthony Dexter in *Colonial Women of Affairs: A Study of Women in Business and the Professions in America before 1776* (New York: Houghton Mifflin, 1924), vii. Richard B. Morris, *Studies in the History of American Law, with Special References to the Seventeenth and Eighteenth Centuries* (New York: Columbia University Press, 1930), 126–200, helped foster this interpretation. See Mary Beth Norton, "The Evolution of White Women's Experience in Early America," *American Historical Review* 89 (June 1984): 593–619.

Chapter 1

1. Stephen Vincent Benét, *Western Star* (New York: Farrar & Rinehart, 1943), 17.

2. In England, the man was considered the head of his family, and its members' lineage was determined through him, a custom that had evolved during the later Middle Ages when surnames, passed from father to son, were adopted. While a daughter also inherited her father's surname at birth, she adopted her husband's name at marriage and became a member of his family. The surname women were known by symbolized their dependence on men. Ralph A. Houlbrooke, *The English Family: 1450–1700* (New York: Longman, 1984), 20.

3. Susan Dwyer Amussen, *An Ordered Society: Gender and Class in Early Modern England* (Oxford: Basil Blackwell, 1988), 22–25, 33, 36–37.

4. Genesis 3:16.

5. Katherine Usher Henderson and Barbara F. MacManus, *Half Human*

Kind: Contexts and Texts of the Controversy about Women in England, 1540–1640 (Urbana: University of Illinois Press), 78.

6. Antonia Fraser, *The Weaker Vessel* (New York: Alfred A. Knopf, 1984), 3.

7. Ibid., 1.

8. Lyle Koehler, *A Search for Power: The "Weaker Sex" in Seventeenth-Century New England* (Urbana: University of Illinois Press, 1980), 29.

9. Sarah Evans, *Born for Liberty: A History of Women in America* (New York: Macmillan), 22.

10. Fraser, *The Weaker Vessel*, 62, 72; I Timothy 2:14–15.

11. Fraser, *The Weaker Vessel*, 62.

12. In 1600, female illiteracy in East Anglia was nearly 100 percent, while in London, where girls had greater access to education, 90 percent of all women were probably illiterate. By 1640 London women's literacy increased slightly, and nearly 20 percent were able to read and write. Outside the urban center, however, the gap between the education of girls and boys continued to grow. Fraser, *The Weaker Vessel*, 129, 137–39.

13. As quoted in Christopher Durston, *The Family in the English Revolution* (New York: Basil Blackwell, 1989), 27.

14. As quoted in Fraser, *The Weaker Vessel*, 122.

15. Hannah Woolley, *The Gentlewoman's Companion; or A Guide to the Female Sex* (1675), as quoted in Angeline Goreau, *The Whole Duty of a Woman: Female Writers in Seventeenth-Century England* (Garden City, N.Y.: Doubleday & Co., 1985), 8.

16. It is doubtful if the writings of Astell or feminist Hannah Woolley, author of *The Gentlewoman's Companion* (1675), influenced more than a few men and women of their time. See Goreau, *The Whole Duty of a Woman*, 1–18, on the controversy over women's intellect during the seventeenth century. Hilda L. Smith, *Reason's Disciples: Seventeenth-Century English Feminists* (Urbana: University of Illinois Press, 1982), discusses the activities of English feminist writers in this period, while Sara Heller Mendelson, *The Mental World of Stuart Women: Three Studies* (Amherst: University of Massachusetts Press, 1987), looks at the lives of Margaret Cavendish, Mary Rich, and Aphra Behn.

17. Fraser, *The Weaker Vessel*, 29.

18. As quoted in Arthur Calhoun, *The Social History of the American Family* (New York: Arthur H. Clark, 1917–19), 1:33.

19. As quoted in Edmund S. Morgan, *The Puritan Family: Religion and Domestic Relations in Seventeenth-Century New England* (New York: Harper & Row, 1966), 29.

20. John R. Gillis, *For Better, for Worse: British Marriages, 1600 to the Present* (New York: Oxford University Press, 1985), 14.

21. Charles Gerbier, *Elogium Heroinum* (London, 1651), 4, as cited in Durston, *The Family in the English Revolution*, 14.

22. As quoted in Calhoun, *The American Family*, 1:42.

23. Sheila Rowbotham, *Hidden from History: Rediscovering Women in History from the Seventeenth Century to the Present* (New York: Vintage Books, 1973), 9–10, and Houlbrooke, *The English Family*, 114.

24. Margaret George, *Women in the First Capitalist Society: Experiences in Seventeenth-Century England* (Urbana: University of Illinois Press, 1988), 2–5.

25. Durston, *The Family in the English Revolution*, 57–62, and Merry E. Weisner, "Women's Work in the Changing City Economy, 1500–1650," in *Connecting Spheres: Women in the Western World, 1500 to the Present*, ed. Marilyn Boxer and Jean H. Quataert (New York: Oxford University Press, 1987), 70.

26. Daughters of the nobility married, on average, at age 20 in the sixteenth century and at age 23 in the eighteenth century. The age that male heirs of squires married rose from 21 in the sixteenth century to 28 by the eighteenth century, while their younger sons often did not marry until they were in their 30s. Houlbrooke, *The English Family*, 29.

27. Houlbrooke, *The English Family*, 102.

28. It was believed that if a man married a woman of higher rank than himself, she would come to dominate him; if a man married a woman of much lower rank, he would be embarrassed by her. While it was more acceptable for a man of high rank to marry a young woman from the merchant class, it was unusual for a young man of the merchant class to marry into the gentry or the nobility. Because the woman assumed the status of her husband, a woman who married a man of inferior social rank lowered herself to his status. Houlbrooke, *The English Family*, 75.

29. Houlbrooke, *The English Family*, 67, Gillis, *For Better, for Worse*, 15, 21–22, and Durston, *The Family in the English Revolution*, 58.

30. As quoted in Julia Cherry Spruill, *Women's Life and Work in the Southern Colonies* (Chapel Hill: University of North Carolina Press, 1938; reprint, New York: W. W. Norton & Co., 1972), 145.

31. Houlbrooke, *The English Family*, 72, 78, Fraser, *The Weaker Vessel*, 38–39, and Durston, *The Family in the English Revolution*, 57. Gillis, *For Better, for Worse*, 21, contends that because of high mortality rates, between two-fifths and two-thirds of all brides marrying in their mid-20s had already lost their fathers.

32. While in the sixteenth century only about 5 percent of the daughters of the landed gentry never married; by the eighteenth century, 25 percent never married. The percentage of women in the nobility who never married also rose. See Clayton Roberts and David Roberts, *A History of England: Prehistory to 1714* (New Jersey: Prentice Hall, 1985), 1:418.

33. During the Commonwealth period, some religious radicals challenged

the belief that sex was sinful and argued that sexual desire, created by God, was good; when expressed toward one's mate, it cemented the marriage bond. A few religious radicals went even further. They challenged the idea that sexuality need be contained within marriage and advocated promiscuity as a glorification of God. Most, however, condemned these radicals for their extremist ideas. The most notable of these religious radical groups were known as the Ranters. Durston, *The Family in the English Revolution*, 20–21.

34. Prenuptial pregnancies are defined as pregnancies that resulted in the birth of a child eight and a half months or less after the wedding. Prenuptial pregnancies declined from 255 per 1,000 in 1550–99 to 228 in 1600–1649 and, finally, to 162 in 1650–99. The numbers increased once more, and during the eighteenth century nearly 40 percent of all first pregnancies were prenuptial. Houlbrooke, *The English Family*, 81–83. See also Roberts and Roberts, *A History of England*, 1:418.

35. A couple could obtain a special license permitting them to marry without this procedure, but this required their parents' consent. Durston, *The Family in the English Revolution*, 66–67.

36. Couples intending to marry during the Commonwealth period were required to submit their names at least 20 days prior to the ceremony to the registrar of their parish, who posted their announcement at their church or the nearest market. The registrar then issued the couple a certificate to be presented to a justice of the peace licensed to conduct the civil ceremony. Because of confusion after the passage of legislation establishing the civil ceremony in 1653, many couples were married in both civil and religious ceremonies to ensure the legality of their union. While one of Lord Protector Oliver Cromwell's daughters was married by a justice of the peace, another was married in a church ceremony. Durston, *The Family in the English Revolution*, 77–86.

37. Mistress Jane Sharp, author of a popular midwife's manual, wrote that a woman's arousal helped produce the "seed" necessary for conception. John D'Emilio and Estelle B. Freedman, *Intimate Matters: A History of Sexuality in America* (New York: Harper & Row, 1988), 5, and Fraser, *The Weaker Vessel*, 51. This theory fell into disfavor by the early eighteenth century, according to Audrey Eccles, *Obstetrics and Gynaecology in Tudor and Stuart England* (Kent, Ohio: Kent State University Press, 1982), 33–42.

38. Houlbrooke, *The English Family*, 22, and Durston, *The Family in the English Revolution*, 18–19, 98–100.

39. Keith Thomas, "The Double Standard," *Journal of the History of Ideas* 22 (April 1959): 210.

40. If a wife was found guilty of adultery, she forfeited her dower rights in her husband's property; an adulterous husband was not penalized in this way. Henderson and MacManus, *Half Human Kind*, 59, and Rowbotham, *Hidden From History*, 4.

41. Many authorities argued that a husband's physical chastisement of his wife was justified only to "correct her faults." William Whatley argued that a wife should not be physically punished by her husband except when "she give just cause, after much bearing and forebearing, and trying all other ways, in case of utmost necessity, so that he exceed hot measure." As quoted in Amussen, *An Ordered Society*, 42.

42. Houlbrooke, *The English Family*, 118–19. On separations, see also, Amussen, *An Ordered Society*, 57.

43. Data about women's death in childbirth in seventeenth-century England is incomplete because parish records rarely included the cause of death. It has been estimated that deaths in childbirth had a range of 125 to 158 per 1,000 during the first half of the century and of 118 to 147 per 1,000 in the second half of the century. Fraser, *The Weaker Vessel*, 76.

44. Fraser, *The Weaker Vessel*, 76–77. Also, Paula A. Treckel, "Breastfeeding and Maternal Sexuality in Colonial America," *Journal of Interdisciplinary History* 20 (Summer 1989): 25–51, and Dorothy MacLaren, "Marital Fertility and Lactation, 1570–1720," in *Women in English Society: 1500–1800*, ed. Mary Prior (New York: Methuen, 1985), 22–53. On infant mortality, see E. A. Wrigley, "Family Limitation in Pre-Industrial England," *Economic History Review*, 2d ser., 19 (April 1966): 82–109. On infant feeding customs in seventeenth century England, see Dorothy MacLaren, "Fertility, Infant Mortality, and Breastfeeding in the Seventeenth Century," *Medical History* 22 (October 1978): 378–96, and Valerie Fildes, *Breasts, Bottles, and Babies: A History of Infant Feeding* (Edinburgh: Edinburgh University Press, 1986).

45. It has been estimated that among the gentry the average number of children born to a wife was four, while studies of specific English villages have found between two and three children per family. See Lawrence Stone, *The Family, Sex, and Marriage in England, 1500–1800*, abridged ed. (New York: Harper & Row, 1979), 52–53. See also E. A. Wrigley and R. S. Scholfied, *The Population History of England, 1541–1871: A Reconstruction* (Cambridge, Mass.: Harvard University Press, 1981), 254–56, 265–69. Philip J. Greven, *Four Generations: Population, Land, and Family in Colonial Andover, Massachusetts* (Ithaca, N.Y.: Cornell University Press, 1970), 24–31, discusses average family size in England and New England in the seventeenth century, as does Richard Archer, "New England Mosaic: A Demographic Analysis for the Seventeenth Century," *William and Mary Quarterly*, 3d ser., 48 (October 1990): 486. See also Durston, *The Family in the English Revolution*, 114–15, Fraser, *The Weaker Vessel*, 68, and E. A. Wrigley, "Family Limitation in Pre-Industrial England," 105.

46. Stone, *The Family, Sex and Marriage*, 149–80.

47. As quoted in Amussen, *An Ordered Society*, 43–44.

48. Sir Anthony Fitzherbert, *Book of Husbandrye* (1555), quoted in Alice

Clarke, *Working Life of Women in the Seventeenth Century* (London: Frank Cass and Co., 1919; reprint, New York: A. M. Kelley, 1968), 49. Also, Fraser, *The Weaker Vessel*, 45.

49. Thomas Tusser, "Five Hundred Points of Good Husbandry," in *The Somers Collection of Tracts*, ed. Walter Scott (New York: AMS Press, 1965), 3:613.

50. Amussen, *An Ordered Society*, 68–70. See also Laurel Thatcher Ulrich, *Good Wives: Image and Reality in the Lives of Women in Northern New England, 1650–1750* (New York: Alfred A. Knopf, 1982), 35–50, for women's activities as deputy husbands in colonial New England. Fraser, *The Weaker Vessel*, 163–204, discusses the role played by women in maintaining and militarily defending their husbands' estates during the Civil War period, as do Durston, *The Family in the English Revolution*, 88–95, and George, *Women in the First Capitalist Society*, 37–136.

51. Clark, *Working Life of Women*, 51.

52. Weisner, "Women's Work in the Changing Economy," in *Connecting Spheres*, 65–66. See also Mary Prior, "Women and the Urban Economy: Oxford, 1500–1800," in *Women in English Society, 1500–1800*, 93–117.

53. Prior, "Women and the Urban Economy," 105–10.

54. During the seventeenth century, however, male brewers prevented women from engaging in this profitable occupation and their numbers were dramatically reduced by the end of the century. Clark, *Working Life of Women*, 147, 221–33.

55. Fraser, *The Weaker Vessel*, 440–463. Clark, *Working Life of Women*, 243–65. On the connection between midwifery and witchcraft in England, see Barbara Ehrenreich and Dierdre English, *Witches, Midwives, and Nurses: A History of Women Healers* (Old Westbury, N.Y.: Feminist Press, 1973), 6–20.

56. Over the course of the century, the Church of England attempted to license midwives and regulate their practice. Upper-class women, or their husbands, chose male doctors to attend the births of their children, and by the eighteenth century male physicians stepped up their effort to drive women out of this profession. Men's scientific knowledge of the birth process increased during the century, and "man-midwives" prevented women from using newly developed obstetric tools. As a result, midwifery was increasingly identified with the lower, uneducated classes. Clark, *Working Life of Women*, 265–85.

57. Prior, "Women and the Urban Economy," 110.

58. There was a decline in life expectancy over the course of the century that is attributed to warfare and the epidemics fostered by urban overcrowding. At the beginning of the century average life expectancy was around 38.1 years, but by 1661 it had fallen to 35.7 years. During the first quarter of the eighteenth century it was 32.5 years. Fraser, *The Weaker Vessel*, 84, and Peter Laslett, *The*

World We Have Lost (New York: Methuen, 1965), 108, table 10. See also Archer, "New England Mosaic," 494.

59. As quoted in Fraser, *The Weaker Vessel*, 5.

60. Susan Staves, *Married Women's Separate Property in England, 1660–1833* (Cambridge: Harvard University Press, 1990), 4.

61. It is estimated that 5 percent of the upper class married three or four times. Fraser, *The Weaker Vessel*, 84.

62. If a woman died before her husband without having producing an heir, he was not entitled to dower lands. Instead, they passed into the hands of her nearest relative by birth. An heiress had greater control over the property she brought to a union and could will her estate as she desired unless it was entailed. Many husbands of heiresses tried to convince their wives to give up their property rights, but some resisted their husbands' efforts and retained control over their property until they died. Houlbrooke, *The English Family*, 83, 100. See also Roger Thompson, *Women in Stuart England and America: A Comparative Study* (Boston: Routledge & Keagan Paul, 1974), 165.

63. Houlbrooke, *The English Family*, 23, Fraser, *The Weaker Vessel*, 11, and Staves, *Married Women's Separate Property*, 31. On p. 42 Staves discusses how men used English law to avoid dower and achieve greater control over the entirety of their estates. Such evasions of the law prompted the development of jointures, trusts, uses, and equity law to safeguard women's property.

64. Ironically, although sons were favored over daughters among all classes in seventeenth-century England, daughters who did not inherit their fathers' estates were sometimes better endowed than their noninheriting brothers. While many fathers distinguished between daughters in the size of their inheritance, equitable endowment among daughters was more common than among younger sons. This was so that all daughters might have an equal opportunity to marry, a woman's prospects for marriage being directly related to the size of her dowry.

Chapter 2

1. The growth of England's population began around 1470, when it numbered about 2 million people. The population numbered 3 million by 1550 and was about 4 million by 1600. It climbed to 5.25 million by the middle of the seventeenth century, when it began to drop gradually. For the rest of the century it remained around 5 million. During the first half of the seventeenth century fertility continued to decline while mortality rose and remained high until the late 1680s. At the end of the seventeenth century, fertility increased. In 1600, 5 percent of the English population lived in London, while in 1700, 10 percent lived there. These changes were influenced by economic trends,

the value of wages, and the age at marriage, and they led to changes in attitudes about the nature of the family. Houlbrooke, *The English Family*, 27.

2. Houlbrooke, *The English Family*, 235, 243.

3. Karen Ordahl Kupperman, *Roanoke: The Abandoned Colony* (Totowa, N.J.: Rowman & Allanheld, 1984), 108–9.

4. White and Raleigh found it difficult to secure a ship to take the necessary supplies to the colony. Shipowners were more interested in the financial rewards of raiding and plundering Spain's Caribbean colonies, especially after the outbreak of England's war with Spain. It is believed that the colonists, who also had contact with the Weapemoc, Moratuck, Choanoke, Secotan, and Neusiok tribes, sought refuge the with the Croatoan tribe when their supplies were depleted. They were probably killed by Powhatan Natives shortly before the English settled at Jamestown in 1607. Kupperman, *Roanoke*, 138–42, discusses the region's tribes. Also see Kupperman, 138–42, for speculation about what happened to these colonists after they disappeared from Roanoke Island.

5. The immediate rewards from privateering raids on Spanish colonies and treasure ships not only risked the fate of the Roanoke settlers but led many investors to scorn Raleigh's attempt to establish a permanent English settlement in the New World. Kupperman, *Roanoke*, 164–74.

6. As quoted in Spruill, *Women's Life and Work in the Southern Colonies*, 3.

7. "General Historie of Virginia by Captain John Smith, 1625," in *Narratives of Early Virginia, 1606–1625*, ed. Lyon Gardiner Tyler (New York: Charles Scribner's Sons, 1907), 295.

8. As quoted in Philip Barbour, *Pocahontas and Her World* (Boston: Houghton Mifflin, 1970), 65.

9. *The Genesis of the United States, 1605–1616*, vol. 1, ed. Alexander Brown (London: William Heineman, 1890), 300. See also sonnet 6 in *The Complete Works of William Shakespeare*, ed. William G. Clark (New York: 1911), 1285.

10. For more on the issue of women's "scarcity value," see Becky Durning, "Where Scarcity Exists, Does Value Follow?" *Canadian Newsletter of Research on Women* 6 (October 1977): 9–11, who states, "If [scarcity value] merely means . . . that men who sought wives had to look harder for them, it is a concept which is irrelevant to understanding women's past."

11. "Kidnapping Maidens to be Sold in Virginia, 1618," *Virginia Magazine of History and Biography* 6 (January 1899): 299. Walter H. Blumenthal, *Brides from Bridewell: Female Felons Sent to Colonial America* (Rutland, Vt.: C. E. Tuttle Co., 1962), 66, and Abbot E. Smith, *Colonists in Bondage: White Servitude and Convict Labor in America, 1607–1776* (Chapel Hill: University of North Carolina Press, 1947), 67–89, discuss the recruitment of women for service in the colony of Virginia, while Gloria Turner Main, *Tobacco Colony: Life in Early Maryland, 1650–1750* (Princeton: Princeton University Press, 1982), 103–4, discusses female indentured servitude in the colony of Maryland.

12. *The Records of the Virginia Company of London*, ed. Susan M. Kingsbury (Washington, D.C.: 1906), 1:269.

13. David R. Ransome, "Wives for Virginia, 1621," *William and Mary Quarterly*, 3d ser., 48 (January 1991): 3–18. The majority of young women shipped to Virginia as Tobacco Brides were married soon after their arrival. Because they adopted their husbands' names, they disappeared from the records of the colony. Single women, too, were referred to as "maids" rather than by their names in the colony's records. As a result, it is not possible to determine with certainty the actual identity of all the Tobacco Brides.

14. *Records*, 1:352, 3:505. Also, Mrs. Henry Lowell Cook, "Maids for Wives," *Virginia Magazine of History and Biography*, 1 (October 1942): 309.

15. Edward Waterhouse, *A Declaration of the State of the Colony of Virginia* (London, 1622), 36–43, and Ransome, "Wives for Virginia, 1621," 18. See also Ivor Noel Hume, *Martin's Hundred: The Discovery of a Lost Colonial Virginia Settlement* (New York: Dell Publishing Co., 1983), 284–95, who discusses the excavation of one woman's grave at Wolstenholme Town and theorizes about the origins of the women residing at this site before the Indian attack on the colony.

16. *Records*, 4:238.

17. Ibid., 4:473, and Mary Newton Stanard, *The Story of Virginia's First Century* (Philadelphia: J. B. Lippincott Co., 1928), 116. For more on women as captives see James Axtell, "The White Indians of Colonial America," *William and Mary Quarterly*, 3d ser., 32 (January 1975): 55–88. Ulrich, *Good Wives*, 204, disagrees with Axtell's assertion that more women than men were captured in New England's wars with Native Americans.

18. Spruill, *Women's Life and Work in the Southern Colonies*, 150–51. See also Stanard, *The Story of Virginia's First Century*, 180–81, for a different version of this incident. *Records*, 4:487, cites the law passed on breach of promise in colonial Virginia.

19. Spruill, *Women's Life and Work in the Southern Colonies*, 11. While the number of women immigrants to the Chesapeake gradually increased during the seventeenth century, it was not until the first decade of the eighteenth century that the population of Maryland was able to reproduce itself. During the heaviest period of immigration to Maryland, from 1640 until 1670, there were two and a half to three times more male immigrants to the colony than female immigrants. Even as late as 1704, men outnumbered women in the colony by a ratio of three to two. Women's scarcity affected their social and economic roles during most of the century. Sex ratio data during the first century in the Chesapeake may be found in Russell R. Menard, "Immigrants and Their Increase: The Process of Population Growth in Early Colonial Maryland," in *Law, Society and Politics in Early Maryland*, ed. Aubrey C. Land, Lois

Green Carr, and Edward C. Papenfuse (Baltimore: Johns Hopkins University Press, 1977), 95, 99.

20. Lois Green Carr and Lorena S. Walsh, "The Planter's Wife: The Experience of White Women in Seventeenth-Century Maryland," *William and Mary Quarterly*, 3d ser., 34 (October 1977): 545.

21. Lorena S. Walsh, " 'Till Death Us Do Part': Marriage and Family in Seventeenth Century Maryland," *The Chesapeake in the Seventeenth Century: Essays on Anglo-American Society and Politics*, ed. Thad W. Tate and David L. Ammerman (New York: W. W. Norton, 1979), 127.

22. Carr and Walsh, "The Planter's Wife," 546. See also Main, *Tobacco Colony*, 108.

23. *Historical Collections of South Carolina Embracing Many Rare and Valuable Pamphlets and Other Documents Relating to the History of that State from its first Discovery to its Independence in the Year 1776*, ed. B. R. Caroll (New York, 1836), 2:17.

24. John Hammond, *Leah and Rachel, or the Two Fruitful Sisters, Virginia, and Maryland* (London: T. Mabb, 1656), in *Tracts and Other Papers, Relating Principally to the Origin, Settlement, and Progress of the Colonies in North America from Discovery of the Country to the Year 1776*, ed. Peter Force (Washington D.C.: William Q. Force, 1844), 3:15, 12.

25. Carr and Walsh, "The Planter's Wife," 547, and Ebenezer Cook, *The Sot-Weed Factor: Or, a Voyage to Maryland. A Satyr* (London, 1708), 6–7, as quoted in Main, *Tobacco Colony*, 178. It was unusual for a wealthy planter to hire a woman servant; only about 5 percent of all indentured women were employed by wealthy planters, who preferred instead to invest their money in slave labor. As a result, the majority of indentured women found employment in the homes of "middling planters," where there were other servants. It is likely that the women employed by these planters spent most of their time at domestic labor and were not regularly put to work in the fields. See, Main, *Tobacco Colony*, 108–9.

26. As quoted in Alice Morse Earle, *Colonial Dames and Good Wives* (Boston: Houghton Mifflin, 1895; reprint, New York: Frederick Ungar Publishing Co., 1962), 14.

27. For examples of the brutal treatment of indentured servants, see Raphael Semmes, *Crime and Punishment in Early Maryland* (Baltimore: Johns Hopkins Press, 1938), 97–98, 108–9, 138–39.

28. Semmes, *Crime and Punishment in Early Maryland*, 240–41.

29. At least 20 percent of all female servants in Somerset County, Maryland, were brought before the court for pregnancy between 1658 and 1705. In this county, 10 percent of all births were illegitimate, the mothers nearly all indentured servants. Carr and Walsh, "The Planter's Wife," 548–49.

30. Semmes, *Crime and Punishment in Early Maryland*, 128–30.

31. Carr and Walsh, "The Planter's Wife," 552.

32. Carr and Walsh, "The Planter's Wife," 561–63. In Maryland, for example, after 1684 only 25 percent of all free white women lived in households with servants or slaves. Main, *Tobacco Colony*, 109–10, 264.

33. These figures do not take into account possible miscarriages and still-births. See Walsh, " 'Till Death Us Do Part,' " 127. Women who migrated with their husbands to the Chesapeake also married in their mid-20s, reflecting the English custom of late marriage at that time. On the rising age at marriage in England, see Wrigley, "Family Limitation in Pre-Industrial England," 86. Seventeen percent of Maryland's 22-year-old male immigrants died before they were 30, 41 percent died before they were 40, and 70 percent died before they reached the age of 50. It has been estimated that men who reached the age of 20 might expect to live around 29 more years, while women could expect to live only another 20 years. Lorena S. Walsh and Russell R. Menard, "Death in the Chesapeake: Two Life Tables for Men in Early Colonial Maryland," *Maryland Historical Magazine* 69 (Summer 1974): 214–17, 219–22; Darrett B. and Anita H. Rutman, " 'Now-Wives and Sons-in-Law': Parental Death in a Seventeenth-Century Virginia County," in *The Chesapeake in the Seventeenth Century*, 157–61; Menard, "Immigrants and Their Increase," 95–97.

34. Carr and Walsh, "The Planter's Wife," 553.

35. This is a hypothetical model, based on statistical averages drawn from recorded marriage, birth, and death records in seventeenth-century Virginia. See Rutman and Rutman, " 'Now-Wives and Sons-in-Law,' " in *The Chesapeake in the Seventeenth Century*, 158–60. Allan J. Kulikoff, *Tobacco and Slaves: The Development of Southern Cultures in the Chesapeake, 1680–1800* (Chapel Hill: University of North Carolina Press, 1986), 45–63, calculates an earlier age at first marriage for native-born women in the Chesapeake than do Rutman and Rutman. He asserts that they married in their late teens but that their average age at first marriage rose to 20 as lands diminished in the tidewater region. He states that early marriage persisted on the piedmont frontier well into the eighteenth century because of the availability of lands there. On remarriage and the sex ratio, see Menard, "Immigrants and their Increase," 95.

36. Walsh, " 'Till Death Us Do Part,' " 128.

37. Neil Larry Shumsky, "Parents, Children, and the Selection of Mates in Colonial Virginia," *Eighteenth Century Life* 2 (1976): 83–88; Walsh, " 'Till Death Us Do Part,' " 133–35; and Daniel Blake Smith, *Inside the Great House: Planter Family Life in Eighteenth-Century Chesapeake Society* (Ithaca: Cornell University Press, 1980), 79–81, 127–28. See also Daniel Blake Smith, "Mortality and Family in the Colonial Chesapeake," *Journal of Interdisciplinary History* 8 (Winter 1978): 403–27, and Rutman and Rutman, " 'Now-Wives and Sons-in-Law,' " 164–68.

38. Remarriage was common for widows in the Chesapeake because of

the high mortality of the colony's men. The mortality of the region's women, however, also meant that 20 percent of all children were orphaned by the time they were 13 and more than 30 percent were orphaned by the time they were 18. For more on the high rate of orphanage in the seventeenth-century Chesapeake, see Rutman and Rutman, " 'Now-Wives and Sons-in-Law,' " 159–62. On the Hanson family, see Semmes, *Crime and Punishment in Early Maryland*, 88–89.

39. As quoted in Spruill, *Women's Life and Work in the Southern Colonies*, 14. For more on disease and the colonization of Carolina, see Peter A. Coclanis, *The Shadow of a Dream: Economic Life and Death in the South Carolina Low Country, 1670–1920* (New York: Oxford University Press, 1989), 41–47. Also, St. Julien Ravenel Childs, *Malaria and Colonization in the Carolina Low Country, 1526–1696*, Johns Hopkins University Studies in Historical and Political Science, ser. 58, no. 1. (Baltimore: Johns Hopkins University Press, 1949).

40. As quoted in Peter Wood, *Black Majority: Negroes in Colonial South Carolina from 1670 through the Stono Rebellion* (New York: W. W. Norton, 1974), 54 n. 75.

41. Spruill, *Women's Life and Work in the Southern Colonies*, 14.

42. Those who voyaged to the Chesapeake were able to command higher wages and shorter terms of service from their masters. Established planters in that region, too, began to turn to an alternate source of labor—African slaves. See Russell Menard, "From Servants to Slaves: The Transformation of the Chesapeake Labor System," *Southern Studies* 16 (Winter 1977): 355–90, for a discussion of the process by which indentured servitude was replaced by plantation slavery.

43. Menard, "Immigrants and their Increase," 99.

44. See Kulikoff, *Tobacco and Slaves*, 23–44, for the best discussion of the factors that transformed the economy and society of the Chesapeake during the seventeenth century.

45. Kulikoff, *Tobacco and Slaves*, 165–204, asserts that during the earliest years of settlement in the Chesapeake, "domestic patriarchialism" was an ideal, virtually impossible to implement because of the economic and demographic problems that plagued this region. See Lois Green Carr and Lorena S. Walsh, "Economic Diversification and Labor Organization in the Chesapeake, 1650–1820," *Work and Labor in Early America*, ed. Stephen Innes (Chapel Hill: University of North Carolina Press, 1988), 145, on the process of economic development and its impact on women's work. English women's acquiescence to male authority might have been superficial, masking their underlying, informal power within colonial society, especially during the seventeenth century. See Susan Carol Rogers, "Female Forms of Power and the Myth of Male Dominance: Model of Female/Male Interaction in Peasant Society," *American Ethnologist* 2 (November 1975): 727–56.

46. William Bradford, *Of Plymouth Plantation, 1620–1647*, ed. Samuel Eliot Morison (New York: Alfred A. Knopf, 1970), 25. Bradford remarked: "many of their children, by . . . the great licentiousness of youth in that country, and the manifold temptations of the place, were drawn away by evil examples into extravagant and dangerous courses, getting the reins off their necks and departing from their parents . . . so that they saw their posterity would be in danger to degenerate and be corrupted."

47. Bradford, *Of Plymouth Plantation*, xxiv.

48. Ibid., 120–21.

49. John Demos, *A Little Commonwealth: Family Life in Plymouth Colony* (New York: Oxford University Press, 1970), 192, table 2, and 193, table 4.

50. Ibid., 192, table 1. See also Menard, "Immigrants and Their Increase," 102–4. Family size in Andover was also large. The first generation of Andover women gave birth to an average of 8.3 children, with 7.2 surviving to adulthood. While the average age at marriage for women of the first generation was only 19, the next generation of women married at the average age of 22.3 years, with 75 percent having married before they reached the age of 25, a pattern similar to that found in Plymouth. These women gave birth to an average of 8.1 children, 6.6 surviving to adulthood. The third generation of Andover women married, on average, at the age of 24.5 years. Despite the risks of childbirth and motherhood, most were strong and lived long lives. As a result of their later age at marriage, these women gave birth to fewer children than their mothers or grandmothers. They bore, on average, 7.2 children, 5.1 of whom lived to adulthood. Data on Andover can be found in Philip J. Greven, Jr., *Four Generations: Population, Land, and Family in Colonial Andover, Massachusetts* (Ithaca: Cornell University Press, 1970), 26–28, 28 n. 6. Also, Richard Archer, "New England Mosaic: A Demographic Analysis for the Seventeenth Century," *William and Mary Quarterly*, 3d ser., 48 (October 1990): 491, 494, asserts that more native-born New England women married before the age of 20 than has been theorized. Their early marriage was not the result of parental death, as in the Chesapeake, but because of demand for them as wives by the single men in the colonies.

51. Although some infants were born within eight or nine months of marriage, the average interval between a couple's marriage and the birth of their first child was 15 months. See Greven, *Four Generations*, 113. His findings contrast with those of John Demos, who in his study of Bristol, Rhode Island, discovered that between 1680 and 1712 no couples had their first child within eight months of their marriage. From 1720 to 1740, however, 10 percent of them did, and between 1740 and 1760, 49 percent had their first child within eight months of marriage. John Demos, "Families in Colonial Bristol, Rhode Island: An Exercise in Historical Demography," *William and Mary Quarterly*, 3d. ser., 25 (January 1968): 40–57. Archer, "New England Mosaic," 491,

discovered that women who married at 17 or older gave birth to their first child within two years. If they were younger than 17, their first child was usually born two and a half years after their marriage.

52. Between 3 and 10 percent of New England women who married between 1630 and 1670 died in childbirth or of birth-related problems. It was unusual for a woman to die following the birth of her first child; most women who died as a result of childbirth did so after bearing between four and six children. For data on death in childbirth, see Archer, "New England Mosaic," 494–95.

53. Greven *Four Generations*, 30, 33, 35–37, 75, 109–11, 120, 193–96, 200–201.

54. As quoted in Earle, *Colonial Dames and Good Wives*, 17.

55. As quoted in David Cressy, "The Vast and Furious Ocean: The Passage to Puritan New England," *New England Quarterly*, 57 (December 1984): 516.

56. Anne Bradstreet, "To My Dear Children," in *The Works of Anne Bradstreet in Prose and Verse*, ed. John Harvard Ellis (New York: Peter Smith, 1932), 5.

57. As quoted in Alice Morse Earle, *Margaret Winthrop* (New York: Charles Scribner's Sons, 1895), 225.

58. Barry Levy, *Quakers and the American Family: British Settlement in the Delaware Valley* (New York: Oxford University Press, 1988), 86–89, 100. For a comparison of the Quaker family with Chesapeake and New England families, see Levy, 144.

59. Large Quaker families were more likely than small ones to migrate to North America. Levy, *Quakers and the American Family*, 114. See also Robert V. Wells, "Quaker Marriage Patterns in a Colonial Perspective," in *A Heritage of Her Own: Toward a New Social History of American Women*, ed. Nancy F. Cott and Elizabeth H. Pleck (New York: Simon & Schuster, 1979), 85.

60. Levy, *Quakers and the American Family*, 146–50, indicates that Quakers' life expectancy was around 67 years, and the average number of children in a family who survived until the age of 21 was between 4.73 and 5.65. Wells, "Quaker Marriage Patterns," 85, 92–102, notes that Quakers continued the English custom of marrying someone nearly their own age, fostering a more egalitarian relationship. He states that in the eighteenth century, Quaker women's age at first marriage began to rise because of economic reasons and equalization of the sex ratio in Pennsylvania, and he compares Quaker marriage patterns with those of other colonists and with those of women and men in England.

61. Tribes classified as costal Algonquin included the Wampanoag and Massachusett of Massachusetts Bay Colony; the Naragansett and Niantic of Rhode Island; the Mohegan and Pequot of eastern Connecticut; the Montauk

of eastern Long Island; the Delawarean groups from western Long Island and southeastern New York, eastern Pennsylvania, and upper Delaware; the Nanticoke, Conoy, and Accomack peoples of the Delmarva Peninsula; and the Powhatan peoples of the Chesapeake Bay. The Creeks, Choctaws, Catawbas, Guales, Chickasaws, and Seminoles in the southeast shared a linguistic base with the coastal Algonquins to the north. Other tribes of the southeast, however, spoke predominantly Muskogean. Tribes in the Great Lakes and along the St. Lawrence River, as well as the Cherokee and the Tuscaroras, spoke an Iroquoian dialect. Robert Steven Grumet, "Sunksquaws, Shamans, and Tradeswomen: Middle Atlantic Coastal Algonquin Women during the Seventeenth and Eighteenth Centuries," in *Women and Colonization: Anthropological Perspectives*, ed. Mona Etienne and Eleanor Leacock (New York: Praeger, 1980), 45–46. Also, Stephanie Coontz, *The Social Origins of Private Life: A History of American Families, 1600–1900* (New York: Verso, 1988), 51. Also, *The Indian Peoples of Eastern America: A Documentary History of the Sexes*, ed. James Axtell (New York: Oxford University Press, 1981), xvii–xviii.

62. David D. Smits, "'Abominable Mixture': Toward the Repudiation of Anglo-Indian Intermarriage in Seventeenth-Century Virginia," *Virginia Magazine of History and Biography* 95 (April 1987): 160.

63. Theda Perdue, *Slavery and the Evolution of Cherokee Society, 1540–1866* (Knoxville: University of Tennessee Press, 1979), 9.

64. In the Algonquin culture that European explorers and settlers encountered along the eastern seaboard, the village was the focus of life. Villages allied themselves in economic districts and allocated lands for hunting, planting, fishing, and gathering for the use of each village. Tribes were groups of villages, usually located around a river or along a shoreline, and it was their governments that usually responded to political, economic, or military crises with the English colonists. Loose alliances between tribes, called confederacies, were sometimes created in response to external threats or problems. Native American confederacies were formed during the late sixteenth and early seventeenth centuries in the Chesapeake, Massachusetts Bay, and upper Hudson River valley regions. Grumet, "Sunksquaws, Shamans, and Tradeswomen," 46–47.

Women were less influential in the hunting and fishing tribes of the Great Lakes and northern New England. Kinship in these tribes was patrilineal because of the greater importance played by men in supporting their people. Judith K. Brown, "Economic Organization and the Position of Women among the Iroquois," *Ethnohistory* 17 (Summer–Fall 1970): 151–67. Also, Elizabeth Tooker, "Women in Iroquois Society," in *Extending the Rafters: Interdisciplinary Approaches to Iroquoian Studies*, ed. Michael K. Foster, Jack Campisi, and Marianne Mithun (Albany: State University of New York Press, 1984), 109–23, and Nancy Shoemaker, "The Rise or Fall of Iroquois Women," *Journal of Women's History* 2 (Winter 1991): 39–41. See also, Joan M. Jensen, "Native

American Women and Agriculture: A Seneca Case Study," in *Women and Power in American History: A Reader*, ed. Kathryn Kish Sklar and Thomas Dublin (Englewood Cliffs, N.J.: Prentice Hall, 1991), 1:8–12. In *The Indian Peoples of Eastern America*, xvii, Axtell indicates that the agricultural central Algonquin tribes of Michigan and Ohio—the Shawnee, Miami, Sauk, Fox, and Potawatomi—were also patrilineal.

65. Grumet, "Sunksquaws, Shamans, and Tradeswomen," 54.

66. Ibid., 50–53.

67. Sara M. Evans, *Born for Liberty: A History of Women in America* (New York: Macmillan, 1989), 13. See also Shoemaker, "The Rise or Fall of Iroquois Women," 40.

68. See Smits, "'Abominable Mixture,'" 158–61, on the preconceived notions about Native American women that English men brought to Virginia in the seventeenth century.

69. Edward Arber, *Travels and Works of Captain John Smith* (Edinburgh: J. Grant, 1910), 64.

70. Smits, " 'Abominable Mixture,' " 158.

71. Ibid., 170, 172, and Judith Reynolds, "Marriage between the English and the Indians in Seventeenth Century Virginia," *Archaeological Society of Virginia Newsletter*, 17 (December 1962): 22.

72. As quoted in J. A. Leo Lemay, *The American Dream of Captain John Smith* (Charlottesville: University Press of Virginia, 1991), 51. For a critical analysis of Smith's relationship with Powhatan and Pocahontas, see also Lemay, *The American Dream*, 146–66, and Jay B. Hubbell, "The Smith-Pocahontas Story in Literature," *Virginia Magazine of History and Biography* 65 (July 1957): 275–300. Grumet, "Sunksquaws, Shamans, and Tradeswomen," 49–50, also discusses the relationship between Smith and Pocahontas.

73. Rayna Green, "The Pocahontas Perplex: The Image of Indian Women in American Culture" in *Unequal Sisters: A Multicultural Reader in U.S. Women's History*, ed. Ellen Carol DuBois and Vicki L. Ruiz (New York: Routledge, 1990), 15–21. For accounts of Pocahontas's life, see Grace Steele Woodward, *Pocahontas* (Norman: University of Oklahoma Press, 1969), and Barbour, *Pocahontas and Her World*.

74. Letter of John Rolfe to Sir Thomas Dale, in *Narratives of Early Virginia*, 239–44.

75. Reynolds, "Marriage between the English and the Indians," 21. See also, Smits, " 'Abominable Mixture,' " 176.

76. Smits, " 'Abominable Mixture,' " 177.

77. As quoted in Levy, *The American Dream*, 125–26.

78. Smits, " 'Abominable Mixture,' " 158, 168. Gary B. Nash, *Red, White, and Black: The Peoples of Early America* (Englewood Cliffs, N.J.: Prentice Hall, 1974), 65, states that intermarriage between the races was rare in early Virginia

"partly because of English squeamishness about women of another culture but probably even more because Indian women, living in tribes not subjugated by the English, had no inclination to consort with men of the intruding culture."

79. Reynolds, "Marriage between the English and the Indians," 21.

80. The Narragansett tribe allied itself with the English colonists and fought against the other tribes, hoping to secure control of the region. Nash, *Red, White, and Black*, 83–85.

81. Nash, *Red, White, and Black*, 122–23.

82. Ibid., 131–34, and John Archdale, "A New Description of . . . Carolina," in *Narratives of Early Carolina, 1650–1708*, ed. Alexander Salley (New York: Charles Scribner's Sons, 1911), 285. An excellent source on the impact of African slavery on the development of South Carolina is Wood, *Black Majority*.

83. James Axtell, "The Vengeful Women of Marblehead: Robert Roules's Deposition of 1677," *William and Mary Quarterly*, 3d ser., 31 (October 1974): 647–52.

84. Nash, *Red, White, and Black*, 158.

85. Lorenzo Johnston Greene, *The Negro in Colonial New England, 1620–1776* (Port Washington, N.Y.: Kennikat Press, 1942), 63.

86. Massachusetts had 2,000 Africans, Connecticut's population included 1,500, while Rhode Island had 500 and New Hampshire had 150 African residents. Greene, *The Negro in Colonial New England*, 74–75.

87. Donald Wright, *African Americans in the Colonial Era: From African Origins through the American Revolution* (Arlington Heights, Ill.: Harlan Davidson, 1990), 11. The region north of Zaire supplied slaves from the Congo, Tio, and Matamba tribes. Southeastern Nigeria provided men and women from the Ibo and Ibibio tribes, while the Mandinka, Fulbe, Serer, Wolof, Bambara, and Jola peoples came from Senegambia. The Ashanti and Fanti people came from the Gold Coast. The Vai, Mende, Kpelle, and Kru tribes were also represented in the slaves sold to North American colonists.

88. On women in the African economy, see Marietta Morrissey, *Slave Women in the New World: Gender Stratification in the Caribbean* (Lawrence: University Press of Kansas, 1989), 29. See also Claire C. Robertson and Martin A. Klein, "Women's Importance in African Slave Systems," *Women and Slavery in Africa* ed. Claire C. Robertson and Martin A. Klein (Madison: University of Wisconsin Press, 1983), 3–28.

89. Wright, *African Americans*, 16–17.

90. Ibid., 18, and Wood, *Black Majority*, 36, 40–42, 131, and 144, table 1.

91. After her husband's death in 1674, Lady Margaret remained in Charles Town where she, too, prospered. Agnes Baldwin, *First Settlers of South Carolina, 1670–1680* (Columbia, S.C.: University of South Carolina Press, 1969), see the last pages under "Yeamans."

92. Russell R. Menard, "The Maryland Slave Population, 1658 to 1730: A Demographic Profile of Blacks in Four Counties," *William and Mary Quarterly*, 3d ser., 32 (January 1975): 31–33. See also Wright, *African Americans*, 40, on the reluctance to sell African women by African slave traders and Morrison, *Women in New World Slavery*, 32–45, on the various theories about gender imbalance in slave imports to plantations in the New World. Philip D. Morgan, "Slave Life in Piedmont Virginia, 1720–1800," in *Colonial Chesapeake Society* ed. Lois Green Carr, Philip D. Morgan and Jean B. Russo (Chapel Hill: University of North Carolina Press, 1988), 435–37, discusses the numbers of African women and female children imported to the region and the role played by native-born slaves in the natural increase of the slave population.

93. Main, *Tobacco Colony*, 124. Morrissey, *Slave Women in the New World*, 31, states: "Where plantation agriculture approached industrial forms of organization, males' and females' labor was not sharply differentiated. The expanded scale and technological apparatus of the plantations increased highly skilled tasks and allocated them to males. Where agriculture was on a smaller scale and processing unmechanized, more traditional, agrarian, gender-based divisions of labor emerged. Men's and women's agricultural work in these settings was both more diversified and differentiated by gender. European and West African farming techniques and modes of agrarian organization influenced the ways in which labor was distributed, both in the production of cash crops and in related aspects of labor."

94. Menard, "Maryland Slave Population," 35.

95. Kulikoff, *Tobacco and Slaves*, 352–53. See also Deborah Gray White, *Ar'n't I a Woman? Female Slaves in the Plantation South* (New York: W. W. Norton, 1985).

96. Greene, *The Negro in Colonial New England*, 119–20.

97. Ibid., 95–96, 127. On African–Native American relations in South Carolina, see Wood, *Black Majority*, 99, 115–17.

98. Greene, *The Negro in Colonial New England*, 139, and Wood, *Black Majority*, 99.

99. Barry Levy, " 'Tender Plants': Quaker Farmers and Children in the Delaware Valley, 1681–1735," *Journal of Family History* 3 (Summer 1978): 124.

100. Kulikoff, *Tobacco and Slaves*, 354–55.

101. Menard, "Maryland Slave Population," 41–43. There is evidence that women enslaved in Africa also demonstrated lower fertility than their free counterparts. See Morrissey, *Slave Women in the New World*, 29, 169 n. 14.

102. In 1725 Virginia merchant Thomas Cable revealed the continuing preference for male slaves. Were he to choose a cargo of 200 African slaves, he remarked, "I would have 100 men able young Slaves, 60 women, 30 Boys and 10 Girls from 10 to 14 years of age. Such a Cargoe I could sell to great

Advantage." Most shipments of slaves to the southern colonies reflected these proportions. Kulikoff, *Tobacco and Slaves*, 66.

103. Menard, "Maryland Slave Population," 45, and Kulikoff, *Tobacco and Slaves*, 352–60. See also Wright, *African Americans*, 55. White, *Ar'n't I a Woman?* 91–118, discusses the life cycle of the female slave in the eighteenth and nineteenth centuries and asserts that African-American women gave birth to their first child at a young age to prove their fertility to their masters.

104. For the discovery that women of Ibo ancestry were most likely to run away, see Daniel C. Littlefield, *Rice and Slaves: Ethnicity and the Slave Trade in Colonial South Carolina* (Baton Rouge: Louisiana State University Press, 1981), 143–44. Littlefield notes that in South Carolina, Ibo women were disproportionately represented in the slave population. He also asserts that, in general, American-born slave women were more likely to run away than those born in Africa. On women in Ibo culture, see Sylvia Leith-Ross, *African Women: A Study of the Ibo of Nigeria* (New York: Frederick A. Praeger, 1965), 21, 75, 87–95, 108–10.

105. On women's resistance to slavery, see White, *Ar'n't I a Woman?* 75–79. The earliest evidence of a slave woman found guilty and executed for poisoning her master was in Charleston, South Carolina, in 1755. See Wood, *Black Majority*, 289–92.

Chapter 3

1. William Cronon, *Changes in the Land: Indians, Colonists, and the Ecology of New England* (New York: Hill and Wang, 1983), 40–41.

2. As quoted in Cronon, *Changes in the Land*, 43.

3. Cronon, *Changes in the Land*, 44.

4. Roger Williams, "A Key into the Language of America," in *The Indian Peoples of Eastern America*, 122–23.

5. As quoted in Alice Morse Earle, *Margaret Winthrop* (New York: Charles Scribner's Sons, 1895), 82.

6. The residents of Martin's Hundred, Virginia, constructed cellars six or seven feet deep lined with saplings to prevent the sides from caving in. These were roofed with bent saplings and covered with bark or sod, much like the long or round houses of Native Americans. See Hume, *Martin's Hundred*, 57.

7. Two-thirds of all Maryland residents in the seventeenth century inhabited homes of only one to three rooms. Main, *Tobacco Colony*, 140–50, 160. Also, Hume, *Martin's Hundred*, 140, 239, 247.

8. John Demos, *A Little Commonwealth: Family Life in Plymouth Colony* (New York: Oxford University Press, 1970), 24–35. On architecture in New Netherlands and New York, see Firth Harding Fabend, *A Dutch Family in the*

Middle Colonies, 1660–1800 (New Brunswick, N.J.: Rutgers University Press, 1991), 57–75.

9. For a discussion of privacy, community values, and architecture in the New England colonies, see David H. Flaherty, *Privacy in Colonial New England* (Charlottesville: University Press of Virginia, 1967), 33–44.

10. Main, *Tobacco Colony*, 151.

11. Flaherty, *Privacy in Colonial New England*, 76–79.

12. Bradstreet, "Some verses upon the burning of our house, July 10, 1666," in *The Works of Anne Bradstreet in Prose and Verse*, 41.

13. John Oldmixon as quoted in Main, *Tobacco Colony*, 177. On the monotonous and exhausting nature of women's work in preindustrial society, see, Ruth Schwartz Cowan, *More Work for Mother: The Ironies of Technology from the Open Hearth to the Microwave* (New York: Basic Books, 1983), 16–25. Also, Main, *Tobacco Colony*, 181.

14. Demos, *A Little Commonwealth*, 40.

15. On how household technology has added to women's workload, see Cowan, *More Work for Mother*, 9–13.

16. On pottery in seventeenth-century Virginia, see Hume, *Martin's Hundred*, 101–2, 106–8, 128.

17. Main, *Tobacco Colony*, 169–70.

18. As quoted in Alice Morse Earle, *Home Life in Colonial Days* (New York: Grosset & Dunlap, 1898; reprint, Stockbridge, Mass.: Berkshire Traveller Press, 1974), 33.

19. Main, *Tobacco Colony*, 264. See also Carr and Walsh, "Economic Diversification and Labor Organization," 145.

20. "Forum: Toward a History of the Standard of Living in British North America," *William and Mary Quarterly*, 3d ser., 45 (January 1988): 116–70.

21. Spruill, *Women's Life and Work in the Southern Colonies*, 133–34.

22. On vestiges of African dress worn by slave women in the New World, the meaning of headcloth tying, and African hairdressing, see Judith Wragge Chase, *Afro-American Art and Craft* (New York: Van Nostrand Reinhold Co., 1971), 61. See Wright, *African Americans in the Colonial Era*, 110–11, on slave attire.

23. Women's methods of hairdressing have not been explored for evidence of continuity from Africa to America. Ethnologists have discovered that among the Ibo people of present-day Nigeria, young women must dress their hair in a different, more elaborate, style each year for a period of eight years before they are considered adults old enough to marry. Sylvia Leith-Ross, *African Women: A Study of the Ibo of Nigeria* (New York, Frederick A. Praeger, 1965), 95.

24. Hume, *Martin's Hundred*, 285–96.

25. Spruill, *Women's Life and Work in the Southern Colonies*, 113.

26. As quoted in Alice Morse Earle, *Two Centuries of Costume in America: 1620–1820* (New York: Macmillan Co., 1903; reprint, New York: Dover Publications, 1970), 1:61.

27. John Winthrop, too, warned his wife, Margaret, not to become preoccupied with her attire or other "trifles," viewing them as signs of vanity and Satan's temptation. Earle, *Two Centuries of Costume in America*, 1:63.

28. Flaherty, *Privacy in Colonial New England*, 184–85.

29. Earle, *Margaret Winthrop*, 89–90. See also Demos, *A Little Commonwealth*, 52–58, on clothing in Plymouth colony.

30. Main, *Tobacco Colony*, 184–90.

31. Madame Sarah Kemble Knight was born in Boston in 1666 and married shipmaster Richard Knight in 1689. His second wife, she bore him a daughter, Elizabeth, before she was widowed. The well-educated Knight may have supported herself for a time as a scrivener. She opened a shop and invested in real estate in the Boston area. Later she moved to Connecticut, where she bought property and ran an inn on one of her farms. In the fall of 1704 she traveled from Boston to New Haven and, finally, New York on business and kept a diary of her journey. It reveals a witty personality as well as a sharp eye for life in the colonies. She died in New London, Connecticut, on 17 March 1735/36. Sarah Knight, *The Journal of Madam Knight* (Boston: David R. Godine, 1972), 30.

32. Bradstreet, "Meditations," in *The Works of Anne Bradstreet in Prose and Verse*, 56–57.

33. On childhood in colonial America, see Ross W. Beales, Jr., "In Search of the Historical Child: Miniature Adulthood and Youth in Colonial New England," *American Quarterly* 27 (October 1975): 379–98; Ross W. Beales, Jr., "The Child in Seventeenth-Century America," in *American Childhood: A Research Guide and Historical Handbook*, ed. Joseph M. Hawes and N. Ray Hiner (Westport, Conn.: Greenwood Press, 1985), 15–56; and especially Karin Calvert, *Children in the House: The Material Culture of Early Childhood, 1600–1900* (Boston: Northeastern University Press, 1992), 19–52.

34. For definition of the terms used here, see Susan Burrows Swan, *A Wintherthur Guide to American Needlework* (New York: Crown Publishers, 1976), 9.

35. As quoted in Morgan, *The Puritan Family*, 67.

36. In cutwork the design is stitched and then the fabric within the design is cut away, its edges reinforced. In drawnwork, also called Dresden work, the warp or the weft threads are cut away or unraveled and the remaining threads are gathered using embroidery thread. It was not until the early eighteenth century that young women included decorative motifs and scenes in their samplers. Then, the sampler's shape changed from a long rectangle to

the more familiar square, framed with a stitchery border. Swan, *American Needlework*, 10–21.

37. Swan, *American Needlework*, 18.

38. Ibid., 26–63.

39. Women seldom manufactured cloth in the Chesapeake during the seventeenth century, buying imported fabric instead and making clothing from it for their families, servants, and slaves. Spinning was much more common in the New England colonies at that time. See Kulikoff, *Tobacco and Slaves*, 179–80, and Walsh and Carr, "Economic Diversification and Labor Organization," 145–46. Also, Ulrich, *Good Wives*, 16, 29, 34, 45–46. On the process of weaving and spinning, see Earle, *Home Life in Colonial Days*, 166–251. Mary Beth Norton, "My Mother/My Friend: Mothers and Daughters in Eighteenth-Century America," Harvey Wish Memorial Lecture Series, 2 (Cleveland: Case Western Reserve University, 1979), 6–7, discusses the dependence of colonial households on imported fabric.

40. On diet in the seventeenth-century Chesapeake see Henry M. Miller, "An Archaeological Perspective on the Evolution of Diet in the Colonial Chesapeake, 1620–1745," in *Colonial Chesapeake Society*, ed. Lois Green Carr, Philip D. Morgan, and Jean B. Russo (Chapel Hill: University of North Carolina Press, 1988), 176–99.

41. As quoted in Earle, *Home Life in Colonial Days*, 134.

42. "A Letter Written in 1711 by Mary Stafford to her Kinswoman in England," *South Carolina Historical Magazine* 81 (January 1980): 4.

43. Peter H. Wood, *Black Majority: Negroes in Colonial South Carolina from 1670 through the Stono Rebellion* (New York: W. W. Norton and Co., 1974), 55–62, 61 n. 97, asserts the important role played by African women in the cultivation of rice. On the other hand, Daniel C. Littlefield, *Rice and Slaves: Ethnicity and the Slave Trade in Colonial South Carolina* (Baton Rouge: Louisiana University Press, 1981), 90, states that in Africa "As a general rule, wherever rice cultivation is a major concern, it is the primary responsibility of men, and wherever . . . it has a supplementary character, it is the responsibility of the women."

44. On baskets and their makers, see Mary Twining, "Harvesting and Heritage: A Comparison of Afro-American and African Basketry," in *Afro-American Folk Art and Crafts* ed. William Ferris (Boston: G. K. Hall & Co., 1983), 259–71. See also John Michael Vlach, *The Afro-American Tradition in Decorative Arts* (Kent, Ohio: Kent State University Press, 1978), 7–9. Vlach, however, assumes that the baskets were made by men during the seventeenth and eighteenth centuries. Chase, *Afro-American Art and Craft*, 40, asserts that basket making was largely women's work in West Africa and that daughters learned the craft from their mothers. Some men practiced the craft, but usually only during the dry season, when there was little agricultural work. In the

American colonies, boys were taught basket making, but they usually abandoned it at puberty when they were put to labor intensively in the fields. They resumed the craft only when they were old and unable to work in the fields. Women, however, performed the craft throughout their lives.

45. For a description of the process, see Twining, "Harvesting and Heritage," 267.

46. As quoted in Demos, *A Little Commonwealth*, 16, and in Earle, *Home Life in Colonial Days*, 438. See also Hume, *Martin's Hundred*, 72–73, 237–38. On kitchen gardens in New York, see Fabend, *A Dutch Family*, 80–82.

47. Thomas Tusser, *His Good Points of Husbandry*, ed. Dorothy Hartley (London: Country Life, 1931), 84.

48. On "change work," see Earle, *Home Life in Colonial Days*, 417. For a discussion of the patterns of women's domestic labor and their interaction with other women in New England, see Laurel Thatcher Ulrich, "'A Friendly Neighbor': Social Dimensions of Daily Work in Northern Colonial New England," *Feminist Studies* 6 (Summer 1980): 392–405, and Laurel Thatcher Ulrich, "Martha Ballard and Her Girls: Women's Work in Eighteenth-Century Maine," *Work and Labor in Early America*, 70–105. Flaherty, *Privacy in Colonial New England*, 72, discusses how women valued the time spent with other women and how only during the winter months did they spend much time with their husbands, confined indoors by the weather.

49. Most written accounts of transactions in colonial America were kept by men; few record the commodities and crafts exchanged by women. While much of the trade within the New England colonies was by barter rather than for cash, entries relating to the enterprise of women are scarce perhaps because men undervalued the importance of women's contribution to the region's economy. Those women whose transactions appear in the records of men were most frequently trading butter and cheese or capitalizing on their skills of sewing and spinning. Most of the women named were also widows, indicating their need to support themselves by their own labors. Ulrich, *Good Wives*, 45. See also Fabend, *A Dutch Family*, 82–83. Gloria L. Main, "Gender, Work, and Wages in Colonial New England," *William and Mary Quarterly*, 3d ser., 51 (January 1994): 39–66, studies how patriarchal values influenced the compensation of women who worked for pay.

50. For an account of soap making, see Earle, *Home Life in Colonial Days*, 254–55. On women's domestic labor in the Chesapeake, see Carr and Walsh, "The Planter's Wife, 561.

51. As quoted in Earle, *Home Life in Colonial Days*, 35.

52. As quoted in Earle, *Margaret Winthrop*, 60.

53. "A Letter Written in 1711 by Mary Stafford," 4.

54. On brewing in colonial New England, see Ulrich, *Good Wives*, 23. On the discovery of the still at Martin's Hundred, see Hume, *Martin's Hundred*,

102. On the diet of colonial southerners, see Spruill, *Women's Life and Work in the Southern Colonies*, 69–71.

55. Earle, *Margaret Winthrop*, 239–40.

56. Morgan, *The Puritan Family*, 67, 77. See also Ulrich, *Good Wives*, 44, on the nature of girls' indentures, and Demos, *A Little Commonwealth*, 120.

57. Morgan, *The Puritan Family*, 70–79.

58. Knight, *The Journal*, 20.

59. Demos, *A Little Commonwealth*, 111.

60. Marietta Morrissey, *Slave Women in the New World: Gender Stratification in the Caribbean* (Lawrence: University Press of Kansas, 1989), 30–31.

61. On women's literacy in colonial New England, see Kenneth Lockridge, *Literacy in Colonial New England* (New York: W. W. Norton, 1974), 38–42. See also E. Jennifer Monaghan, "Literacy Instruction and Gender in Colonial New England," *American Quarterly* 40 (March 1988): 18–41, for a critique of localized studies. Linda Auwers, "Reading the Marks of the Past: Exploring Female Literacy in Colonial Windsor, Connecticut," *Historical Methods* 13 (Fall 1980): 204–14, asserts that the percentage of women able to write dramatically improved to include 90 percent of those women born in 1740. While the percentage of women who could write improved by the eighteenth century, the meaning of that improvement is not entirely clear. For more on the literacy of women in the eighteenth century, see Joel Perlmann and Dennis Shirley, "When Did New England Women Acquire Literacy?" *William and Mary Quarterly*, 3d ser., 48 (January 1991): 50–67.

62. Bradstreet, "The Prologue" to *The Tenth Muse*, in *The Works of Anne Bradstreet in Prose and Verse*, 101.

63. John Winthrop, as quoted in Morgan, *The Puritan Family*, 44.

64. Bradstreet, "In Honor of That High and Mighty Princess Queen Elizabeth of Happy Memory," in *The Works of Anne Bradstreet in Prose and Verse*, 361.

65. Bradstreet, "In Reference to her Children," in *The Works of Anne Bradstreet in Prose and Verse*, 400.

66. Bradstreet, "To My Dear and Loving Husband," in *The Works of Anne Bradstreet in Prose and Verse*, 394.

67. *The Works of Anne Bradstreet in Prose and Verse*, xi–lxxi. Also *The Works of Anne Bradstreet*, ed. Jeanine Hensley, with a foreword by Adrienne Rich (Cambridge: Harvard University Press, 1967), ix–xxxv; Jennifer R. Waller, "'My Hand a Needle Better Fits: Anne Bradstreet and Women Poets in the Renaissance," *Dalhousie Review* 54 (Autumn 1974): 436–50. For a feminist interpretation of Bradstreet's poetry, see Wendy Martin, "Anne Bradstreet's Poetry: A Study of Subversive Piety," in *Shakespeare's Sisters: Feminist Essays on Women Poets*, ed. Sandra M. Gilbert and Susan Grubar (Bloomington: University of Indiana Press, 1979), 19–31.

68. As quoted in Morgan, *The Puritan Family*, 29.

69. Walsh, " 'Till Death Us Do Part,' " 138–39.

70. On bundling, see: Henry Reed Stiles, *Bundling: Its Origin, Progress, and Decline in America* (Albany: Knickerbocker Publishing Co., 1871; reprint, New York: Book Collectors Assn., 1934), E. S. Turner, *A History of Courting* (New York: E. P. Dutton and Co., 1955), 122–27, and Dana Doten, *The Art of Bundling* (New York: Countryman Press, 1938), 40, who says the custom was also familiar to Dutch settlers, who imported it from the Netherlands, where it was called *queesting*.

71. As quoted in Fabend, *A Dutch Family*, 41.

72. James Axtell, *The School upon a Hill: Education and Society in Colonial New England* (New Haven: Yale University Press, 1974), 54–55.

73. Morgan, *The Puritan Family*, 31.

74. Walsh, " 'Till Death Us Do Part,' " 129–31.

75. Morgan, *The Puritan Family*, 63–64, says the Puritans saw sex as a pleasurable and necessary part of married life. Consequently, both impotence and refusal to have intercourse were grounds for divorce in New England. Ulrich, *Good Wives*, 95–96, 108, 110–13, argues that Puritan men feared women's sexuality and tried to control it through marriage. An inability to do so was, therefore, grounds for divorce. Koehler, *A Search for Power*, 74–80, also believes misogyny was at the heart of the Puritans' divorce policy. On Puritans' attitudes about sex, see Edmund S. Morgan, "The Puritans and Sex," *New England Quarterly* 15 (December 1942): 591–607, and Kathleen Verduin, " 'Our Cursed Natures': Sexuality and the Puritan Conscience," *New England Quarterly* 56 (June 1983): 220–37.

76. On Puritan attitudes about marriage, see Edmund Leites, "The Duty to Desire: Love, Friendship, and Sexuality in Some Puritan Theories of Marriage," *Journal of Social History* 15 (Spring 1982): 383–408, and Edmund Leites, *The Puritan Conscience and Modern Sexuality* (New Haven: Yale University Press, 1986).

77. As quoted in Morgan, *The Puritan Family*, 46.

78. Earle, *Margaret Winthrop*, 38–39. The couple had been married for 29 years when Margaret died in 1647. Winthrop married his fourth wife, Martha Coytmore, in 1648, and died in 1649.

79. As quoted in Koehler, *A Search for Power*, 32.

80. Earle, *Margaret Winthrop*, 130.

81. For accounts of women's "Coming of Age" in Native American culture, see *The Indian Peoples of Eastern America*, 55–69.

82. Father Gabriel Sagard, "The Long Journey to the Country of the Hurons," in *The Indian Peoples of Eastern America*, 7.

83. Roger Williams, "A Key into the Language of America," in *The Indian Peoples of Eastern America*, 20–21.

84. John Long, "John Long's Voyages and Travels in the Years 1768–1788," *The Indian Peoples of Eastern America*, 17.

85. "The Autobiography of a Fox Indian Woman," in *The Indian Peoples of Eastern America*, 29.

86. For Native American birth practices, see *The Indian Peoples of Eastern America*, 4–30.

87. White, *Ar'n't I a Woman?* 94–99, discusses African women's reproductive lives and their work on eighteenth- and early nineteenth-century plantations.

88. Richard Archer, "New England Mosaic: A Demographic Analysis for the Seventeenth Century," *William and Mary Quarterly*, 3d ser., 48 (October 1990): 491–92, on women's fertility in seventeenth-century New England.

89. Bradstreet, "To My Dear Children," *The Works of Anne Bradstreet in Prose and Verse*, 5.

90. Dexter, *Colonial Women of Affairs*, 60–67.

91. On lying-in customs, see Ulrich, *Good Wives*, 127. Also, Axtell, *The School upon a Hill*, 65–70, discusses childbirth in New England.

92. Thomas Tusser, as quoted in Earle, *Margaret Winthrop*, 81.

93. Regina Markell Morantz-Sanchez, *Sympathy and Science: Women Physicians in American Medicine* (New York: Oxford University Press, 1985), 12. On childbirth and the role of the midwife in seventeenth-century England, see Eccles, *Obstetrics and Gynaecology*, 86–108. On midwifery in America, see Irving S. Cutter and Henry R. Viets, *A Short History of Midwifery* (Philadelphia: W. B. Saunders Co., 1964), 143–44; Catherine Scholten, " 'On the Importance of the Obstetrick Art': Changing Customs of Childbirth in America, 1760–1825," *William and Mary Quarterly*, 3d ser., 34 (July 1977): 426–45; and Jane Bauer Donegan, *Women and Men Midwives: Medicine, Morality, and Misogyny in Early America* (Westport, Conn.: Greenwood Press, 1978). Also, Richard W. and Dorothy C. Wertz, *Lying In—A History of Childbirth in America* (New York: Free Press, 1977), 1–28, discuss the role of midwives in colonial America. Cotton Mather, *The Angel of Bethesda*, ed. Gordon W. Jones (Marre, Mass.: Barre Publishers and the American Antiquarian Society, 1972), 245–48, provided his readers with herbal remedies for pain in childbirth.

94. Mather, *The Angel of Bethesda*, 236.

95. Bradstreet, "Before the Birth of one of her Children," *The Works of Anne Bradstreet in Prose and Verse*, 393.

96. Tusser, *His Good Points of Husbandry*, 162.

97. Cotton Mather, *Ornaments for the Daughters of Zion* (Delmar, N.Y.: Scholars' Facsimiles & Reprints, 1987), 105–6. See also Axtell, *The School upon a Hill*, 76–84.

98. Treckel, "Breastfeeding and Maternal Sexuality, 25–51.

99. Ibid. For more on pregnancy, childbirth, and nursing, see Claire

Fox, "Pregnancy, Childbirth, and Early Infancy in Anglo-American Culture, 1675–1830" (Ph.D. diss., University of Pennsylvania, 1966), and Axtell, *The School upon a Hill*, 86–88.

100. Bradstreet, "Meditations," in *The Works of Anne Bradstreet in Prose and Verse*, 56. See Ulrich, *Good Wives*, 140–44, on the "weaning journey." Valerie Fildes, *Breasts, Bottles, and Babies: A History of Infant Feeding* (Edinburgh: Edinburgh University Press 1986), 377–82, indicates that both gradual and abrupt weaning were common during this era, the abrupt method being used with older children.

101. Ross Beales, "Ebenezer Parkman's Children," paper presented at the Charles Rieley Armington Research Center, Case Western Reserve University (Cleveland, 1979), 61–63. Also, Ross Beales, "Nursing and Weaning in an Eighteenth-Century New England Household," Dublin Seminar for New England Folklife, *Annual Proceedings*, 1985, ed. Peter Benes (Boston, 1987), 121–23.

102. Bradstreet, "An Epitaph on my dear and ever honoured Mother Mrs. Dorothy Dudley," in *The Works of Anne Bradstreet in Prose and Verse*, 369.

103. Women's preoccupation with childbearing and rearing has been attributed to economic and religious changes in the colonies after 1660. See Norton, "The Evolution of White Women's Experience," 604–8.

104. As quoted in Ulrich, *Good Wives*, 36.

105. The author is indebted to Bradford L. Rauschenberg for this information on Henrietta Johnston and her works. See the exhibit catalog *Henrietta Johnston: "Who greatly helped . . . by drawing pictures,"* ed. Forsyth Alexander (Museum of Early Southern Decorative Arts, Winston-Salem, N.C., 12 October–8 December 1991; the Gibbes Museum of Art, Charleston, S.C., 12 December 1991–2 February 1992), 1–16.

106. On the role of women in Bacon's Rebellion, see Stephen S. Webb, *Sixteen-hundred-seventy-six: The End of American Independence* (New York: Knopf, 1984), 5–7, 20–21, 49, 63.

107. As quoted in Earle, *Colonial Dames and Goodwives*, 53.

108. "A Letter Written in 1711 by Mary Stafford," 1–7.

109. Knight, *The Journal*, 48.

110. Dexter, *Colonial Women of Affairs*, 49, 53, 55–56, provides other examples of widows who continued their husbands' work.

111. As quoted in Dexter, *Colonial Women of Affairs*, 18.

112. Dexter, *Colonial Women of Affairs*, 166–69.

113. As quoted in Earle, *Colonial Dames and Good Wives*, 74–75.

114. Mather, *Ornaments for the Daughters of Zion*, 112–13.

115. These wars, following the costly war against chief King Philip in 1676, seriously hurt the Massachusetts economy and undermined the sense of community in the colony. On the widows of King Philip's War, see William F. Ricketson, "To Be Young, Poor, and Alone: The Experience of Widowhood

in the Massachusetts Bay Colony, 1675–1676," *New England Quarterly* 64 (March 1991): 113–27. On widows of the later wars, see Gary B. Nash, *The Urban Crucible: Social Change, Political Consciousness, and the Origins of the American Revolution* (Cambridge: Harvard University Press, 1979), 58–59.

116. On the relative youth of war widows, see Ricketson, "To Be Young, Poor, and Alone," 116. On widows' postwar migration to urban centers, see Nash, *The Urban Crucible,* 65.

117. Auwers, "Reading the Marks of the Past," 206.

Chapter 4

1. Fraser, *The Weaker Vessel,* 147.

2. William Blackstone, as quoted in Linda Biemer, *Women and Property in Colonial New York: The Transition from Dutch to English Law, 1643–1727* (Ann Arbor: UMI Research Press, 1983), ix.

3. While many English men who wrote wills granted their children more than the law prescribed, few willed their widows a larger share in their estate. Carole Shammas, Marylynn Salmon, and Michael Dahlin, *Inheritance in America from Colonial Times to the Present* (New Brunswick, N.J.: Rutgers University Press, 1987), 25, 28.

4. Carol F. Karlsen, *The Devil in the Shape of a Woman: Witchcraft in Colonial New England* (New York: Random House, 1987), 82. In the American colonies, South Carolina, New York, Virginia, and Maryland adopted the custom of primogeniture. In these colonies, if a man died without a will, his eldest son was entitled to all his real estate, while his personal property was divided equally among all his children. If a man had no son, then the estate was divided equally among his daughters. Primogeniture could, however, be superseded by a will, and many men wrote wills to divide their estates among all their children.

5. Shammas, Salmon, and Dahlin, *Inheritance in America,* 28–29, and, Fraser, *The Weaker Vessel,* 97.

6. For example, English laws on dower rights changed during the course of the seventeenth century, so the colony of Maryland, founded in 1634, granted women dower in personal property, while South Carolina, founded in 1670, permitted men to bequeath personal property to whomever they pleased, reflecting changes in English dower law during the nearly four decades between the settlement of these two colonies.

7. As quoted in Koehler, *A Search for Power,* 31.

8. Massachusetts lawmakers required a wife's signature on deeds authorizing the sale or mortgaging of her property, but she was not required to publicly approve of her husband's actions or privately affirm that her consent was freely given. In Connecticut, widows had dower rights only in property owned by

their husbands at death, and the colony did not require the wife's signature on deeds of sale or mortgages until 1723. Marylynn Salmon, *Women and the Law of Property in Early America* (Chapel Hill: University of North Carolina Press, 1986), 5–6.

9. Evidence from the probate records of Essex County, Massachusetts, and Hartford, Connecticut, shows that widows were frequently named executors by their husbands and were awarded substantial amounts of land and movable goods. Kim Lacy Rogers, "Relicts of the New World: Conditions of Widowhood in Seventeenth-Century New England," in *Woman's Being, Woman's Place: Female Identity and Vocation in American History*, ed. Mary Kelley (Boston: G. K. Hall & Co., 1979), 26–52. Also, Shammas, Salmon, and Dahlin, *Inheritance in America*, 59–60.

10. On separate estates and jointures in New England, see Salmon, *Women and the Law of Property*, 83, 146. The common law courts of Quaker Pennsylvania enforced marriage settlements that established separate estates for women within marriage. Such marriage settlements were administered by equity courts in other colonies. Without equity courts, married women in Pennsylvania had less chance of having their right to separate estates acknowledged and protected. Salmon, 82.

11. While couples could request that wives be examined privately to ensure the validity of a deed, it was not required by law. Transfers of land or property in Pennsylvania throughout the colonial period merely required the signature of the wife.

William Penn was more concerned about creditors than wives in his colony. Initially, according to "The Great Law of 1683," if a man died in debt, leaving a widow with children, half of his lands were set aside for his creditors. In 1688, the Pennsylvania Assembly passed legislation that placed all lands for use in payment of creditors. See Linda Ford, "William Penn's Views on Women: Subjects of Friendship," *Quaker History* 72 (February 1983): 91. Also, Shammas, Salmon, and Dahlin, *Inheritance in America*, 51.

12. The Puritans' and Quakers' belief in the marital unity of husband and wife also meant that there were no chancery courts, also known as courts of equity, in the colonies of Massachusetts, Connecticut, and Pennsylvania. English chancery courts managed property held in trust for women, free from their husbands' control. For more on the legal rights of *femes covert* in Pennsylvania, see Marylynn Salmon, "Equality or Subversion? Feme Covert Status in Early Pennsylvania," in *Women of America: A History*, ed. Carol R. Berkin and Mary Beth Norton (Boston: Houghton Mifflin, 1979), 92–113.

13. Lorena S. Walsh, "The Experiences and Status of Women in the Chesapeake, 1750–1775," in *The Web of Southern Social Relations: Women, Family, and Education*, ed. Walter J. Fraser, Frank R. Saunders, and Jon L. Wakelyn (Athens: University of Georgia Press, 1985), 5.

Men's high mortality rate and women's scarcity do not completely explain women's greater legal rights in the region. In Jamaica, England's Caribbean island colony, men's mortality was higher and there were even fewer English women than in the Chesapeake. Yet Jamaican planters were far less willing than southern planters to trust their wives as executors of their estates and so appointed male friends. In this colony where African slaves performed most domestic labor, English women's principle purpose was biological—to bear their husbands' male heirs—and they were valued for little else. Consequently, few planters granted their wives more than the dower required by law, and many widows faced destitution unless they quickly remarried. Trevor Burnard, "Inheritance and Independence: Women's Status in Early Colonial Jamaica," *William and Mary Quarterly*, 3d ser., 48 (January 1991): 93–114.

14. In Maryland during the 1660s, nearly 20 percent of men with children left their entire estates to their wives, trusting them to grant their children fair portions of the estate. Some willed their widow all or most of their estate for use during her lifetime, although they specified how it should be distributed after her death. Few men ended their widow's control of the estate if she remarried or when their children came of age. And if a husband did not leave his wife his entire estate, he gave her land, outright, or more than her dower right to one third of his property. Carr and Walsh, "The Planter's Wife," 555–57. Also, Walsh, "Women in the Chesapeake," 4–5.

15. On premarital agreements in the Chesapeake, see Carr and Walsh, "The Planter's Wife," 561. Equity courts administered these estates for women, free from their husbands' control. South Carolina also established equity courts, as did the colony of New York. Salmon, "Equality or Subversion?" in *Women of America*, 92–113.

16. A similar change was reflected in Connecticut, where a law was passed in 1656 that entitled women to dower in both real and personal property. By 1673, however, the law was changed limiting women to dower in real property, only.

In Virginia, women received dower rights in both real and personal property, but by 1673 their dower rights in personal property were restricted. Although the widow retained her one-third share of real property, her right to personal property was limited to a child's portion. The law changed again in 1705. A widow whose husband died without a will was entitled to a full one-third of his personal as well as his real property, regardless of the number of children who survived him, while the minimum personal property that a wife could be willed by her husband was a child's portion if there were two or more surviving children. This act also stated that if the couple was childless, the widow was entitled to half her husband's real and personal property.

In Virginia a man could entail both land and slaves, ensuring that sons who inherited land possessed the slaves to work it. His widow had the use of his slaves only during her lifetime and could not sell them. If she remarried, her husband could use them but not sell them. When she died, these slaves and her dower lands went to her first husband's children. In Maryland, however, widows owned their slaves outright. Both policies resulted from the belief that land without slaves was worthless. The goal was to permit the inheritor to improve the lands during her or his lifetime.

The custom of willing land to sons and slaves to daughters even became the norm on the frontier, where land was abundant. Walsh, "Women in the Chesapeake," 10.

In South Carolina, the largest and richest slave economy in North America, planters relied on the use of jointures, wills, and settlements more often than their northern peers. While usually providing generously for their wives, men frequently placed restrictions on their inheritance. Fearing that his widow's remarriage might deprive his children of their rights to his estate, a husband often limited his widow's use of inherited property. Other provisions prohibited the widow's next husband from outright ownership of inherited slaves, keeping them for the children of the first marriage.

Many South Carolina planters also secured their daughters' inheritance— land and slaves—in trusts to protect it from misuse by their sons-in-law. Other trusts even provided for the descent of property to grandchildren and prohibited sons-in-law from selling the property or slaves. In this way planters controlled property even after they died, reinforcing patriarchy and patrilineality in England's North American colonies.

17. The number of Chesapeake widows named sole heirs of their husbands' estates declined by the end of the century, as did the number of widows named executors and guardians of their children. Carr and Walsh, "The Planter's Wife," 569. Also, Shammas, Salmon, and Dahlin, *Inheritance in America*, 59.

18. As quoted in Salmon, *Women and the Law of Property*, 41.

19. Spruill, *Women's Life and Work in the Southern Colonies*, 347.

20. Ibid.

21. Sophie Drinker, "Women Attorneys of Colonial Times," *Maryland Historical Magazine* 56 (December 1961): 337–38, 347.

22. Drinker, "Women Attorneys of Colonial Times," 347.

23. Ibid., 349–50. See also Spruill, *Women's Life and Work in the Southern Colonies*, 236–41.

24. As quoted in Spruill, *Women's Life and Work in the Southern Colonies*, 239.

25. Spruill, *Women's Life and Work in the Southern Colonies*, 268, 345–46.

26. Other colonies also recognized this problem. Initially, South Carolina courts absolved husbands of the debts incurred by wives who were *feme sole* traders. Later, however, the courts recognized that the working wives needed

their support. They then authorized these women to recover debts themselves, without their husbands' assistance or permission. Most colonies, however, made no special provisions for *feme sole* traders. Instead they utilized other legal customs and laws to address women's need to support their families. A woman whose husband left her, either temporarily or permanently, could draw upon his estate for basic support, and the estate was liable for her debts. If her husband failed to pay her debts, his estate could be seized. It was the responsibility of husbands to support their wives and families unless the wife deserted her husband or was guilty of adultery.

27. Spruill, *Women's Life and Work in the Southern Colonies*, 394. See also, Drinker, "Women Attorneys of Colonial Times," 342–43.

28. Norton, "The Evolution of White Women's Experience," 605.

29. Only about 200 absolute divorces were granted in England by Act of Parliament before 1857. In that year the Matrimonial Causes Act was passed, making divorce available to the general population. Of the absolute divorces granted by Parliament, only six were suits brought by wives. It is believed that more men secured divorces than women because of a sexual double standard: a wife's adultery was viewed as sufficient grounds for divorce, while a man's adultery was not. The Matrimonial Causes Act continued this double standard, granting men divorces on the grounds of their wives' adultery but requiring women to demonstrate their husbands' cruelty or desertion in addition to adultery before granting them divorces.

In England, some unhappy couples privately contracted to live apart rather than legally separate, and they divided their property in agreements drawn up by a third party. Official separations were enforced in equity courts because common law courts did not recognize the validity of a contract between a husband and his wife. Fraser, *The Weaker Vessel*, 297. Also, K. Kelly Weisberg, " 'Under Greet Temptations Heer': Women and Divorce in Puritan Massachusetts," *Feminist Studies* 2 (1975): 185.

30. This settlement was in either personal property or real estate or both. Spruill, *Women's Life and Work*, 342–44.

31. South Carolina women probably had greater autonomy to live separately from their husbands and control their own property within marriage because they were denied the right to absolute divorce. Lawmakers there protected the property of married women, and some widows utilized marriage settlements to protect their property when they remarried in the colony. Lawmakers also permitted postnuptial agreements that allowed couples to live apart and divide their property. The agreement had to be made by a third party, or trustee, because the law did not recognize contracts made between a husband and a wife.

32. Salmon, *Women and the Law of Property*, 68.

33. As quoted in Roger Thompson, *Sex in Middlesex: Popular Mores in a*

Massachusetts County, 1649–1699 (Amherst: University of Massachusetts Press, 1986), 126.

34. New Hampshire also permitted absolute divorces, though fewer were granted there than in the other New England colonies. A part of the colony of Massachusetts until it became a royal province in 1679, New Hampshire assigned the responsibility of hearing divorce proceedings to its county courts, the General Court, and the Court of Assistants. When it became a royal colony in 1681, this authority was delegated to the governor and his council. Though a royal colony, New Hampshire continued to permit annulment for bigamy and sexual incapacity, and absolute divorce for desertion and adultery.

The first divorce petition heard in New Hampshire was brought by Sarah Pearce Mattoon, who accused her husband of "notorious fornication," physical and mental cruelty, and desertion. Although the New Hampshire governor and council did not rule on her petition, she was eventually granted an absolute divorce by the colony of Massachusetts and remarried. The first divorce in the colony was granted to Elizabeth Smart in July 1697, on the grounds of her husband's admitted bigamy. Only two other petitions for divorce were heard before 1754, and both were brought by men: Thomas Holland was granted a divorce from his wife, Elizabeth, on the grounds of her adultery, while Joseph Randall's petition was withdrawn because of insufficient evidence of his wife's adultery. Sheldon S. Cohen, "What Man Hath Put Asunder: Divorce in New Hampshire, 1681–1784," *Historical New Hampshire* 41 (Fall/Winter 1986): 120, 122.

35. Weisberg, " 'Under Greet Temptations Heer,' " 185, says that there were 40 divorces granted in Massachusetts from 1639 to 1692, but Koehler, *A Search For Power*, 153, asserts that during this same period, Massachusetts courts permitted 43 divorces and courts in Connecticut granted 36 petitions. During the period from 1665 to 1689, 19 women in Connecticut petitioned for and received divorces, and one woman received a separation from her husband. While women were 80.9 percent of the petitioners for divorce in Massachusetts, in Connecticut they were 70.5 percent of all petitioners. In New Haven and New Hampshire, only women petitioned for divorce, while in Plymouth Colony, they were just 22.2 percent of all petitioners.

New England women who sued for divorce cited desertion (61.8 percent), adultery and bigamy (44.7 percent), impotence (9.2 percent), a failure to provide (3.8 percent), cruelty or excessive violence (four cases), incest and heresy (one case each) in their petitions. More than one reason was mentioned in almost 30 percent of the women's petitions for divorce. Men cited adultery or bigamy (79 percent), desertion (44.8 percent), cruelty (two cases), refusal to have sex (two cases), incest (one case) in their petitions. Koehler, *A Search for Power*, 152.

Women received divorces in the majority of cases brought before the courts in these colonies. See Koehler's appendix listing all known petitions for divorce by women and men in New England from 1620 until 1690.

Men's embarrassment kept them from seeking legal assistance in ending their wives' adultery with other men. Mary Beth Norton, "Gender, Crime, and Community in Seventeenth-Century Maryland," in *The Transformation of Early American History: Society, Authority, and Ideology,* ed. James Henretta, Michael Kammen, and Stanley Katz (New York: Knopf, 1991), 131.

36. Weisberg, " 'Under Greet Temptations Heer,' " 188.

37. As quoted in Glenda Riley, *Divorce: An American Tradition* (New York: Oxford University Press, 1991), 12. See also Weisberg, " 'Under Greet Temptations Heer,' " 188.

38. William Penn also recognized women's right to divorce on grounds of adultery in the colony of Pennsylvania, but no court was ever created there to grant divorces. A first offense of adultery was punished by a public whipping and one year's imprisonment, and the second offense was punishable by divorce and life imprisonment. Later, the laws against adultery were strengthened. Those found guilty were to be branded with the letter *A,* yet there is little evidence these harsh punishments were ever enforced. Instead, adulterers were fined and sentenced to stand in a public place carrying a sign indicating their offense. Only two women were granted divorces by the Pennsylvania legislature before the American Revolution, one in 1769 and the other in 1772. Ford, "William Penn's Views on Women," 93.

39. Koehler, *A Search for Power,* 147.

40. Offenders in Plymouth Colony and New Hampshire were severely whipped and required to wear the letters *AD* on their clothing, a punishment adopted by New Hampshire in 1680. By 1673, Connecticut had modified its punishment for adultery, whipping offenders and requiring them to wear a halter around their neck. They were also branded on their forehead with the letter *A.* Massachusetts began to modify its punishment for adultery as early as 1638. Severe whipping and banishment from the colony replaced the death penalty for adultery. By 1694, adulterers in Massachusetts were punished by being whipped and being required to stand on the gallows for a few hours, wearing the letter *A* on their clothing. Whipping, branding, public humiliation, and banishment gradually replaced the death penalty and by the end of the century, adulterers in most colonies were merely fined for their offense. See Koehler, *A Search for Power,* 148. Also, Thompson, *Sex in Middlesex,* 203 n. 15.

41. As quoted in Norton, "Gender, Crime, and Community in Seventeenth-Century Maryland," 132. Thompson, *Sex in Middlesex,* 142, identifies the origins of the term *cuckold* in the habit of the cuckoo bird: "The illicit introduction into the nest of a cuckoo which would deprive legitimate fledglings of their rightful inheritance was commonly dwelt on as a peculiarly feminine

act of injustice. Indeed, in folklore, that perennial figure of derision and unease—the cuckold—had no female equivalent."

42. As quoted in Elizabeth Pleck, *Domestic Tyranny: The Making of American Social Policy against Family Violence from Colonial Times to the Present* (New York: Oxford University Press, 1987), 21–22.

43. Koehler, *A Search for Power*, 49.

44. As quoted in Pleck, *Domestic Tyranny*, 18.

45. As quoted in Flaherty, *Privacy in Colonial New England*, 59.

46. As quoted in Pleck, *Domestic Tyranny*, 21. See also, Pleck, 22–25, 27–29.

47. Flaherty, *Privacy in Colonial New England*, 59. On the Dutton case, see Thompson, *Sex in Middlesex*, 121–22, and on wife beating in general, 119–23.

48. In the colony of Rhode Island couples could sue for separation or divorce on the grounds of the husband's physical abuse as well as the wife's failure to be an adequate "helpmeet." Of the 24 petitioners seeking divorce or separation in Rhode Island from 1644 to 1697, 16 were granted their request. There, unlike the other New England colonies, abusive husbands were punished more severely than abusive wives. Koehler, *A Search for Power*, 320–21. But Pleck, *Domestic Tyranny*, 29, asserts that as religious orthodoxy declined in New England during the seventeenth century, so too did prosecutions for family violence. Without a community to support or defend them, battered women were isolated in abusive households, with little hope of escape. And, as the English government insisted on conformity to its laws in the region, men regained complete authority over their wives and children.

49. As quoted in Barbara S. Lindemann, "'To Ravish and Carnally Know': Rape in Eighteenth-Century Massachusetts," *Signs: Journal of Women in Culture and Society* 10 (Autumn 1984): 64. Seven-year-old Elizabeth Stowe was accused of encouraging her Native American rapist by her "wanton & uncivill carridges." See Thompson, *Sex in Middlesex*, 74, for a discussion of this case.

50. Rape was also viewed as a property crime in Pennsylvania. There the convicted rapist of an unmarried woman was sentenced to forfeit one-third of his estate to her father. If she had no parents, or was a widow, she received his estate. If she was married, it was granted to her husband. The rapist was also whipped and served a year of hard labor. In 1700 the law was revised to include castration and branding with the letter *R*. Ford, "William Penn's Views on Women," 93.

51. At least 72 men were brought before Puritan authorities in seventeenth-century New England on charges of rape or attempted rape. Their unconsenting accusers included 26 unwed servants, 35 wives, and 8 children between the ages of 3 and 13. Only 6 men were executed for their crime, 5 in Massachusetts and 1 in Connecticut. Factors influencing conviction and

punishment of rapists were the age and marital status of the victim. Damages were awarded to victims of rape in only four known cases in New England, and the amounts awarded to these women were quite low. When the crime was committed against a man's wife, however, the husband received a much higher award. Catherine Baker, "Sexual Assaults in Seventeenth-Century Massachusetts," first draft of an unpublished manuscript, 12 December 1974, 19–20.

Thompson, *Sex in Middlesex*, 75–80, sees rape as an erotic act rather than an expression of power or dominance. He minimizes its violence and states that women were often "less than unwilling" victims. He interprets women's attempts to defend themselves from their attackers as proof that New England was not a patriarchy and that women were not cowed into submission by men.

It is probable that rape victims understood that their charges would be taken more seriously if they testified that they tried to resist their attackers. This was because the courts were reluctant to implement the death penalty and inclined to charge both parties—the rapist and his victim—with fornication, instead. Thus, many women were doubly victimized—by their male attacker and by the courts reluctant to condemn him to death for his crime. Little wonder, then, that rape was probably underreported in New England, especially during the latter part of the century as Puritan influence in the region declined.

52. Koehler, *A Search for Power*, 91–107. Lindemann, " 'To Ravish and Carnally Know,' " 80–81, found there was a higher conviction rate when the alleged rapist was of lower social standing than his victim, when he was non-white, or when the victim was a married woman who resisted her attacker. She asserts that the higher conviction rate of men accused of raping married women affirms the theory that rape was viewed as an offense "not against a woman so much as against her father or husband."

53. Connecticut had the most liberal divorce policy in England's American colonies. There women were also granted absolute divorces with the right to remarry on the grounds of cruelty, adultery, a three-year desertion, or seven years' absence without word. (In the latter case, the absence was presumed unintentional and possibly indicated an unreported death.) Absolute divorce permitted women to act as *feme sole* traders, and this minimized the need for special legislation permitting married women to support themselves or to control property. As a result, however, the courts of the colony did not recognize a married woman's right to an estate separate from her husband. Alison Duncan Hirsch, "The Thrall Divorce Case: A Family Crisis in Eighteenth-Century Connecticut," in *Women, Family, and Community in Colonial America: Two Perspectives*, with an introduction by Carol Berkin (New York: Haworth Press, 1983), 43–75.

54. Between 1656 and 1664, seven women petitioned the Massachusetts

Court for divorce, as compared with seven between the years 1630 and 1655 and three from 1665 to 1675. One of the two women in Plymouth Colony who petitioned for divorce did so in 1661 during the era of Quaker unrest. In Connecticut, where Quakers chose not to challenge the established authorities, there was no significant increase in female divorce petitions. Koehler, *A Search for Power*, 254.

55. Norton, "The Evolution of White Women's Experience," 61, Koehler, *A Search for Power*, 345–54, and Karlsen, *The Devil in the Shape of a Woman*, 273–93.

56. Koehler, *A Search for Power*, 347–49, discusses this upsurge in the prosecution of female criminals in New England. Before 1644, Massachusetts women were tried for less than 15 percent of all crimes, but from 1665 to 1689 women were charged with nearly 23 percent of all crimes. The increase in the number of women tried for crimes was disproportionate to their number in New England's population.

57. Norton, "The Evolution of White Women's Experience," 611.

58. As quoted in Koehler, *A Search for Power*, 354.

59. Norton, "Gender, Crime, and Community in Seventeenth-Century Maryland," 141.

60. Ibid., 144–48. On the role of midwives in New England trials, see Thompson, *Sex in Middlesex*, 22–24, 33, 196.

61. In fact, the 1692 Salem witchcraft trials were remarkable for the number of men executed for witchcraft. There were 14 women and 5 men hanged for their crime. Many other women and some men died in prison while awaiting trial, and Giles Corey died while being tortured. Although the majority of women accused at Salem were married, their percentage of the accused was actually lower than the norm. This was because more young, single women—often related to the suspected witch—were accused during that outbreak. Karlsen, *The Devil in the Shape of a Woman*, 41, 47–51, 64, 71.

62. Although separated, divorced, widowed, and deserted women made up only about 20 percent of all women in seventeenth-century New England, they were disproportionately represented among the accused. Karlsen, *The Devil in the Shape of a Woman*, 73. Demos, *Entertaining Satan: Witchcraft and the Culture of Early New England* (New York: Oxford University Press, 1982), 246–47, explores the role of gossip in New England witchcraft accusations.

63. Karlsen, *The Devil in the Shape of a Woman*, 101.

64. Women whose marriages produced only daughters or no children at all were also vulnerable to accusation. For data on the relationship between women's family background, their inheritance status, and their vulnerability to witchcraft accusation, see Karlsen, *The Devil in the Shape of a Woman*, 77–116, especially, 102. On patterns of paternal longevity, land availability, and the inheritance of sons, see Daniel S. Smith, "Parental Power and Marriage Pat-

terns: An Analysis of Historical Trends in Hingham, Massachusetts," *Journal of Marriage and the Family* 35 (August 1973): 422–24, and Greven, *Four Generations*, 125–72. On the psychology of men in young adulthood and their role in witchcraft accusations, see Demos, *Entertaining Satan*, 156–57.

65. On the economic basis for witchcraft accusation, see Karlsen, *The Devil in the Shape of a Woman*, 77–116. For a case study of Katherine Harrison, see Karlsen, 84–89.

66. Dutch men transported many legal customs from the Netherlands to North America. They trusted the financial abilities of their wives and typically willed all of their property to them for their widowhood. They postponed their children's inheritance until their widows' remarriage or death. A Dutch widow inherited at least one-half of the estate if the couple had children and often the entire estate if the children were young. When she died, the estate was divided equally between her children, regardless of their gender. In a joint will written by Lawrence Zacharison Sluijs and his wife, Annetie Oenen, for example, the couple acknowledged that they had "gained together their estate," and they together gave the survivor of their marriage all their common property. Their two children, then both minors, were to inherit only after both parents died. This will was drawn up in 1685 and enforced by the English court in the colony of New York. David E. Narrett, "Men's Wills and Women's Property Rights in Colonial New York," in *Women in the Age of the American Revolution*, ed. Ronald Hoffman and Peter J. Albert (Charlottesville: University Press of Virginia, 1989), 100, 104–5.

67. Dutch women's rights were derived from the Justinian Code of the sixth century, which was adopted in parts of the Netherlands during the seventh century. Dutch jurists had incorporated aspects of Roman law into their legal system because they admired its logic, clarity, and comprehensiveness. The Dutch merchants of the provinces of Friesland and Holland adopted this law, and, because they were deeply involved in the trade of both the Dutch East and West India Companies, they transported it to the colonies and trading posts they established around the world. Although many women in New Netherland had *manus* marriages, they could change their marital status by renouncing "all laws, statutes, and customs which have been made in favor of woman," meaning those which granted her the protection of her husband. Biemer, *Women and Property in Colonial New York*, 3.

68. Biemer, *Women and Property in Colonial New York*, 6, 7, and Narrett, "Men's Wills and Women's Property," 103.

69. Biemer, *Women and Property in Colonial New York*, 56.

70. Narrett, "Men's Wills and Women's Property," 106–9.

71. With English conquest, the property rights of a widow whose husband died without a will were defined in accordance with the English common law. She received one-third of his personal property after his estate honored his

debts and was entitled to use of one-third of his real estate during her lifetime. While a husband could not deprive his wife of dower without her permission, he could grant her personal property in lieu of dower. She, however, could claim her dower rights instead of this grant on his death.

Between 1664 and 1725, Dutch men who wrote wills gave their wives all or most of their property as long as they remained widows and required that their children wait for their inheritance until their mother had either remarried or died. It was understood that widows would continue the practice of giving all children, regardless of gender, an equal portion of the property when they reached the age of 21 or married to assist them in establishing their own household. Some husbands granted their wives the power to manage their estates, permitting them to sell the land, but it was assumed a widow's property was held in trust for the next generation rather than hers alone. Narrett, "Men's Wills and Women's Property," 104–5.

72. During the first 30 years of English control, three-fourths of all men of Dutch ancestry named their wives as sole executors of their estates, but by the middle of the eighteenth century fewer than one-quarter of all men did so. Narrett, "Men's Wills and Women's Property," 101.

73. Narrett, "Men's Wills and Women's Property," 112–18, and Biemer, *Women and Property in Colonial New York*, 9.

74. Staves, *Married Women's Separate Property in England*, 4.

75. The major proponent of the golden age theory regarding English women's legal status in the American colonies was Morris, *Studies in the History of American Law*, 126–200.

Chapter 5

1. On women's attraction to Puritanism, see Amanda Porterfield, *Female Piety in Puritan New England: The Emergence of Religious Humanism* (New York: Oxford University Press, 1992), 108. On the models for Puritan women in northern New England see Ulrich, *Good Wives*. On Quaker women see Levy, *Quakers and the American Family*, 193–230.

2. Bradstreet, "To My Dear Children," *The Works of Anne Bradstreet in Prose and Verse*, 5.

3. Ibid. On Bradstreet's perceptions of God, see Wendy Martin, "Anne Bradstreet's Poetry: A Study of Subversive Piety," in *Shakespeare's Sisters: Feminist Essays on Women Poets*, ed. Sandra M. Gilbert and Susan Gubar (Bloomington: Indiana University Press, 1979), 22–23.

4. As quoted in Martin, "Anne Bradstreet's Poetry," 23.

5. Bradstreet, "To My Dear Children," *The Works of Anne Bradstreet in Prose and Verse*, 5.

6. Bradstreet, "Meditations," *The Works of Anne Bradstreet in Prose and Verse*, 56.

7. In 1618, Mary Robinson, a wealthy London widow, designated £200 toward building a church in the young colony of Virginia, while in 1684 Elizabeth Daniell purchased and distributed Bibles to men in the colony in hopes of improving their spiritual condition. Other women were benefactors of their local churches, donating money, plate, and furnishings for use by the minister and congregation. For example, in 1689 Affra Coming of Charles Town, South Carolina, donated 17 acres of land as a parish lot for use by the Anglican minister. Spruill, *Women's Life and Work in the Southern Colonies*, 247, and Alice E. Mathews, "The Religious Experience of Southern Women," in *Women and Religion in America: The Colonial and Revolutionary Periods, A Documentary History*, ed. Rosemary Radford Ruether and Rosemary Skinner Keller (San Francisco: Harper & Row, 1983), 2:195.

8. As quoted in Spruill, *Women's Life and Work in the Southern Colonies*, 246. In 1685, colonist Mary Taney chastised the Archbishop of Canterbury for neglecting his "stray flock" in Maryland, requesting that he allocate monies for building and staffing an Anglican church there. Allegedly the king contributed money for building the first Anglican church in the colony. But in 1691 the Maryland assembly voted to make the Church of England the established church in the colony and in 1715 passed an act denying widows the right to rear their own children if they were Catholic or had married men of the Catholic faith. Mathews, "The Religious Experience of Southern Women," 2:195.

9. On the role played by women in fostering the expansion of religion in New England, see Ulrich, *Good Wives*, 215–35.

10. While initially church membership decisions rested with the church elders, by the end of the seventeenth century ministers assumed this responsibility. By 1700, men were also examined privately, their testimony read before the Congregation by the church elders. Flaherty, *Privacy in Colonial New England*, 143–44.

11. As quoted in Flaherty, *Privacy in Colonial New England*, 140–41.

12. On "tales of grace," see Charles Lloyd Cohen, *God's Caress: The Psychology of Puritan Religious Experience* (New York: Oxford University Press, 1986), 201–41. Cohen also explores gender differences in conversion narratives. He found that women's narratives were shorter than men's and that women referred to their children more often than men. Women more often confessed to the sin of sloth, while men confessed to the sin of pride. Cohen, *God's Caress*, 222.

13. 1 Cor. 14:34

14. Ulrich, *Goodwives*, 219–23.

15. As quoted in Koehler, *A Search for Power*, 216–17.

16. Ibid., 222.

17. Titus 2:3–4.

18. Koehler, *A Search for Power*, 223, 230.

19. As quoted in Koehler, *A Search for Power*, 224.

20. Ibid., 226.

21. John Winthrop, *Winthrop's Journal*, *"History of New England,"* *1630–1649*, ed. James Kendall Hosmer (New York, 1908), 2:138. For an account of Anne Hutchinson's life, see Emery Battis, *Saints and Sectaries: Anne Hutchinson and the Antinomian Controversy in the Massachusetts Bay Colony* (Chapel Hill: University of North Carolina Press, 1962).

22. Koehler, *A Search for Power*, 227.

23. For the transcript of Hibbens's excommunication from the First Church of Boston, see "Proceedings of Excommunication against Mistress Ann Hibbens of Boston (1640)," in *Remarkable Providences: 1600–1760*, ed. John Demos (New York: George Braziller, 1972), 222–39. For a discussion of the Hibbens case see Koehler, *A Search for Power*, 206.

24. A woman of wealth, she bequeathed most of her £344 estate to three sons living in England. Karlsen, *The Devil in the Shape of a Woman*, 28.

25. Lady Moody established a cooperative relationship with Dutch governor Peter Stuyvesant, much to the annoyance of New England authorities. Biemer, *Women and Property in Colonial New York*, 11–31. See also Koehler, *A Search for Power*, 240–43.

26. In seventeenth-century England and America, *thou* was used when speaking to someone of inferior station. Its use by members of the Society of Friends emphasized the equality of all people, regardless of class or gender. The Society of Friends also liberated its members from the authority of both ministers and magistrates. They espoused the separation of church and state, refused to swear oaths, opposed payment of tithes to support an established church, and insisted on their own form of marriage. Mary Maples Dunn, "Women of Light," in *Women of America: A History*, ed. Carol R. Berkin and Mary Beth Norton (Boston: Houghton Mifflin, 1979), 125–26.

27. As quoted in Fraser, *The Weaker Vessel*, 264.

28. Levy, *Quakers and the American Family*, 193.

29. Of the 59 Quaker missionaries in North America between 1656 and 1663, 26 were women, all but four of whom were unmarried. Spinsters and older women free from family responsibilities were the religious group's greatest proselytizers. Dunn, "Women of Light," in *Women of America: A History*, 118.

30. As quoted in Fraser, *The Weaker Vessel*, 358.

31. The greatest influence on the role of women in the Society of Friends was Margaret Fell. The "nursing mother" of the Quaker faith, Fell personally inspired George Fox's beliefs about women's spirituality, and her writings influenced the actions of many Quaker women and men who traveled to and settled in the American colonies. Born in 1614, Margaret Askew was a wealthy young woman of good family when she married a much older man, Judge Fell.

Her marriage was happy, and she bore her husband eight children—seven daughters and one son. But, after hearing George Fox preach, she concluded, "either I must displease my husband, or offend God," and joined the Society of Friends. Although Judge Fell never became a Quaker, he supported his wife's beliefs and activities in behalf of the Friends. Margaret's social position and her modest manner helped dispel the image of Quakers as disorderly women. After she was widowed in 1658, she devoted her life and her considerable fortune to the advancement of the Quaker faith. In 1669 she married Fox and served as the society's executive secretary, corresponding with women missionaries in the American colonies. H. Larry Ingle, "A Quaker Woman on Women's Roles: Mary Penington to Friends, 1678," *Signs: Journal of Women in Culture and Society* 16 (Spring 1991): 588. See also Fraser, *The Weaker Vessel,* 357.

32. Koehler, *A Search for Power,* 247.

33. Horatio Rogers, *Mary Dyer of Rhode Island, the Quaker Martyr that Was Hanged on Boston Common* (Providence, R.I.: Preston and Rounds, 1896), 96–97.

34. Dyer's death inspired another Quaker woman to voyage to New England. Elizabeth Hooten was nearly 50 years of age when she joined the Society of Friends after hearing George Fox preach. The wife of a prosperous farmer, she left her husband and family to testify to her faith throughout England and was often imprisoned for disturbing the peace. When word of Mary Dyer's execution in Massachusetts reached England, she resolved to challenge the authorities there. Her husband's death in 1661 left her a wealthy widow and enabled her to make the voyage. But when she arrived in Boston, she was taken to Governor Endicott, who proclaimed her a witch and ordered her imprisonment.

King Charles II, angered by this brutal treatment, barred the Massachusetts Court from administering corporal and capital punishment in cases involving Quakers. Instead, the court ordered Hooten and other imprisoned Quakers "to be driven out of [Boston] by men and horses, armed with swords and staffs and weapons of war, who went along with us near two days' journey in the wilderness." There they were abandoned to fend for themselves. Eventually, Hooten and the others reached the colony of Rhode Island. She continued her missionary activities in the Caribbean, Virginia, and England, and eventually returned to Massachusetts, armed with a permit issued by Charles II, himself. Although she was arrested many times and severely punished for her activities, she preached in the colony for five years. Hooten returned to England in 1670, but the New World beckoned the septuagenarian once more. In 1671, she returned to the West Indies with George Fox, visiting Barbados and Jamaica, where she died. Fraser, *The Weaker Vessel,* 358–65.

35. Kai T. Erikson, *Wayward Puritans: A Study in the Sociology of Deviance* (New York: John Wiley and Sons, 1966), 125.

36. As quoted in Ingle, "A Quaker Woman on Women's Roles," 595. The foundation of the Society of Friends in England and America was the local meeting. At the local level, Quakers met on a regular basis for worship and meditation at their meetinghouse, where seating was segregated by sex. There male and female Friends in good standing met to discuss business matters on a monthly basis. The monthly meeting disciplined its members, aided those in need of spiritual as well as temporal assistance, reviewed marriage petitions, and oversaw maintenance of the meeting house. The monthly meeting sent representatives to a quarterly meeting, and the quarterly meeting sent representatives to a yearly meeting. During the late seventeenth and early eighteenth centuries New Jersey and Pennsylvania Quakers created separate men's and women's meetings at the monthly, quarterly, and yearly meeting levels. For more on women's meetings in England, see Ingle, "A Quaker Woman on Women's Roles," 591.

37. While women's meetings were never completely accepted by English Quakers, North American Quakers were more enthusiastic about the practice. Women who presided over the meetings were empowered through their traditional roles as wives and mothers. Most were wives of prominent Quaker men. They tended to be relatively affluent and employed servants or slaves to assist them with their household chores. Most became active as their childbearing and childrearing responsibilities waned, and some served as elders at the women's meetings for 20 years or more. Jean R. Soderlund, "Women's Authority in Pennsylvania and New Jersey Quaker Meetings, 1680–1760," *William and Mary Quarterly*, 3d ser., 44 (October 1987): 722–49. On William Penn's attitudes and beliefs about women, see Ford, "William Penn's Views on Women," 75–102.

38. Charles Town, South Carolina, and Savannah, Georgia, also attracted settlers of all faiths, even Sephardic and Ashkenazic Jews. A ritual bath, a *mikveh*, was built for the women of Savannah by the men of their religious faith in 1738. Although many of these Jewish settlers later left the southern colonies, they established ties with others of their faith in North America and in England's Caribbean colonies. Mathews, "The Religious Experience of Southern Women," 2:197.

39. On the role of religion in the enslavement of Africans by Europeans, see Winthrop D. Jordan, *White over Black: American Attitudes Towards the Negro, 1550–1812* (Chapel Hill: University of North Carolina Press, 1968), 17–19, 20–24, 50, 73, 179–87, 190–93.

40. Lillian Ashcraft Webb, "Black Women and Religion in the Colonial Period," in *Women and Religion in America*, 2:235–36.

41. Warren Billings, "The Cases of Fernando and Elizabeth Key: A Note on the Status of Blacks in Seventeenth-Century Virginia," *William and Mary Quarterly*, 3d. ser., 30 (July 1973): 467–74. See also Mathews, "The Religious Experience of Southern Women," 2:209–10.

42. Webb, "Black Women and Religion," 2:237.

43. The great Puritan migration from England to North America lasted from 1620 until the outbreak of the Civil Wars in England. Immigration slowed during the Commonwealth period when some colonists even returned to the mother country. Migration resumed with the Restoration in 1661, but these new colonists did not share the religious zeal of their predecessors.

The population of Massachusetts in 1634 was 15,000 and by 1665 had grown to 23,467. In 1680 there were 42,000 residents in the colony; by 1690 nearly 50,000 people lived there. Boston, 25 percent larger than any other city in New England's North American colonies, had approximately 5,000 residents by 1690. Koehler, *A Search for Power*, 339, 376 n. 8.

44. From 1660 until 1689, women were between 55.2 and 67.1 percent of all new church members in Massachusetts; by the end of the century they dominated membership lists of the region's churches. Koehler, *A Search for Power*, 379 n. 76. See also Martha Tomhave Blauvelt and Rosemary Skinner Keller, "Women and Revivalism: The Puritan and Wesleyan Traditions," in *Women and Religion in America*, 2:317. On the feminization of New England church membership, see Gerald F. Moran, " 'Sisters' in Christ: Women and the Church in Seventeenth-Century New England," in *Women in American Religion*, ed. Janet Wilson James (College Park: University of Pennsylvania Press, 1980), 47–65. On women's church membership and the half-way covenant, see Robert G. Pope, *The Half-Way Covenant: Church Membership in Puritan New England* (Princeton: Princeton University Press, 1969), 213–14, 217–18, 225.

45. Mary Rowlandson, "The Narrative of the Captivity and Restoration of Mrs. Mary Rowlandson," as quoted in Nancy Woloch, *Women and the American Experience* (New York: Alfred A. Knopf, 1984), 4.

46. Rowlandson, "The Narrative," 15. See also Ulrich, *Good Wives*, 174, 202–35, on Mary Rowlandson's captivity. Porterfield, *Female Piety in Puritan New England*, 138–44, discusses how Rowlandson viewed her captivity as a vehicle for salvation, likening her suffering to the suffering of Christ.

47. During the first 26 years of settlement, there were no formal accusations of witchcraft made in New England. The first was made in Virginia, where the settlers' anxieties about witchcraft were probably fueled in part by their fears of the region's Native Americans, who nearly destroyed the colony in 1622. Richard Beale Davis, "The Devil in Virginia in the Seventeenth Century," *The Virginia Magazine of History and Biography* 65 (April 1957): 138–41.

48. The authorities on witchcraft in colonial New England, including the outbreak at Salem, Massachusetts, in 1691–92, include Erikson, *Wayward Puritans*, Karlsen, *The Devil in the Shape of a Woman*, and Paul Boyer and Stephen Nissenbaum, *Salem Possessed: The Social Origins of Witchcraft* (Cambridge: Harvard University Press, 1974).

49. "Religion is supplicative, magic is manipulative," according to Richard Godbeer, *The Devil's Dominion: Magic and Religion in Early New England* (Cambridge: Cambridge University Press, 1992), 9. For an excellent discussion of the fine line between religion and magic in New England, see especially, Godbeer, 24–54. Most people ignored the incompatibility of these two belief systems, and few attempted to reconcile them. For further information on the role of witchcraft belief and its relationship to religion in colonial New England, see Richard Weisman, *Witchcraft, Magic, and Religion in Seventeenth-Century Massachusetts* (Amherst: University of Massachusetts Press, 1984), and David D. Hall, *Worlds of Wonder, Days of Judgment: Popular Religions Belief in Early New England* (Cambridge, Mass.: Harvard University Press, 1989).

50. As quoted in Ehrenreich and English, *Witches, Midwives, and Nurses,* 12–13.

51. Davis, "The Devil in Virginia," 138–41.

52. John Winthrop as quoted in *Witch-hunting in Seventeenth-Century New England: A Documentary History, 1638–1692* ed. David D. Hall (Boston: Northeastern University Press, 1991), 20. Although Anne Hutchinson and Mary Dyer were informally accused of witchcraft, neither was brought to trial. Alice Young was the first woman tried as a witch in Puritan New England. She was found guilty and executed in Windsor, Connecticut, on 26 May 1647. Between 1647 and 1663, a period of extreme anxiety about witchcraft in New England, at least 79 people, 61 of them women, were accused of witchcraft in Hartford, Connecticut. Of those, 15—including 13 women—were found guilty of the crime and executed. The two men executed were husbands of women found guilty of witchcraft. Karlsen, *The Devil in the Shape of a Woman,* 20.

53. On the vulnerability of women with unusual childbearing histories to witchcraft accusation, see Demos, *Entertaining Satan,* 73. Margaret Jones, who in 1648 became the first woman executed for witchcraft in Boston, was, like Jane Hawkins, a midwife and healer. But, Demos, 80–81, argues that women identified as nurses and midwives were no more suspect than their peers. In his study of pre-Salem witchcraft, he states that "only two people in the entire suspect-group can be plausibly associated with the regular practice of midwifery" and that the majority of midwives were never charged with witchcraft. He concedes, however, that many women later accused of witchcraft might have served their communities as unofficial midwives and healers and that witchcraft charges often developed from childbirth cases where the accused was present in a supportive capacity.

54. Demos, *Entertaining Satan,* 84–86, 285–92. For more on the class of accused witches, see Karlsen, *The Devil in the Shape of a Woman,* 77–79. Karlsen, 298 n. 6, disputes Demos's contention that there was a marked change in the economic status of those accused of witchcraft from the earlier years to the Salem outbreak. She contends that social and economic status can be different

things and remarks on the difficulties of determining women's economic status during the colonial period.

55. The trials resulted in the deaths of 22 people: 19 were executed for the crime of witchcraft, one man, Giles Corey, died as a consequence of torture used to force him to plead his guilt or innocence, and two of the accused died in jail before standing trial. Erikson, *Wayward Puritans*, 149.

56. Ann Carr Putnam, her daughter, and her servant, Mercy Lewis, soon fell victim to mysterious disorders. While the young Ann was one of the most vocal of the "afflicted girls," her mother was the first adult prostrated by fits. Thomas Putnam also played a central role in the outbreak. Eager to blame others for his problems and to reclaim a position of authority in the community, he testified against 12 people accused of witchcraft and signed petitions against 24 of the accused. His daughter accused more than 21 people during the course of the outbreak. Many of those accused by the Putnams were related, directly or indirectly, to the Porter family. Anne Kibbey, "Mutations of the Supernatural: Witchcraft, Remarkable Providences, and the Power of Puritan Men," *American Quarterly* 34 (Summer 1982): 143–45.

57. Karlsen, *The Devil in the Shape of a Woman*, 226–27.

58. Ibid., 36–37, and Boyer and Nissenbaum, *Salem Possessed*, 1–3.

59. Boyer and Nissenbaum, *Salem Possessed*, 204–6.

60. Tituba was not the first woman of color accused of witchcraft in colonial New England. Earlier, an African servant named Marja had been accused of arson in Roxbury, Massachusetts. Unlike the men accused with her, she was executed for her crime because it was believed her actions were "instigated by the divil." Webb, "Black Women and Religion," 2:237.

61. On the use of countermagic in New England, see Godbeer, *The Devil's Dominion*, 24–55, esp. 44.

62. On Mary Black, see Robert C. Twombly and Robert H. Moore, "Black Puritan: The Negro in Seventeenth-Century Massachusetts," *William and Mary Quarterly*, 2d ser., 24 (April 1967): 228–29. On Tituba, see Karlsen, *The Devil in the Shape of a Woman*, 37, and Webb, "Black Women and Religion," 2:237–38, 246–48. Also, Boyer and Nissenbaum, *Salem Possessed*, 181. Tituba was eventually freed but sold to pay her jail expenses.

The imagery found in accounts of the afflicted girls' behavior has a strong Caribbean flavor. Their repeated references to yellow birds and snakes, images prevalent in Caribbean and West African religions, demonstrate they had some contact with these religions, possibly through Tituba. Also, their references to being pricked by pins give evidence of familiarity with the sympathetic magic, voodoo, practiced by many in the Caribbean islands.

The conspicuous role played by Tituba in the Salem trials later inspired Cotton Mather to address the spiritual needs of the colony's slaves. In 1693, Mather organized a weekly school and worship service for them, perhaps hoping to minimize the threat they appeared to pose as "heathens" in a Christian community.

63. How Puritan colonists in New England used "deviant" behavior to affirm their own values is discussed by Erikson, *Wayward Puritans*, 3–29.

64. Karlsen, *The Devil in the Shape of a Woman*, 248, discusses the relationship between the afflicted or possessed girls and the accused. She states: "[d]uring their brief respite from powerlessness, the possessed continued to blame both themselves and other (older, seemingly more independent and powerful) women for their condition. In their fits, most of their anger was directed inward, on themselves, and, more overtly, outward on women their culture designated as their arch-enemies."

65. That a quarter of those accused were men distinguishes this outbreak from others, in which men were much less likely to be targeted. Believed more susceptible to Satan's lure since Eve's temptation in the Garden of Eden, women were four times more likely than men to be accused of witchcraft. And their husbands, sons, and daughters were also more likely to be accused of the crime than nonrelatives. Karlsen, *The Devil in the Shape of a Woman*, xii, also estimates that four-fifths of the tens of thousands of women executed as witches in Europe and North America were women. See also *Witch-hunting in Seventeenth-Century New England*, 6–7, for estimates on the ratio of accused women to men.

66. As quoted in Flaherty, *Privacy in Colonial New England*, 230.

67. It is possible that the afflicted girls were led by their male interrogators to identify as witches men whose behavior violated the norms of the community. If so, the girls were manipulated by some men to accuse other men, and the women with whom the men were associated, of witchcraft. Kibbey, "Mutations of the Supernatural," 148.

68. Cotton Mather as quoted in Blauvelt and Keller, "Women and Revivalism," 2:318.

69. Cotton Mather, *Ornaments for the Daughters of Zion*, 47.

70. Proverbs 31:10–31.

71. Laurel Thatcher Ulrich, "'Vertuous Women Found': New England Ministerial Literature 1578–1735," *American Quarterly* 28 (January 1976): 34–35.

72. On Hannah Dunston's experience and Mather's sanitized interpretation of it see, Ulrich, *Good Wives*, 167–83.

73. For a wonderful telling of Eunice Williams's tale, see John Demos, *The Unredeemed Captive: A Family Story from Early America* (New York: Alfred A Knopf, 1994).

74. Margaret W. Masson, "The Typology of the Female as a Model for the Regenerate: Puritan Preaching, 1690–1730." *Signs: Journal of Women in Culture and Society* 2 (Winter 1976): 309.

75. Jonathan Edwards, "Sarah Pierrepont," in *Jonathan Edwards: Basic*

Writings, ed. Ola Elizabeth Winslow (New York: New American Library, 1966), 66–67. On how Sarah Pierrepont Edwards was the model for the conversions Edwards sought to inspire during the Great Awakening, see Patricia J. Tracy, *Jonathan Edwards, Pastor: Religion and Society in Eighteenth-Century Northampton* (New York: Hill and Wang, 1979), 62. Tracy contends that Edwards envied his wife's holiness and was never able to achieve the "blissful resignation to God's will" that Sarah experienced, 140–41.

Afterword

1. This sentiment was best expressed about women on a much later frontier by John Mack Faragher, *Women and Men on the Overland Trail* (New Haven: Yale University Press, 1979), 174, who wrote: "If we are to judge them not by our standards but their own, we will not resurrect and applaud every little act of womanly resistance and mean feminine spirit but examine and attempt to understand the powers of endurance that permitted them to act out the role of goodwife through the whole hated experience." On confronting the problem of reading back into earlier eras the sentiments of our own, Julie Roy Jeffrey, *Frontier Women: The Trans-Mississippi West, 1840–1880* (New York: Hill and Wang, 1979), xv–xvi, remarked: "I hoped to find that pioneer women used the frontier as a means of liberating themselves from stereotypes and behaviors which I found constricting and sexist. I discovered that they did not . . . I now have great sympathy for the choices these women made and admiration for their strength and courage. I have continually wondered whether any of us would have done as well."

BIBLIOGRAPHICAL ESSAY

Prior to publication of Mary Beth Norton's article "The Evolution of White Women's Experience in Early America" in the *American Historical Review* 89 (June 1984), historians theorized that the seventeenth century was a golden age for women in the American colonies. Chief among those advocating this view of women's experience were Elisabeth Anthony Dexter, *Colonial Women of Affairs* (New York: Houghton Mifflin, 1924)), and Richard B. Morris, *Studies in the History of American Law* (New York: Columbia University Press, 1930). More recently, Roger Thompson, *Women in Tudor and Stuart England and America* (Boston: Routledge & Kegan Paul, 1974), also asserted this theory. Later historians have recognized that the subject of women's lives in early America requires closer scrutiny.

The search for women's experience in seventeenth-century American history has utilized archaeological studies as well as demographic data to reconstruct women's lives. It requires an understanding of family history in England and America, for the family was the centerpiece of women's lives in this era. It also requires investigation of precolonial Native Americans and the cultures of preslavery West Africa. Women's experience may also be extrapolated from studies of the law and religion in seventeenth-century England and America, and the legal and church records of the colonies they helped establish. Although primary materials written by and for women, and the artifacts they produced, are scarce, those that have survived reveal the richness and complexity of the lives they led in early America.

General Works on Women and Families in Seventeenth-Century England

The best studies devoted to understanding women's lives in England prior to the English colonization of North America include Antonia Fraser, *The Weaker Vessel* (New York: Alfred A. Knopf, 1984), and *Women in English Society: 1500–1800*, edited by Mary Prior (New York: Methuen, 1985), which contains a number of articles exploring a wide variety of issues shaping women's lives in England during this period. *Connecting Spheres: Women in the Western World, 1500 to the Present*, edited by Marilyn Boxer and Jean H. Quataert (Oxford University Press, 1987), also contains articles written about women in the English economy and society during this century, and Alice Clarke, *Working Life of Women in the Seventeenth Century* (London: Frank Cass and Co., 1919; reprint, New York: A. M. Kelley, 1968), although dated, remains valuable on the subject of women in the economy. Susan Staves, *Married Women's Separate Property in England, 1600–1833* (Cambridge: Harvard University Press, 1990), explores women's rights under the law in seventeenth-century England, while *Marriage and Society: Studies in the Social History of Marriage*, edited by R. B. Outhwaite (New York: St. Martin's Press, 1981), contains articles on women and marriage in England during this period.

Lawrence Stone, *The Family, Sex, and Marriage in England, 1500–1800* (New York: Harper and Row, Publishers, 1979), was a pathbreaking work in its effort to establish a basic understanding of the forces affecting the English family in this period. Refining, and often contradicting, Stone's theories on family development in England are Ralph A. Houlbrooke, *The English Family: 1450–1700* (New York: Longman, 1984), John R. Gillis, *For Better, for Worse: British Marriages, 1600 to the Present* (New York: Oxford University Press, 1985), Susan Dwyer Amussen, *An Ordered Society: Gender and Class in Early Modern England* (Oxford: Basil Blackwell, 1988), Christopher Durston, *The Family in the English Revolution* (New York: Basil Blackwell, 1989), and Alan Macfarlane, *Marriage and Love in England: Modes of Reproduction, 1300–1840* (New York: Basil Blackwell, 1986). These authors also expanded the study of women's changing role within the family over time and explored how the forces of the law, religion, and economic change during the seventeenth century shaped their responsibilities in the family.

Keith Wrightson *Poverty and Piety in an English Village: Terling, 1525–1700* (New York: Academic Press, 1979), and Jeremy Boulton, *Neighborhood and Society: A London Suburb in the Seventeenth Century* (Cambridge: Cambridge University Press, 1987), studied women's experience in two geographic areas, while Wrightson's more general work, *English Society: 1580–1680* (New Brunswick, N.J.: Rutgers University Press, 1982), and those of Peter Laslett, *The World We Have Lost* (New York: Methuen, 1965), *Household and Family Structure in*

Past Time (New York: Cambridge University Press, 1972), and *Family Life and Illicit Love in Earlier Generations* (New York: Cambridge University Press, 1977), are also valuable for the light they shed on women's lives in seventeenth-century England.

Primary works by and about women in England are collected in Katherine Usher Henderson and Barbara F. MacManus, *Half Human Kind: Contexts and Texts of the Controversy about Women in England, 1540–1640* (Urbana: University of Illinois Press, 1985), and in *The Whole Duty of a Woman: Female Writers in Seventeenth-Century England*, edited by Angeline Goreau (Garden City, N.Y.: Dial Press, 1984). Thomas Tusser, "Five Hundred Points of Good Husbandry," in *The Somers Collection of Tracts*, edited by Walter Scott, vol. 3 (New York: AMS Press, 1965), was one of the most popular domestic manuals in the century, describing and prescribing women's household duties.

General Works on Women, Population, and Families in Seventeenth-Century America

Edmund S. Morgan, *The Puritan Family: Religion and Domestic Relations in Seventeenth-Century New England* (New York: Harper and Row, 1966; reprint, Westport, Conn.: Greenwood Press, 1980), and John Demos, *A Little Commonwealth: Family Life in Plymouth Colony* (New York: Oxford University Press, 1970), were important early works recognizing the role played by women in the settlement of New England. The best source to date on women's lives in the New England colonies is Laurel Thatcher Ulrich, *Good Wives: Image and Reality in the Lives of Women in Northern New England, 1650–1750* (New York: Alfred A. Knopf, 1982).

John Demos, "Families in Colonial Bristol, Rhode Island: An Exercise in Historical Demography," *William and Mary Quarterly* 3d ser., 25 (January 1968), and Philip J. Greven, Jr., *Four Generations: Population, Land and Family in Colonial Andover, Massachusetts* (Ithaca: Cornell University Press, 1970), discuss the impact of women's presence in the region on these communities' development. Other demographic sources on New England women's lives include Richard Archer, "New England Mosaic: A Demographic Analysis for the Seventeenth Century," *William and Mary Quarterly* 3d ser., 48 (October 1990).

On Quaker families in the Old World and the New, see Barry Levy, *Quakers and the American Family: British Settlement in the Delaware Valley* (New York: Oxford University Press, 1988), and Robert V. Wells, "Quaker Marriage Patterns in a Colonial Perspective," in *A Heritage of Her Own: Toward a New Social History of American Women*, edited by Nancy F. Cott and Elizabeth H. Pleck (New York: Simon & Schuster, 1979).

Julia Cherry Spruill, *Women's Life and Work in the Southern Colonies* (Chapel Hill: University of North Carolina Press, 1938; reprint, New York: W. W.

Norton, 1972), was a pioneering work in the study of women's history in the southern colonies and remains a valuable source. Since the 1970s, however, more detailed demographic studies of women's experience have expanded our understanding of women in the settlement of the southern colonies. See especially Lois Green Carr and Lorena S. Walsh, "The Planter's Wife: The Experience of White Women in Seventeenth Century-Maryland," *William and Mary Quarterly* 3d ser., 34 (October 1977); Lorena S. Walsh, " 'Till Death Us Do Part': Marriage and Family in Seventeenth-Century Maryland," in *The Chesapeake in the Seventeenth Century: Essays on Anglo-American Society and Politics*, edited by Thad W. Tate and David L. Ammerman (New York: W. W. Norton, 1979), Darret B. and Anita H. Rutman, " 'Now-Wives and Sons-in-Law': Parental Death in a Seventeenth-Century Virginia County," in *The Chesapeake in the Seventeenth Century*, and Daniel Blake Smith, "Mortality and Family in the Colonial Chesapeake," *Journal of Interdisciplinary History* 8 (Winter 1978). See also Russell R. Menard, "Immigrants and Their Increase: The Process of Population Growth in Early Colonial Maryland," in *Law, Society, and Politics in Early Maryland*, edited by Aubrey C. Land, Lois Green Carr, and Edward C. Papenfuse (Baltimore: Johns Hopkins University Press, 1977), Lorena S. Walsh and Russell R. Menard, "Death in the Chesapeake: Two Life Tables for Men in Early Colonial Maryland," *Maryland Historical Magazine* 69 (Summer 1974), and Alan J. Kulikoff, *Tobacco and Slaves: The Development of Southern Cultures in the Chesapeake, 1680–1800* (Chapel Hill: University of North Carolina Press, 1986).

On the "Tobacco Brides" in Virginia see Mrs. Henry Lowell Cook, "Maids for Wives," *Virginia Magazine of History and Biography* 1 (October 1942), and David R. Ransome, "Wives for Virginia, 1621," *William and Mary Quarterly* 3d ser., 48 (January 1991).

Native American and African Women

Sources on Native American women's lives prior to English colonization are scarce. Historians must rely on the biased accounts of Jesuit missionaries and early English observers for their view of Native American society, and women's roles within it, prior to conquest by European cultures. For a critical view of how Native American women have been portrayed, see Rayna Green, "The Pocahontas Perplex: The Image of Indian Women in American Culture," in *Unequal Sisters: A Multicultural Reader in U.S. Women's History*, edited by Ellen Carol DuBois and Vicki L. Ruiz (New York: Routledge, 1990), and "Native American Women," *Signs: Journal of Women in Culture and Society* 6 (Winter 1980).

The best collection of documents for students of Native American women's history is *The Indian Peoples of Eastern America: A Documentary History of the Sexes*, edited by James Axtell (New York: Oxford University Press, 1981). More is known about women in the Iroquois culture than any other tribe in eastern America. See articles in *Extending the Rafters: Interdisciplinary Approaches to Iroquoian Studies*, edited by Michael K. Foster, Jack Campisi, and Marianne Mithun (Albany: State University of New York Press, 1984), and in *Women and Colonization: Anthropological Perspectives*, edited by Mona Etienne and Eleanor Leacock (New York: Praeger, 1980); also see Anthony F. C. Wallace, *Death and Rebirth of the Seneca* (New York: Random House, 1969). Joan M. Jensen, "Native American Women and Agriculture: A Seneca Case Study," in *Women and Power in American History: A Reader*, vol. 1, edited by Kathryn Kish Sklar and Thomas Dublin (Englewood Cliffs, N.J.: Prentice Hall, 1991), and Judith K. Brown, "Economic Organization and the Position of Women among the Iroquois, *Ethnohistory* 17 (Summer–Fall 1970), discuss women's power in Native American society as a function of their agricultural work, as does Nancy Shoemaker, "The Rise and Fall of Iroquois Women," *Journal of Women's History* 2 (Winter 1991). Theda Perdue, *Slavery and the Evolution of Cherokee Society, 1540–1866* (Knoxville: University of Tennessee Press, 1979), is the recognized authority on women in Cherokee society. For a more general exploration of the conflict between Native American and English cultures, see Gary B. Nash, *Red, White, and Black: The Peoples of Early America* (Englewood Cliffs, N.J.: Prentice Hall, 1974), and William Cronon, *Changes in the Land: Indians, Colonists, and the Ecology of New England* (New York: Hill and Wang, 1983).

Biographers of the most famous Native American woman in the colonial period include Philip Barbour, *Pocahontas and Her World* (Boston: Houghton Mifflin, 1970), and Grace Steele Woodward, *Pocahontas* (Norman: University of Oklahoma Press, 1969).

Works on the role of women in African society that shed light on their experience as slaves in the American colonies during the seventeenth century include Donald Wright, *African Americans in the Colonial Era: From African Origins through the American Revolution* (Arlington Heights, Ill.: Harlan Davidson, 1990), Marietta Morrissey, *Slave Women in the New World: Gender Stratification in the Caribbean* (Lawrence: University Press of Kansas, 1989), and articles in *Women and Slavery in Africa*, edited by Claire C. Robertson and Martin A. Klein (Madison: University of Wisconsin Press, 1983), and *Sea Island Roots: African Presence in the Carolinas and Georgia*, edited by Mary A. Twining and Keith E. Baird (Trenton, N.J.: Africa World Press, 1991). See also Deborah Grey White, *Ar'n't I a Woman? Female Slaves in the Plantation South* (New York: W. W. Norton, 1985), for her insights on slavery in the postrevolutionary South, which raise questions about the experience of African women in the first years of that institution.

On African women in Africa, see Sylvia Leith-Ross, *African Women: A Study of the Ibo of Nigeria* (New York: Frederick A. Praeger, 1965). For information about African women's skills and artistry, see Judith Wragge Chase, *Afro-American Art and Craft* (New York: Van Nostrand Reinhold Co., 1971), and articles in *Afro-American Folk Art and Crafts*, edited by William Ferris (Boston: G. K. Hall & Co., 1983), as well as John Michael Vlach, *The Afro-American Tradition in Decorative Arts* (Kent, Ohio: Kent State University Press, 1978). Susan Westbury, "Slaves of Colonial Virginia: Where They Came From," *William and Mary Quarterly* 3d. ser., 42 (April 1985), investigates the origins of slaves imported to the Chesapeake region.

The African women's role in the growth of the Maryland slave population is discussed by Russell R. Menard, "The Maryland Slave Population, 1658–1730: A Demographic Profile of Blacks in Four Counties," *William and Mary Quarterly* 3d ser., 32 (January 1975), and Gloria T. Main, *Tobacco Colony: Life in Early Maryland, 1650–1750* (Princeton: Princeton University Press, 1982). Philip D. Morgan, "Slave Life in Piedmont Virginia, 1720–1800," in *Colonial Chesapeake Society*, edited by Lois Green Carr, Philip D. Morgan, and Jean B. Russo (Chapel Hill: University of North Carolina Press, 1988), as well as Kulikoff, *Tobacco and Slaves*, discuss their experience in Virginia. Peter A. Coclanis, *The Shadow of a Dream: Economic Life and Death in the South Carolina Low Country, 1670–1920* (New York: Oxford University Press, 1989), Peter Wood, *Black Majority: Negroes in Colonial South Carolina from 1670 through the Stono Rebellion* (New York: W. W. Norton, 1974), and Daniel C. Littlefield, *Rice and Slaves: Ethnicity and the Slave Trade in Colonial South Carolina* (Baton Rouge: Louisiana State University Press, 1981), discuss the role played by African women in the colonization and development of South Carolina.

Lorenzo Johnston Greene, *The Negro in Colonial New England, 1620–1776* (Port Washington, N.Y.: Kennikat Press, 1942), discusses the lives of African women in the Puritan colonies, as do Robert C. Twombly and Robert H. Moore in "Black Puritan: The Negro in Seventeenth-Century Massachusetts," *William and Mary Quarterly* 3d. ser., 24 (April 1967), and Winthrop D. Jordan, "The Influences of the West Indies on the Origins of New England Slavery," *William and Mary Quarterly* 3d. ser., 18 (April 1961). Jean R. Soderlund, "Black Women in Colonial Pennsylvania," *Pennsylvania Magazine of History and Biography* 107 (January 1983), discusses their presence there, while Gary B. Nash, "Slaves and Slaveowners in Colonial Philadelphia," *William and Mary Quarterly* 3d. ser., 30 (April 1973), analyzes the growth of slavery in this Pennsylvania city. Ira Berlin, "Time, Space, and the Evolution of Afro-American Society on British Mainland North America," *American Historical Review* 85 (February 1980), discusses the origins of slavery in seventeenth-century America. Lillian Ashcraft Webb, "Black Women and Religion in the Colonial Period," in *Women and Religion in America*, vol. 2, edited by Rosemary Radford Ruether and Rosemary Skinner Keller (San Francisco: Harper & Row, 1983), and Warren M. Billings, "The Cases of Fernando and Elizabeth Key: A Note on the Status of

Blacks in Seventeenth-Century Virginia," *William and Mary Quarterly* 3d. ser., 30 (July 1973), discuss the role of religion in defining African women's status in the colonies.

Women and Domesticity

Among the oldest, and most entertaining, works on women's domestic lives in early America are those written by Alice Morse Earle, including *Colonial Dames and Good Wives* (New York: 1895; reprint, New York: Frederick Ungar Publishing Co., 1962), *Margaret Winthrop* (New York: Charles Scribner's Sons, 1895), and *Home Life in Colonial Days* (New York: Grosset & Dunlap, 1898; reprint, Stockbridge, Mass.: Berkshire Traveler Press, 1974). Earle's *Two Centuries of Costume in America: 1620–1830*, vol. 1 (New York: Macmillan Co., 1903; reprint, New York: Dover Publications, 1970), remains the authority on fashions in the American colonies. On women's needlework skills, see Susan Burrows Swan, *A Winterthur Guide to American Needlework* (New York: Crown Publishers, 1976). The best recent work on women's domestic labors in seventeenth-century New England is Ulrich, *Good Wives*. See also Ulrich, " 'A Friendly Neighbor': Social Dimensions of Daily Work in Northern Colonial New England," *Feminist Studies* 6 (Summer 1980).

Archaeological evidence found by Ivor Noel Hume, *Martin's Hundred: The Discovery of a Lost Virginia Settlement* (New York: Dell Publishing Co., 1979), illuminates the domestic lives of English women in Virginia. His findings are confirmed by estate inventories in Main, *Tobacco Colony*. On the material culture in seventeenth-century America, see "Forum: Toward a History of the Standard of Living in British North America," *William and Mary Quarterly* 3d ser., 45 (January 1988).

On the domestic responsibilities of women in the southern colonies, see Main, *Tobacco Colony*, Spruill, *Women's Life and Work in the Southern Colonies*, and Carr and Walsh, "The Planter's Wife." Lois Green Carr and Lorena S. Walsh, "Economic Diversification and Labor Organization in the Chesapeake, 1650–1820," *Work and Labor in Early America*, edited by Stephen Innes (Chapel Hill: University of North Carolina Press, 1988), discuss how women's work changed in the colonial period as the result of the settlement process and economic development. Russell Menard, "From Servants to Slaves: The Transformation of the Chesapeake Labor System," *Southern Studies* 16 (Winter 1977), discusses how slavery shaped English women's domestic labors.

There are few works on women in the middle colonies during the seventeenth and early eighteenth centuries. Firth Harding Fabend, *A Dutch Family in the Middle Colonies, 1660–1800* (New Brunswick, N.J.: Rutgers University Press, 1991), indirectly discusses the domestic lives of Dutch women in New Netherland, as does Linda Biemer, *Women and Property in Colonial New York: The*

Transition from Dutch to English Law, 1643–1727 (Ann Arbor: UMI Research Press, 1983).

On women's education and literacy in the American colonies, see James Axtell, *The School upon a Hill: Education and Society in Colonial New England* (New Haven: Yale University Press, 1974), Kenneth Lockridge, *Literacy in Colonial New England* (New York: W. W. Norton, 1974), E. Jennifer Monaghan, "Literacy Instruction and Gender in Colonial New England," *American Quarterly* 40 (March 1988), and Linda Auwers, "Reading the Marks of the Past: Exploring Female Literacy in Colonial Windsor, Connecticut," *Historical Methods* 13 (Fall 1980). Also, Joel Perlmann and Dennis Shirley, "When Did New England Women Acquire Literacy?" *William and Mary Quarterly* 3d ser., 48 (January 1991), provide a helpful review of the literature on this important question.

On Puritan attitudes about marriage, see Morgan, *The Puritan Family*, with emphasis on the prescriptive literature for marriages written by Puritan ministers. Demos, *A Little Commonwealth*, contends the Pilgrims were more egalitarian in their relationships than other English men and women. Lyle Koehler, *A Search for Power: The 'Weaker Sex' in Seventeenth-Century New England* (Urbana: University of Illinois Press, 1980), sees the Puritans as misogynistic and fearful of women's sexuality. On Puritans and sexuality, see Edmund S. Morgan, "The Puritans and Sex," *New England Quarterly* 15 (December 1942), and Kathleen Verduin, " 'Our Cursed Natures': Sexuality and the Puritan Conscience," *New England Quarterly* 56 (June 1983). Roger Thompson, *Sex in Middlesex: Popular Mores in a Massachusetts County, 1649–1699* (Amherst: University of Massachusetts Press, 1986) and Robert F. Oaks, " 'Things Fearful to Name': Sodomy and Buggery in Seventeenth-Century New England," *Journal of Social History* 12 (Winter 1978), discuss violators of the sexual mores in New England.

On midwifery and childbearing in colonial America, see Audrey Eccles, *Obstetrics and Gynaecology in Tudor and Stuart England* (Kent, Ohio: Kent State University Press, 1982), which discuses seventeenth-century beliefs about the birth process and women's anatomy. Most works on childbirth in the colonies focus on the replacement of midwives by physicians in the eighteenth century. Catherine Scholten, " 'On the Importance of the Obstetrick Art': Changing Customs of Childbirth in America, 1760–1825," *William and Mary Quarterly* 3d ser., 34 (July 1977), does discuss customs in the seventeenth-century colonies, as do Richard W. and Dorothy C. Wertz, *Lying In—A History of Childbirth in America* (New York: Free Press, 1977), and Jane Bauer Donegan, *Women and Men Midwives: Medicine, Mortality, and Misogyny in Early America* (Westport, Conn.: Greenwood Press, 1978). Barbara Ehrenreich and Dierdre English, *Witches, Midwives, and Nurses: A History of Women Healers* (Westbury, N.Y.: Feminist Press, 1973), discuss the connection between women healers and witchcraft.

Dorothy MacLaren, "Fertility, Infant Mortality, and Breastfeeding in the

Seventeenth Century," *Medical History* 22 (October 1978), Valerie Fildes, *Breasts, Bottles, and Babies: A History of Infant Feeding* (Edinburgh: Edinburgh University Press, 1986), and Paula A. Treckel, "Breastfeeding and Maternal Sexuality in Colonial America," *Journal of Interdisciplinary History* 20 (Summer 1989), discuss the affect of infant nursing on fertility in seventeenth-century England and America, while Ulrich, *Good Wives*, explores the weaning process.

On childrearing in early America, see Morgan, *The Puritan Family*, and Demos, *A Little Commonwealth*. Ross W. Beales, Jr., "In Search of the Historical Child: Miniature Adulthood and Youth in Colonial New England," *American Quarterly* 27 (October 1975), and "The Child in Seventeenth-Century America," in *American Childhood: A Research Guide and Historical Handbook*, edited by Joseph M. Hawes and N. Ray Hiner (Westport, Conn.: Greenwood Press, 1985), asserts that children were not just viewed as "miniature adults" by their parents in the seventeenth century. See also Philip Greven, *The Protestant Temperament: Patterns of Child-Rearing, Religious Experience, and the Self in Early America* (New York: Knopf, 1977).

The poetry of Anne Bradstreet offers insight into the daily lives of women in colonial New England. See *The Works of Anne Bradstreet*, edited by Jeanine Hensley, with a foreword by Adrienne Rich (Cambridge: Harvard University Press, 1967). Another early woman writer was Sarah Kemble Knight, *The Journal of Madam Knight* (Boston: David R. Godine, 1972). Her journal is an interesting, humorous account of a trip through New England from Boston to New Haven in 1704 that describes the people and the countryside.

Mary Rowlandson, "The Narrative of the Captivity and Restoration of Mrs. Mary Rowlandson," provides insight into the experiences of a woman captured by Narragansetts during King Philip's War. The experience of Eunice Williams, who after being captured by Mohawks in Deerfield, Massachusetts, as a girl in 1704 chose to remain with her captors as a young adult, is recounted in John Demos, *The Unredeemed Captive: A Family Story from Early America* (New York: Alfred A. Knopf, 1994).

The prescriptive works of Cotton Mather, especially *Ornaments for the Daughters of Zion* (Delmar, N.Y.: Scholars' Facsimiles and Reprints, 1978), and *The Angel of Bethesda*, edited by George W. Jones (Barre, Mass.: Barre Publishers and the American Antiquarian Society, 1972), give evidence of the role Puritan ministers believed women should play in New England.

The Legal Status of Women

One of the earliest discussions of women's legal status in seventeenth-century America is found in Morris, *Studies in the History of America Law*. In recent years, more specific works have explored dimensions of women's rights to hold property, sue for divorce, and operate businesses in early America. The best source on the property rights of women in the American colonies is Marylynn Salmon, *Women and the Law of Property in Early America* (Chapel Hill: University of North Carolina Press, 1986). See also Carol Shammas, Marylynn Salmon, and Michael Dahlin, *Inheritance in America from Colonial Times to the Present* (New Brunswick, N.J.: Rutgers University Press, 1987).

On women's legal rights in the Chesapeake region, see Carr and Walsh, "The Planter's Wife." See also Linda Spaeth, "More than Her 'Thirds': Wives and Widows in Colonial Virginia," *Women and History* 4 (1982). For an assessment of the changes in women's rights over time in the region, see Lorena S. Walsh, "The Experiences and Status of Women in the Chesapeake, 1750–1775," *The Web of Southern Social Relations: Women, Family, and Education*, edited by Walter J. Fraser, R. Frank Saunders, and Jon L. Wakelyn (Athens: University of Georgia Press, 1985).

For a comparison of women's rights under Dutch law and under English law in seventeenth-century New York, see Biemer, *Women and Property in Colonial New York*. Joan R. Gundersen and Gwen Victor Gampel, "Married Women's Legal Status in Eighteenth-Century New York and Virginia," *William and Mary Quarterly* 3d ser., 39 (January 1982), contrasts the rights of women in these two regions, focusing on changes in the eighteenth century. David E. Narrett, "Men's Wills and Women's Property Rights in Colonial New York," in *Women in the Age of the American Revolution*, edited by Ronald Hoffman and Peter J. Albert (Charlottesville: University Press of Virginia, 1989), discusses women's rights in that colony in the early eighteenth century. See Trevor Burnard, "Inheritance and Independence: Women's Status in Early Colonial Jamaica," *William and Mary Quarterly*, 3d ser., 48 (January 1991), for a comparison of women's rights in England's Caribbean colonies with those in the Chesapeake region. On women's property rights in South Carolina, see Marylynn Salmon, "Women and Property in South Carolina: The Evidence from Marriage Settlements, 1730 to 1830," *William and Mary Quarterly* 3d ser., 39 (October 1982).

On women's rights in the New England colonies and in Pennsylvania, see Kim Lacy Rogers, "Relicts of the New World: Conditions of Widowhood in Seventeenth-Century New England," in *Woman's Being, Woman's Place: Female Identity and Vocation in American History*, edited by Mary Kelley (Boston: G. K. Hall & Co., 1979), and Alexander Keyssar, "Widowhood in Eighteenth-Century Massachusetts: A Problem in the History of the Family," *Perspectives in American History* 8 (1974). Marylynn Salmon, "Equality or Subversion? Feme Covert Status in Early Pennsylvania," *Women of America: A History* (Boston: Houghton Mifflin, 1979), discusses women's rights in the Quaker colony. See also Linda Ford, "William Penn's Views on Women: Subjects of Friendship," *Quaker History* 72 (February 1983), for more on women's right to dower in Pennsylvania.

On *feme sole* traders and professional women in colonial America, see Spruill, *Women's Life and Work in the Southern Colonies*, Sophie Drinker, "Women Attorneys of Colonial Times," *Maryland Historical Magazine* 56 (December 1961), and Dexter, *Colonial Women of Affairs*. On women and divorce in seventeenth-century New England, see K. Kelly Weisberg, " 'Under Greet Temptations Heer': Women and Divorce in Puritan Massachusetts," *Feminist Studies* 2 (1975), and Koehler, *A Search for Power*. Nancy Cott, "Divorce and the Changing Status of Women in Eighteenth-Century Massachusetts," *William and Mary Quarterly* 3d ser., 33 (October 1976), and "Eighteenth-Century Family and Social Life from Massachusetts Divorce Records," *Journal of Social History* 10 (Fall 1976), discusses seventeenth-century divorce as well. Sheldon S. Cohen, "What Man Hath Put Asunder: Divorce in New Hampshire, 1681–1784," *Historical New Hampshire* 41 (Fall/Winter 1986), and Alison Duncan Hirsch, "The Thrall Divorce Case: A Family Crisis in Eighteenth-Century Connecticut," *Women, Family and Community in Colonial America: Two Perspectives*, with an introduction by Carol Berkin (New York: Haworth Press, 1983), look at divorce in two other Puritan colonies. See also Roger Thompson, *Sex in Middlesex: Popular Mores in a Massachusetts County, 1649–1699* (Amherst: University of Massachusetts Press, 1986). For more general works on women, divorce, and family violence in America see Glenda Riley, *Divorce: An American Tradition* (New York: Oxford University Press, 1991), and Elizabeth Pleck, *Domestic Tyranny: The Making of American Social Policy against Family Violence from Colonial Times to the Present* (New York: Oxford University Press, 1987).

Mary Beth Norton, "Gender and Defamation in Seventeenth-Century Maryland," *William and Mary Quarterly* 3d ser., 44 (January 1987), and "Gender, Crime, and Community in Seventeenth-Century Maryland," in *The Transformation of Early American History: Society, Authority, and Ideology*, edited by James Henretta, Michael Kammen, and Stanley Katz (New York: Knopf, 1991), discusses women's gossip and the defamation suits brought against them in the Maryland court records. C. Dallett Hemphill, "Women in Court: Sex Role Differentiation in Salem Massachusetts, 1636 to 1683," *William and Mary Quarterly* 3d ser., 39 (January 1982), discusses the changes in women's legal status that occurred as the Salem economy became more commercial.

Women and Religion in Colonial America

On women and religion in colonial New England, see Morgan, *The Puritan Family*, and Gerald Moran and Maris Vinovskis, "The Puritan Family and Religion: A Critical Appraisal," *William and Mary Quarterly* 3d ser., 39 (January 1982). See also Gerald Moran, "Sisters in Christ: Women and the Church in Seventeenth-Century New England," in *Women in American Religion*, edited by Janet Wilson James (Philadelphia: University of Pennsylvania Press, 1980), and

Rosemary Skinner Keller, "New England Women: Ideology and Experience in First-Generation Puritanism, 1630–1650," *Women and Religion in America,* vol. 2. Ulrich, *Good Wives,* and Koehler, *A Search for Power,* provide an interesting contrast in their assessment of Puritanism and women's roles. Laurel Thatcher Ulrich, "Vertuous Women Found: New England Ministerial Literature, 1678–1735," *American Quarterly* 28 (January 1976), discusses the prescriptive literature regarding women's spiritual nature. Margaret Masson, "The Typology of the Female as a Model for the Regenerate: Puritan Preaching, 1690–1730," *Signs* 2 (Winter 1976), also analyzes this literature. Robert G. Pope, *The Half-Way Covenant: Church Membership in Puritan New England* (Princeton: Princeton University Press, 1969), and Richard D. Sheils, "The Feminization of American Congregationalism, 1730–1835," *American Quarterly* 33 (Spring 1981), discuss the impact of women's domination of New England church membership in the seventeenth and eighteenth centuries. On women's attraction to the Puritan faith, see Amanda Porterfield, *Female Piety in Puritan New England: The Emergence of Religious Humanism* (New York: Oxford University Press, 1992). Charles Lloyd Cohen, *God's Caress: The Psychology of Puritan Religious Experience* (New York: Oxford University Press, 1986), addresses women's "tales of grace." On women as spiritual role models for men, see Margaret W. Masson, "The Typology of the Female as a Model for the Regenerate: Puritan Preaching, 1690–1730," *Signs: Journal of Women in Culture and Society* 2 (Winter 1976). Patricia J. Tracy, *Jonathan Edwards, Pastor: Religion and Society in Eighteenth-Century Northampton* (New York: Hill and Wang, 1979), discusses Sarah Pierrepont Edwards as the archetype of the "awakened" soul.

For assessments of Anne Hutchinson, see Emery Battis, *Saints and Sectaries: Anne Hutchinson and the Antinomian Controversy in Massachusetts Bay Colony* (Chapel Hill: University of North Carolina Press, 1962), Edmund S. Morgan, "The Case against Anne Hutchinson," *New England Quarterly* 10 (March 1937), Ann Fairfax Withington and Jack Schwartz, "The Political Trial of Anne Hutchinson," *New England Quarterly* 51 (June 1978), and J. F. Maclear, "Anne Hutchinson and the Mortalist Heresy," *New England Quarterly* 54 (March 1981). See also Lyle Koehler, "The Case of the American Jezebels: Anne Hutchinson and Female Agitation during the Years of the Antinomian Turmoil, 1636–1640," *William and Mary Quarterly* 3d ser., 31 (January 1974), and Ben Barker-Benfield, "Anne Hutchinson and the Puritan Attitude toward Women," *Feminist Studies* 1 (Fall 1972). For primary materials dealing with Hutchinson's trial, see *The Antinomian Controversy, 1636–1638: A Documentary History,* edited by David D. Hall (Middletown, Conn.: Wesleyan University Press, 1968).

On Margaret Fox and other Quaker women in England, see Fraser, *The Weaker Vessel,* and Levy, *Quakers and the American Family.* On the Quaker threat to New England, see Kai T. Erikson, *Wayward Puritans: A Study in the Sociology of Deviance* (New York: John Wiley and Sons, 1966). Mary Maples Dunn,

"Women of Light," in *Women of America: A History*, edited by Carol R. Berkin and Mary Beth Norton (Boston: Houghton Mifflin, 1979), and Levy, *Quakers and the American Family*, discuss the role of Quaker women in the American colonies. See also Ford, "William Penn's Views on Women." For materials on Mary Dyer, see Horatio Rogers, *Mary Dyer of Rhode Island, the Quaker Martyr that Was Hanged on Boston Common* (Providence, R.I.: Preston and Rounds, 1896). The women's meetings of the Society of Friends are discussed by Jean R. Soderlund, "Women's Authority in Pennsylvania and New Jersey Quaker Meetings, 1680–1760," *William and Mary Quarterly* 3d ser., 44 (October 1987), and by H. Larry Ingle, "A Quaker Woman on Women's Roles: Mary Penington to Friends, 1678," *Signs: Journal of Women in Culture and Society* 16 (Spring 1991). On women and revivalism in the late seventeenth century, see Martha Tomhave Blauvelt and Rosemary Skinner Keller, "Women and Revivalism: The Puritan and Wesleyan Traditions," in *Women and Religion in America*, vol. 2.

Little has been written on the religious beliefs of women in the southern colonies during the seventeenth century. See Spruill, *Women's Life and Work in the Southern Colonies*, and the articles by Alice E. Mathews, "The Religious Experience of Southern Women," and Lillian Ashcraft Webb, "Black Women and Religion in the Colonial Period," in *Women and Religion in America* vol. 2.

Carol Karlsen, *The Devil in the Shape of a Woman: Witchcraft in Colonial New England* (New York: Random House, 1989), is the best source on the relationship between gender and witchcraft accusation in seventeenth-century New England. Richard Weisman, *Witchcraft, Magic, and Religion in Seventeenth-Century Massachusetts* (Amherst: University of Massachusetts Press, 1984), discusses how religion and magic were intertwined in the Puritans' minds, as do Jon Butler, "Magic, Astrology, and the Early American Religious Heritage, 1600–1760," *American Historical Review* 84 (April 1979), David D. Hall, *Worlds of Wonder, Days of Judgment: Popular Religious Belief in Early New England* (New York: Knopf, 1989), and Richard Godbeer, *The Devil's Dominion: Magic and Religion in Early New England* (Cambridge: Cambridge University Press, 1992). Anne Kibbey, "Mutations of the Supernatural: Witchcraft, Remarkable Providences, and the Power of Puritan Men," *American Quarterly* 34 (Summer 1982), discusses how men's sense of powerlessness led them to project their fears on women, leading to accusations of witchcraft.

Other sources on witchcraft in America are John Demos, *Entertaining Satan: Witchcraft and the Culture of Early New England* (New York: Oxford University Press, 1982), and "Underlying Themes in the Witchcraft of Seventeenth Century New England," *American Historical Review* 75 (June 1972), as well as Erikson, *Wayward Puritans*. The authorities on the outbreak in Salem, Massachusetts, are Paul Boyer and Stephen Nissenbaum, *Salem Possessed: The Social Origins of Witchcraft* (Cambridge: Harvard University Press, 1974).

For documents on witchcraft in New England, see *Witch-hunting in Seventeenth-Century New England: A Documentary History, 1638–1692*, edited by David D. Hall (Boston: Northeastern University Press, 1991), and *The Salem Witchcraft Papers: Verbatim Transcripts of the Legal Documents of the Salem Witchcraft Outbreak of 1692*, 3 vols., edited by Paul Boyer and Stephen Nissenbaum (New York: DeCapo Press, 1977).

INDEX

Page numbers in *italics* refer to illustrations.

adultery: double standard in, 17,
141–42, 145–46, 230n29; punishment
for, 145, 232nn38,40
African women, in slavery, 29, 66,
67–72, 127, 128, 195; and
Christianity, 178; and family
formation, 68, 69–70, 72, 76, 113–14;
and hairdressing, 86; headcloths of,
86, *87*; resistance of, 71, 72, 86;
sexual exploitation of, 71, 145; and
witchcraft, 186–87, 244n60 (*see also*
Tituba; voodoo); work of, 68, 98,
103–4, 114
Algonquin tribes, 51, 53, 113,
212–13n61, 213–14n64; matrilineal
family structure in, 53. *See also*
Powhatan Confederacy
American colonies, 3, 26; class structure
in, 26; and England's overpopulation,
29; household implements in, 82–84,
97; housewives' role in, 43, 46, 76,
79–80, 82, 96–98, 99–102, 119–20,
127–28; housing/furnishings in,
79–81; imports, 101; legal position of
women in, 130–59; life expectancy in,
41; scarcity value of women in, 33,
135; slavery, introduction into, 32,
64–65 (*see also* individual colonies); and
younger sons of English families,

29–30. *See also* Chesapeake colonies;
middle colonies; New England
Anabaptists, 167, 172
Anglican Church, 3, 4, 10, 15–16, 44,
238n8; and divorce, 16; and
midwifery, 23
annulments, 16
Antinomian Controversy, 167–68
apprenticeships, 102–3, 115
Astell, Mary, 8–9
Austin, William, 6

Bacon, Elizabeth (Duke), 13–14
Bacon, Francis, on colonization, 31
Bacon, Nathaniel, 13, 121
Bacon's Rebellion, 121, 123
Baltimore, Lord. *See* Calvert, George
banns, posting, 16, 109–10
barter, by women, 22, 100
basket making, 98, 220–21n44
Berkeley, Frances (Culpeper), 123
birth rate: among African slaves in
colonies, 70; in 17th-century England,
18
Blackstone, William, on marriage, 24,
131, 136
Bland, Sarah, 137
Bradford, Dorothy May, 45
Bradford, William, 45
Bradstreet, Anne (Dudley), 91, 106–8,

Bradstreet, Anne (Dudley) (*cont.*)
111, 118; arrival of in America, 47,
49; and infertility, 114–15; poems of,
81, 106–7, 117, 119–20, 164; and
religious faith, 163–65
breastfeeding, 19, 114, 116–18; and
control of fertility, 18, 117; lengthy,
70, 77, 78, 113; and weaning, 117
brewing, 23, 101
Brewster, William, 45
bundling, 109

Calvert, George (Lord Baltimore),
138–39
Calvert, Leonard, 138
Calvin, John, 6
capitalism, 3–4
"change work," 100
Charles I, 4
Charles II, 5, 123, 175, 181, 240n34
Chesapeake colonies, 31–44, 46, 50,
58–59, 132, 210nn42,45; adultery in,
145–46; changing economy in, 43;
divorce in, 142; housing in, 79–80;
Jews in, 241n38; marriage in, 108–9,
110; mortality in, 41, 135, 175;
property rights in, 135–36,
228–29nn16–17; religion in, 176–79;
rice in, 97–98; slavery in, 65, 66–67,
132, 176; wives' roles in, 79, 97–98,
220n39. *See also* Maryland; South
Carolina; Virginia
childbearing, 6, 7, 77, 112–19, 127;
among African women, 76, 113–14; in
the Chesapeake colonies, 40; as life-
threatening, 17–18, 40, 76, 115, 116,
118; among Native American women,
112–13; in New England colonies,
46–47, 211–12nn50–52; and
witchcraft, 184
childrearing: among African women,
69–70; class differences in, 19; of
daughters, 9, 20, 75, 93, 97, 102 (*see
also* needlework); in New England,
102–3, 119; in northern vs. southern
colonies, 76; in 17th-century England,
18–19
church building, 165

church membership, 165–66, 179–80,
194, 195
Church of England. *See* Anglican Church
clothing, 86, 88–91; children's, 91, *93*;
Dutch women's, 91, *92*; Puritan rules
concerning, 88
Coming, Affra (Harleston), 42, 238n7
common law, 24, 25, 131, 136
common law wives, 71
Connecticut: adultery laws in, 232n40;
divorce in, 148–50, 231–32n35,
234n53; property rights in, 141,
226–27nn8–9,12; 235n54; witchcraft
trials in, 243n52
contracts, 136–37, 139; marriage (*see*
banns, posting)
conversion narratives, 165–66
Cook, Ebenezer: *The Sot-Weed Factor*, 38
Cooper, Susannah, 140–41
Corey, Giles, 187
Corey, Martha, 187, 189
corn, in colonial diets, 96, 98
Cotton, John, 10, 46, 108, 165, 168; and
Anne Hutchinson, 169, 170
courtship rituals, 109
Cromwell, Oliver, 4, 5, 14, 202n36

dame schools, 104, 126
Dare, Virginia, 31
Davenport, Mrs. John, 123
deputy husbands, 21, 42, 120–23, 126,
127, 136–38
desertion, 17, 140, 144, 230n26
divorce: absolute, 141–42, 143, 230n29,
234n53; grounds for, 110, 142,
143–44, 146, 231–32n35; and
remarriage, 142; in 17th-century
England, 16; in Thrall case, 148–50
domestic service, for women, 12. *See also*
indentured servants
domestic violence, 17, 146–48
dower rights, 24, 31, 134, 149,
226–27n6, 228–29n16
Downing, Lucy (Winthrop), 49
dowries, 14, 132, 205n64; goods as, 14,
81, 116; for widows, 133
Drake, Francis, 30
Drummond, Sarah, 123

Dudley, Dorothy, 119
Dunston, Hannah, 192–93
Dyer, Mary, 174–75, 243n52
Dyer, William, 174–75

eating utensils, 83
education, of women: in American
  colonies, 104–5, 126; in 17th-century
  England, 7–8
Edwards, Jonathan, 194
Edwards, Sarah (Pierrepont), 194
Elizabeth I, 7–8, 30
empowering acts, 140–41
English women: duties of, 1–2, 19–21,
  43, 82; on farms, 20, 33; legal status
  of, 24–25; in the marketplace, 22–24;
  migration of to America, 2–3, 5, 26,
  27–28, 44, 46, 48–49, 196; and
  obedience in marriage, 5
equity law, 25, 227n10, 228n15
espousal, 15–16
Eve, 162, 190; and childbirth, 116; and
  original sin, 6, 7, 173

families, 3–5; importance of in American
  colonies, 30, 31, 33–36; importance of
  in 17th-century England, 4–5, 33; in
  New Netherland, 156; Quaker,
  49–50; 17th-century ideal, 11–12,
  133; as units of production, 12, 24,
  81; and urbanization, 18
Fell, Margaret (Askew), 239–40n31
feme sole, 137, 138–41; and divorce, 143
feminine vs. masculine attributes, 7
fertility, restraints on, 18, 70, 77, 117.
  See also breastfeeding
Fitzherbert, Sir Anthony: *Book of
  Husbandrye*, 22
Fox, George, 173–74, 239–40n31,
  240n34
Franklin, Anne, 125
Freake, Elizabeth, 89, *90*
Friends, Society of, 11, 49–50, 150, 172,
  173–75, 239n26, 241n36; life
  expectancy among, 212n60; and
  marriage, 107, 108, 134; persecution
  of, 174–175; and slavery, 69; in

southern colonies, 178–79; women's
  meetings in, 175
friendships, women's, 100, 127

Gerbier, Charles, 10
Gilbert, Humphrey, 30
Giton, Judith, 42–43
Good, Sarah, 186, 187
Gouge, William, 133, 145
Great Awakening, 161, 194
Greensted, William, 177–78

hairdressing, 51, 86–88
half-way covenants, 179–80
Hammond, John: *Leah and Rachel*, 37
Hammond, Phillipa, 171
Hardenbroeck, Margaret, 155–56
Hariot, Thomas, 50
Harrison, Katherine, 153–54
Hawkins, John, 30
healing skills, 23, 56. *See also* medicines;
  midwifery
Heathersall, Rebecca, 137–38
Henry VIII, 3
Hibbens, Anne, 171–72
Hooten, Elizabeth, 240n34
hornbooks, 104
Hutchinson, Anne (Marbury), 106,
  168–71, 174, 184, 243n52

indentured servants, 37–40, 43, 76, 102;
  brutal treatment of, 38–39
infant mortality: among African slaves,
  70; in 17th-century England, 18, 19
infanticide, 40
infertility, 7, 70, 114–15, 216n101
inn/tavernkeeping, 124
"Invective against the Pride of Women,
  An," 8
Iroquois tribe, 56

Jamaica, 227–28n13
James I, 4, 8, 45
Jamestown settlement, 31, 32, 123; first
  women in, 32; Indian attacks on, 35
Johnston, Henrietta (de Beaulieu),
  120–21
jointure, 25, 133–34, 157

Key, Elizabeth, 177–78
King Philip's War, 63, 180, 225–26n115
King William's War, 126
kitchen gardens, 23, 75, 99
Knight, Sarah (Kemble), 91, 103, 124, 219n31

literacy, female, 7–8, 104, 200n12; Puritan encouragement of, 8; in urban centers, 126
London, 12, 29, 205–6n1

magic, belief in, 160–61, 182–83. *See also* witchcraft
Markham, Gervaise, 9
marriage, 13–17, 108–12; age at first, 12, 13, 40, 46, 209n35, 211n50, 212n60; Anne Bradstreet's 163; contract (*see* banns, posting); as economic union, 12, 14; interracial, 58, 60, 61, 63; love in, 15, 110–11; parental permission for, 13–14, 108; physical abuse in (*see* domestic violence); and property rights, 133–34 (*see also* property rights); in Puritan religion (*see* Puritans, and marriage); as religious metaphor, 195; among slaves, 68; and social class, 13, 201n28; among Society of Friends, 49, 212n60
Martin's Hundred, Virginia, 35, 88, 217n6
Maryland, 36–37, 110, 138–39, 165, 207n19; contract law in, 136–37; dower rights in, 226n6; primogeniture laws in, 226n4; religion in, 238n8
Massachusetts, 144, 235n56; adultery laws in, 232n40; divorce in, 144, 231–32nn34–35; 234–35n54; and domestic violence, 146–47; and Indian wars, 126; population of, 242n43; property rights in, 141, 226–27nn8,12; religious toleration imposed in, 175; Salem, 167 (*see also* Salem witchcraft trials)
Mather, Cotton, 125–26, 150, 167, 244–45n62; on breastfeeding, 117; on domestic violence, 146–47; and Hannah Dunston, 192–93; *Ornaments*

for the Daughters of Zion, 191–92; on witchcraft, 190–91
matrilineal family systems: in Africa, 66; among Native Americans, 53
medicines, 23, 113, 115–16, 183
middle colonies, 50, 76. *See also* New York; Pennsylvania
midwifery, 23, 113, 115; male physicians' usurpation of, 204n56; and witchcraft, 183–84, 243n53
Milton, John, 10, 16
Moody, Lady Deborah, 172
mother-daughter bond, 20, 102

Narragansett tribe, 113, 180, 215n80
Native American women, 52, 53, 54–55, 56–64, 72, 128, 197; and African men, 68; authority of, 53, 56, 59, 78; and childbirth, 112–13; and cultural traditions, 28–29, 127; enslavement of, 63, 68; and fur trade, 57, 77–78; and menstruation, 112; and religion, 195; work of, 51, 57, 77–79
Native Americans, 212–13n61; in conflict with settlers, 35, 50, 63, 179; enslavement of, 63–64; kinship systems among, 53, 213–14n64; lifestyles of, 51, 77–79; in Plymouth Colony, 45; in Roanoke, 50–53; women captured by, 35–36, 180–81, 192–93. *See also* individual tribes
needlework, 23, 74, 93–94, 95, 97, 104–5; as trade, 124
New England, 44–49; adultery laws in, 232n40; divorce in, 143–45, 231–32nn34–35; "female crime wave" in, 150; housewives' role in, 76, 80, 97, 103, 119–20; housing in, 80–81; slavery in, 65, 68, 103–4; life expectancy in, 47; literacy in, 104; marriage laws in, 133; migration waves in, 242n43; and relations with Native Americans, 45, 63–64; trade in, 221n49. *See also* Connecticut; Massachusetts; New Hampshire; Rhode Island
New England Primer, 105
New Hampshire, 231n34, 232n40

New Jersey, Society of Friends in, 175, 241n36

New Netherland, rights of women in, 236nn66–67

New York, 142; Dutch in, 91, 154–57; primogeniture laws in, 226n4; and rescission of women's rights under English rule, 155; "news wives," 123

Nurse, Rebecca, 184, 188

orgasm, 16

original sin, doctrine of, 6, 7, 18

orphaned children, 41, 108–9, 126, 209–10n38

Osborne, Dorothy, 17

Osborne, Sarah (Price), 187

Parkman, Hannah, 119

Parkman, Mary, 118, 119

patriarchal family, 3, 5, 162; challenges to, 11; in the New World, 28, 43, 44, 130, 132, 133; and primogeniture, 25–26

patrilineal family, 3, 4, 26, 28, 178, 199n2, 213n64; in West Africa, 66

Penn, William, 50, 227n11, 232n38

Pennington, Mary, 175

Pennsylvania: banning of slave trade in, 69; divorce in, 232n38; literacy in, 104; Quaker settlement of, 50; rape laws in, 233n50; and women's rights, 134, 140, 227nn10–12

Pequot tribe, 63

Phips, Lady Mary, 188

Pilgrims. *See* Separatists

Plymouth Colony, 44–49, 146–47, 232n40

Pocahontas, 59–61, *62*

Pollard, Anne, *48*

polygamy: in Africa, 66; among Native Americans, 60

population growth, in England, 29, 205–6n1

Powhatan Confederacy, 32, 35, 58–60, 206n4

pregnancy, 6, 118; in indentured servants, 39–40; premarital, 15, 108–9. *See also* childbearing

primogeniture, 25–26, 226n4

printing, women in, 22, 125

Procter, Elizabeth, 188

Procter, John, 188

property rights, 228–29n16; liberalization of, 140–41, 158; and protective laws for women, 132, 134, 157; and remarriage, 135; through wills, 157. *See also* dower rights; jointure

Protestantism: and nationalism/ capitalism, 3; nonconformist sects in, 167 (*see also* Anabaptists; Puritans; Separatists)

Puritan Commonwealth, in England, 4–5, 15; childrearing in, 17; divorce in, 16; marriage ceremonies in, 16

Puritans: beliefs of, 4, 5, 10–11; and conversion narratives, 165–66; and distrust of women, 190; and marriage, 5, 10, 15, 16, 107–8, 109, 110–11, 162; in New England (*see* New England); radical, 11, 16, 201–2n33

Putnam, Ann (Carr), 185–86

Putnam, Thomas, 185

Quakers. *See* Friends, Society of

Queen Anne's War, 126

Raleigh, Walter, 30, 31

Ranters, 201–2n33

rape, 148, 233–34nn50–52

Reformation, 3, 162

Rhode Island, 233n48, 240n34

Roanoke settlement, 30–31, 50–53

Rolfe, John, 59–60

Rowlandson, Mary (White), 180–81

Salem witchcraft trials, 152, 182, 184–91, 195; confessions in, 187, 188; and Putnam-Porter families, 185–86

samplers, 74, 93–94, *95. See also* needlework

seeds, transported to America, 98–100

separation, marital, 16–17; grounds for, 17, 145; support granted in, 142–43

Separatists, 44–46

servants, 12, 102–4. *See also* indentured servants; slavery

sesame seeds, 98–99
sexual activity: in marriage, 16, 110, 201–2n33; among Native American women, 53, 58; premarital, 15, 47, 110; and social class, 15; women's, fear of, 6–7, 170
sexual double standard, 15; and adultery (*see* adultery); in punishment for crimes, 151; in rape trials, 148
Sharp, Jane, 202n37
slave trade, 63–65, 66
slavery, 28, 29, 64–71, 103; Christian baptism in, 177–78; as defining colonial Englishwomen's roles, 76; and fears of miscegenation, 69; introduction of to colonies, 32, 43, 64–65; kinship networks in, 70; and religion, 177–79; in West Africa, 66, 67. *See also* African women; slave trade
Smith, Captain John, 32, 57, 59, 60
Smith, Martha, 125–26
Society for the Propagation of the Gospel in Foreign Parts, 178
South Carolina, 36, 42, 120–21; Charles Town, 241n38; dower rights in, 226n6; fears of miscegenation in, 69; primogeniture laws in, 226n4; property control in, 228–29n16; 230n31; slave trade in, 63, 66–67
spinning, 22, 96, 102, 220n39
spousal abuse, 17, 147–48
Stuyvesant, Peter, 239n25

Thrall, Hannah and William, 148–50
Tilney, Edmund, 19–20
Tituba, 160–61, 186, 187, 189, 244–45n62
Tobacco Brides, 34–35
Tusser, Thomas, 21, 101, 116, 117

Venderdonck, Mary, 140
Virginia, 27–28, 31, 32–36, 141, 178, 196; deputy husbands in, 137–38; dower rights in, 228–29n16; primogeniture laws in, 226n4. *See also* Jamestown settlement; Martin's Hundred; Roanoke settlement
Virginia Company of London, 31, 32,

33, 59, 60; and recruitment of Tobacco Brides
Virginia Massacre, 35–36
virginity, 15, 17, 58
voodoo, 244–45n62
vote, right of, 139

Wampanoag tribe, 45, 63, 180, 212n61
"weaker vessel," 6–7
West African peoples, 65–66, 196–97; Ibo tribe, 71, 218n23; kinship networks in, 69–70; religious heritage of, 176, 244–45n62
wet nurses, 18, 116–17
Whately, William, 6, 143, 203n41
White, John, 30, 31, 50–53
widows, 22, 24, 41, 72–73, 124–27, 127; continuing husbands' trades, 22–23, 124–25; dower rights of, 24, 25, 131, 158; Dutch, 157, 236n66; legal position of, 129–30, 135; and remarriage, 24–25, 41, 42, 132, 135, 136, 158, 209–10n38; and wars, 126
Willard, Samuel, 110, 189
Williams, Eunice, 193
Williams, Roger, 78, 89, 97, 113, 167
Winthrop, John, 46, 47, 49; and Anne Hutchinson, 169, 183; marriage of, 111–12; and women's education, 105
Winthrop, John Jr., 123
Winthrop, Margaret (Tyndall), 102, 111–12
witchcraft, accusations of, 23, 151, 152–54, 160–62, 182–91; executions for, 172, 188, 189, 190, 191; and property control, 153; and Quaker women, 174; in Virginia, 183, 242n47; of women vs. man, 245n65. *See also* Salem witchcraft trials
women: and control of property, 24–25, 129, 131–32, 135 (*see also* deputy husbands; dower rights); and crafts, 22–23, 124; and crime, 150–51; education of, 7, 104–5; emotionality of, 6; health risks of, 17–18, 40; inferiority attributed to, 5–6, 162; legal status of, 24–26, 120, 130–59; in the marketplace, 22–24, 125, 155–56;

in professions, 137–39, 140; racial antagonism in, 64; in religious life, 11, 76, 161–95, 238n7; and rice cultivation, 98. *See also* African women; English women; Native American women

Woolley, Hannah, 8, 9

Yeamans, Lady Margaret, 67
Young, Alice, 243n52

Zenger, John Peter, 125

THE AUTHOR

Paula A. Treckel is a graduate of Kent State University and received her Ph.D. from Syracuse University. She has taught at the College of St. Benedict and St. John's University in Minnesota and is currently Professor of History at Allegheny College in Meadville, Pennsylvania. She has published articles on women and family life in seventeenth- and early eighteenth-century America and on the history of sexuality. She is currently writing a biography of eighteenth-century South Carolina planter Eliza Lucas Pinckney and researching the ritual and romance of American weddings.